GERMAN GRAMMAR DRILLS

Ed Swick

McGraw Hill

New York   Chicago   San Francisco   Lisbon   London   Madrid   Mexico City
Milan   New Delhi   San Juan   Seoul   Singapore   Sydney   Toronto

7 8 9 10 11 12 13 14 15 16 17 18 19 20 21 22 23 24 25   QDB/QDB   10

ISBN 978-0-07-147514-3
MHID   0-07-147514-1
Library of Congress Control Number: 2006939978

This book is printed on acid-free paper.

Contents

Preface

If you've picked up this book, you know that to learn a language well—that is, to read, write, understand others, and be understood yourself—at some point you have to buckle down and deal with the grammar. *German Grammar Drills* will enable you to take charge of the grammar that you need to know German well. It does so by providing you with plenty of writing drills that will reinforce your knowledge and enhance your ability to speak, read, and write with finesse.

This book shows you how each grammatical structure functions by giving you comprehensive descriptions and practical examples. It is divided into three groupings of nine chapters each that will help you organize your studies. At the end of each group of chapters there is a review of the concepts you encountered in that section's chapters, and at the end of the book is a Final Review. The exercises in the reviews serve as an aid in determining which concepts you have learned well and which ones you might need to go over again. Answers for all the exercises are provided in the Answer Key. The language emphasis is on contemporary spoken German, and the German reflects the latest orthography used in the German-speaking world.

When you've worked your way through *German Grammar Drills,* not only will you find yourself confidently on your way to fluency, but also this book will remain a unique resource anytime you need to clarify or review essential grammatical concepts.

Acknowledgment

With much gratitude to Sabine McNulty for all her help and suggestions.

1

Determining Gender

For the most part, the gender of English nouns is based upon being male, female, or an inanimate object. German is similar only in a small degree. Many nouns that refer to males or females are masculine or feminine respectively. But this similarity to English soon ends. The gender of most German nouns can be determined by examining their makeup. Certain prefixes, suffixes, and structural elements are signals that a noun is a specific gender. And that gender doesn't necessarily have to do with the noun being male, female, or inanimate.

Masculine nouns can be identified by the following characteristics:

1. Nouns that refer to males: **der Vater, der Junge** (*father, boy*)
2. Many nouns that end in -er, -en, and -el: **der Lehrer, der Wagen, der Mantel** (*teacher, car, coat*)
3. Days of the week, months, and seasons: **der Montag, der Januar, der Herbst** (*Monday, January, autumn*)
4. Foreign words with the accent on the last syllable: **der Soldat, der Elefant** (*soldier, elephant*)
5. Nouns formed from an infinitive minus the -en ending: **der Besuch (besuchen), der Lohn (lohnen)** (*visit, wages*)
6. Many nouns that form their plural by (umlaut) + e: **der Brief (die Briefe), der Satz (die Sätze)** (*letter, sentence*)
7. Nouns that end in -ich, -ig, -ismus, -ist, -ling, and -us: **der Teppich, der Käfig, der Kommunismus, der Kapitalist, der Lehrling, der Rhythmus** (*carpet, cage, communism, capitalist, apprentice, rhythm*)

Feminine nouns can be identified by the following characteristics:

1. Nouns that refer to females: **die Mutter, die Frau** (*mother, woman* or *wife*)
2. Names of numerals: **die Eins, die Hundert** (*one, hundred*)
3. Names of many rivers: **die Elbe, die Mosel** (*the Elbe, the Moselle*)
4. Many nouns ending in -e: **die Lampe, die Ernte** (*lamp, harvest*)
5. Nouns ending in **-in** that identify females in professions: **die Lehrerin, die Ärztin** (*teacher, physician*)
6. Many nouns ending in -a: **die Kamera, die Pizza** (*camera, pizza*)
7. Many nouns that form their plural by -(e)n: **die Tante (die Tanten), die Zeitschrift (die Zeitschriften)** (*aunt, magazine*)

8. Nouns that end in -ei, -heit, -keit, -ie, -ik, -nz, -schaft, -ion, -tät, -ung, and -ur: die Schweinerei, die Einheit, die Einsamkeit, die Fotografie, die Topik, die Konferenz, die Landschaft, die Position, die Universität, die Prüfung, die Natur (*mess, unity, loneliness, photography, topic, conference, landscape, position, university, test, nature*)

Neuter nouns can be identified by the following characteristics:

1. Diminutive nouns that end in **-chen** or **-lein: das Mädchen, das Röslein** (*girl, little rose*)
2. Nouns formed from an infinitive: **das Einkommen, das Singen** (*income, singing*). These nouns do not have a plural form.
3. Most nouns that end in **-nis: das Bekenntnis, das Gedächtnis** (*confession, memory*)
4. Many nouns with the prefix **Ge-: das Gemälde, das Gelächter** (*painting, laughter*)
5. Nouns that refer to metals: **das Gold, das Silber** (*gold, silver*)
6. Nouns that end in **-ment: das Regiment, das Experiment** (*regiment, experiment*)
7. Most nouns that form their plural by (umlaut) + er: **das Haus (die Häuser), das Kind (die Kinder)** (*house, child*)
8. Nouns that end in **-tel, -tum,** and **-um: das Viertel, das Königtum, das Gymnasium** (*quarter, monarchy, prep school*)

Exercise 1

Identify the gender of the following nouns by supplying the missing definite article (**der, die,** or **das**).

1. _der_ Apfel
2. _der_ Bruder
3. _die_ Übung
4. _das_ Gesetz
5. _die_ Reise
6. _das_ Album
7. _die_ Krankheit
8. _der_ Eisen
9. _die_ Schwester
10. _das_ Eigentum
11. _das_ Appartement
12. _der_ Qualität
13. _der_ Eleganz

14. <u>der</u> Onkel

15. _____ Explosion

16. <u>die</u> Eigenschaft

17. <u>das</u> Schwimmen

18. _____ Lehre

19. <u>der</u> Schlag

20. _____ Ereignis

21. <u>die</u> Donau

22. <u>das</u> Museum

23. <u>der</u> Honig

24. <u>der</u> Sozialismus

25. <u>der</u> Regen

Exercise 2

Provide nouns that exemplify the characteristics shown in parentheses. For example:

      (-ung)   die *Untersuchung*

  1. (-nis)   das _____

  2. (-heit)   die _____

  3. (Ge-)   das _____

  4. (-e)   die _____

  5. (-um)   das _____

  6. (-er)   der _____

  7. (-el)   der _____

  8. (-keit)   die _____

  9. (-ling)   der _____

10. (-ig)   der _____

11. (-tum)   das _____

12. (-in)   die _____

13. (-en)   der _____

14. (-lein)   das _____

15. (-ion)   die _____

Exercise 3

Rewrite the following plural nouns as singular nouns. Provide the appropriate definite article.

1. die Tannen _____
2. die Flüsse _____
3. die Bücher _____
4. die Übungen _____
5. die Zeiten _____
6. die Bäume _____
7. die Arme _____
8. die Kinder _____
9. die Freundinnen _____
10. die Könige _____
11. die Zeitungen _____
12. die Länder _____
13. die Bälle _____
14. die Finger _____
15. die Mädchen _____

Exercise 4

Rewrite the following singular nouns as plural nouns.

1. der Mantel   die _____
2. die Frau   die _____
3. das Haus   die _____
4. das Fräulein   die _____
5. die Küste   die _____
6. das Schwimmen   die _____
7. der Wagen   die _____
8. der Lehrer   die _____
9. die Richterin   die _____
10. der Bleistift   die _____

11. der Platz   die _____

12. die Sitte   die _____

13. das Lachen   die _____

14. die Nase   die _____

15. der Lautsprecher die _____

Exercise 5

1. List ten masculine nouns, five of which refer to males and five of which are inanimate objects.

male   **object**

der _____   der _____

der _____   der _____

der _____   der _____

der _____   der _____

der _____   der _____

2. List ten feminine nouns, five of which refer to females and five of which are inanimate objects.

female   **object**

die _____   die _____

die _____   die _____

die _____   die _____

die _____   die _____

die _____   die _____

3. List ten neuter nouns, five of which refer to living persons or things and five of which are inanimate objects.

living thing   **object**

das _____   das _____

das _____   das _____

das _____   das _____

das _____   das _____

das _____   das _____

2

Forming Plurals

Singular nouns are those that describe one person or object: *a boy, a girl, my house, their teacher, our party.* Plural nouns describe more than one person or object: *five boys, the women, a few windows, your parents, these flowers.* In English, most nouns become plural by adding an *-s.* Some English nouns form their plural in other ways, such as *one woman* becomes *ten women, a mouse* becomes *the mice.*

A few German nouns form their plural by adding an -s like English. These nouns tend to be foreign words, such as:

singular	plural	English
das Auto	die Autos	*cars*
das Baby	die Babys	*babies*
das Kino	die Kinos	*movie theaters*
der Streik	die Streiks	*strikes (by workers)*
das Hotel	die Hotels	*hotels*
der Park	die Parks	*parks*

Most German nouns, however, form their plural in other ways. Although there are general rules to follow when forming the plural of a German noun, it is best to consult a dictionary for complete accuracy. Masculine nouns ending in **-er**, **-en**, or **-el** do not require an ending to form the plural. But some require the addition of an umlaut.

no umlaut required

der Lehrer	die Lehrer	*teachers*
der Wagen	die Wagen	*cars*
der Onkel	die Onkel	*uncles*

umlaut required

der Vater	die Väter	*fathers*
der Garten	die Gärten	*gardens*
der Mantel	die Mäntel	*coats*

Other masculine nouns add an **-e** to form the plural. Some of these also require an umlaut.

no umlaut required

der Arm	die Arme	*arms*
der Tisch	die Tische	*tables*
der Hund	die Hunde	*dogs*

umlaut required

der Sohn	die Söhne	*sons*
der Stuhl	die Stühle	*chairs*
der Kopf	die Köpfe	*heads*

Some masculine nouns *traditionally* form their plural with the addition of **-en**. Those masculine nouns that end in **-e** in the singular as well as those that are foreign words with the accent on the last syllable also form their plural by adding **-(e)n**.

traditional -*en* plural

der Bär	die Bären	*bears*
der Mensch	die Menschen	*people*
der Held	die Helden	*heroes*

words ending in -*e* in the singular

der Junge	die Jungen	*boys*
der Affe	die Affen	*apes*
der Glaube/der Glauben	die Glauben	*beliefs, faith*

foreign words with accent on last syllable

der Student	die Studenten	*students*
der Soldat	die Soldaten	*soldiers*
der Komponist	die Komponisten	*composers*

A few masculine nouns form their plural by adding **-er**. Many also require an umlaut.

der Geist	die Geister	*spirits*
der Gott	die Götter	*gods*
der Mann	die Männer	*men*
der Wald	die Wälder	*woods*

Feminine nouns in the plural generally end in **-n** or **-en**.

die Frau	die Frauen	*women*
die Arbeit	die Arbeiten	*jobs, labors*
die Regel	die Regeln	*rules*
die Lampe	die Lampen	*lamps*
die Sitte	die Sitten	*customs, habits*
die Schule	die Schulen	*schools*

But a small group of feminine nouns forms its plural by adding **-e** and an umlaut.

die Bank	die Bänke	*benches*
die Hand	die Hände	*hands*
die Luft	die Lüfte	*airs*
die Nacht	die Nächte	*nights*
die Kuh	die Kühe	*cows*
die Stadt	die Städte	*cities*

A few feminine nouns that end in **-er** in the singular form their plural by an umlaut or the addition of an **-n**.

die Mutter	die Mütter	*mothers*
die Tochter	die Töchter	*daughters*
die Schwester	die Schwestern	*sisters*

Feminine nouns having the suffix **-in** form their plural by adding **-nen**.

| die Ärztin | die Ärztinnen | *physicians* |
| die Studentin | die Studentinnen | *students* |

Neuter nouns that are diminutives with the suffix **-chen** or **-lein** do not require an ending to form the plural.

| das Mädchen | die Mädchen | *girls* |
| das Röslein | die Röslein | *little roses* |

This is also true of neuter nouns that end in **-er**, **-en**, or **-el**. However, infinitives, which end in **-en** and are used as nouns, are always neuter. But they do not form plurals.

das Messer	die Messer	*knives*
das Mädel	die Mädel	*girls*
das Kissen	die Kissen	*pillows*
das Einkommen (*an infinitive, no plural*)		*income*

A large group of neuter nouns forms the plural by adding -er. This plural form requires an umlaut when an umlaut vowel (**a, o, u**) is present in the noun.

no umlaut vowel

das Kind	die Kinder	*children*
das Ei	die Eier	*eggs*
das Rind	die Rinder	*cattle*

umlaut vowel

das Haus	die Häuser	*houses*
das Buch	die Bücher	*books*
das Dorf	die Dörfer	*villages*

Another large group of neuter nouns adds the ending -e to form the plural.

das Boot	die Boote	*boats*
das Jahr	die Jahre	*years*
das Haar	die Haare	*hairs* or *hair*
das Geschäft	die Geschäfte	*businesses*
das Gedicht	die Gedichte	*poems*
das Klavier	die Klaviere	*pianos*

All plurals, no matter from what gender they are derived, use the definite article **die**.

Exercise 6

Rewrite the following masculine nouns as plural nouns.

1. der Vogel _____

2. der Spiegel _____

3. der Gärtner _____

4. der Brief _____

5. der Lehrling _____

 6. der Physiker _____

 7. der Laden _____

 8. der Käfig _____

 9. der Hammer _____

10. der Schuh _____

Exercise 7

Rewrite the following feminine nouns as plural nouns.

 1. die Maus _____

 2. die Schülerin _____

 3. die Kasse _____

 4. die Landkarte _____

 5. die Hausarbeit _____

 6. die Macht _____

 7. die Wurst _____

 8. die Schwester _____

 9. die Tafel _____

10. die Tanne _____

Exercise 8

Rewrite the following neuter nouns as plural nouns.

 1. das Heft _____

 2. das Wort _____

 3. das Hotel _____

 4. das Kind _____

 5. das Rad _____

 6. das Gesicht _____

 7. das Bein _____

 8. das Blatt _____

9. das Büchlein _____

10. das Zimmer _____

Exercise 9

Rewrite the following plural nouns as singular nouns. Provide the appropriate definite article to identify the gender of the noun.

1. die Schulen _____

2. die Lehrer _____

3. die Kinos _____

4. die Hütten _____

5. die Bände _____

6. die Würstchen _____

7. die Eulen _____

8. die Namen _____

9. die Würmer _____

10. die Straßen _____

11. die Sachen _____

12. die Läden _____

13. die Wölfe _____

14. die Schweine _____

15. die Franzosen _____

Exercise 10

In the space provided, write the letter **P** if the noun shown is plural. Write the letter **S** if the noun shown is singular. Write the letter **B** if the noun can be either plural or singular.

1. _____ Leute

2. _____ Häuser

3. _____ Brille

4. _____ Haar

5. _____ Nase

6. _____ Wanderer

7. _____ Rechtsanwälte

8. _____ Hunde

9. _____ Katze

10. _____ Dichterinnen

11. _____ Lehrer

12. _____ Wagen

13. _____ Anzug

14. _____ Spielzeug

15. _____ Fenster

16. _____ Lehrlinge

17. _____ Mädchen

18. _____ Bäume

19. _____ Touristin

20. _____ Bilder

21. _____ Büchlein

22. _____ Bein

23. _____ Soldaten

24. _____ Mäntel

25. _____ Städte

3

Pronouns

In German, pronouns must have the same gender as the noun they replace. But remember that gender is determined not by reference to males, females, or inanimate objects but rather by the structure of the noun. Since some German masculine nouns are inanimate objects, the German masculine pronoun can mean *it* when referring to something inanimate, or it can mean *he* when referring to a male. The same thing occurs with feminine and neuter pronouns. Look at the following examples for masculine, feminine, neuter, and plural nouns and their respective pronouns.

masculine noun		**masculine pronoun**	
der Lehrer	*teacher*	er	*he*
der Gärtner	*gardener*	er	*he*
der Wald	*forest*	er	*it*
der Bleistift	*pencil*	er	*it*

feminine noun		**feminine pronoun**	
die Tante	*aunt*	sie	*she*
die Dame	*lady*	sie	*she*
die Zeitung	*newspaper*	sie	*it*
die Vase	*vase*	sie	*it*

neuter noun		**neuter pronoun**	
das Kind	*child*	es	*he* or *she*
das Mädchen	*girl*	es	*she*
das Land	*country*	es	*it*
das Bild	*picture*	es	*it*

plural noun		**plural pronoun**	
die Kinder	*children*	sie	*they*
die Leute	*people*	sie	*they*
die Häuser	*houses*	sie	*they*
die Blumen	*flowers*	sie	*they*

Besides the third-person pronouns that substitute for nouns (**er, sie, es,** and plural **sie**), there are also first-person, second-person informal, and second-person formal pronouns.

singular pronoun		plural pronoun	
ich	*I*	wir	*we*
du	*you* informal	ihr	*you* informal
Sie	*you* formal	Sie	*you* formal

There is another third-person singular pronoun: **man**. This pronoun is used where English uses *one* or *you* when referring to people in general. Often **man** is used where the general terms *people* or *they* are said.

Hier spricht man nur Deutsch.	*One only speaks German here.*
Man hat von dort eine gute Aussicht.	*You have a good view from there.*
Man fährt in Europa oft mit dem Fahrrad.	*People often use a bike in Europe.*
Hat man Ihnen das nicht mitgeteilt?	*Didn't they tell you about that?*

There are two important indefinite pronouns. They are **jemand** (*someone*) and **niemand** (*no one*). They are the replacements for unknown or unspecified persons.

Ich habe jemand an der Ecke gesehen.	*I saw someone on the corner.*
Niemand kann es verstehen.	*No one can understand it.*

Exercise 11

In the space provided, write the pronoun that would be a substitute for the noun shown. Use **er, sie s., es,** or **sie pl.**

1. Lehrerin   Sie s.
2. Wald _____
3. Haus   es
4. Kinder   sie pl.
5. Schule   sie
6. Kino   es
7. Mutter   sie s.
8. Mütter   Sie pl.
9. Keller   er
10. Kellner   er

Exercise 12

In the space provided, give the pronoun that appropriately replaces the noun or phrase in bold print. For example:

Der Mann hat uns geholfen. _Er_

1. **Meine Schwester** wohnt jetzt in der Hauptstadt. Sie
2. Wo sind **die Kinder**? sie
3. **Viele Leute** wollen eine Deutschlandreise machen. Sie
4. **Mein Bruder und ich** sind Mitglieder der Fußballmannschaft. Wir
5. Ist **das Mädchen** eine Bekannte von dir? es
6. **Diese Bücher** sind sehr interessant. _____
7. **Die Frauen** haben es von einem Fremden gehört. _____
8. **Der Schüler** lernt oft dumme Sachen. _____
9. Ist **Ihr Volkswagen** neu? _____
10. **Das Land, das ich am meisten liebe,** ist meine Heimat. _____
11. **Die neue Wohnung** ist ziemlich klein. _____
12. Warum ist **diese Tür** zu? _____
13. **Der Dieb** behauptete, den Ring auf der Straße gefunden zu haben. _____
14. **Dieser rote Apfel** ist für dich. _____
15. **Meine Freunde und ich** fahren morgen in die Stadt. _____

Exercise 13

Replace the pronoun in bold print with any appropriate noun. For example:

Sie tanzt gut. _**Meine Mutter** tanzt gut._

1. **Er** ist alt aber fährt gut.

_____

2. Ist **er** ein guter Freund von euch?

_____

3. **Sie** spielen gern Schach.

_____

4. Wo wird **sie** wohnen?

_____

5. **Es** ist nur sechs Jahre alt und kann schon lesen und schreiben.

_____

6. **Sie** kann Englisch und Arabisch.

_____

7. Liegt **es** auf dem Tisch?

_____

8. **Er** hat sein Fahrrad verkaufen müssen.

_____

9. **Es** glaubt mir nicht.

_____

10. Ist **sie** kaputt?

_____

11. Wo ist **es**?

_____

12. **Sie** will uns nicht stören.

_____

13. **Wir** wohnen in der Goethestraße.

_____

14. Ist **sie** grün?

_____

15. **Er** schläft in einer Ecke der Küche.

_____

Exercise 14

Change the subject of each sentence to the pronoun **man**. For example:

> Du sollst nicht schreien.   _Man soll nicht schreien._

1. Ich kann nicht jedem gefallen.

_____

2. In unserem Klassenzimmer sprechen wir nur Deutsch.

_____

3. Was du versprichst, das musst du halten.

_____

4. Hat jemand an die Tür geklopft?

_____

5. Warum müssen Sie so lange warten?

_____

6. Bei grün dürfen wir über die Straße gehen.

_____

7. Damals wart ihr großzügiger.

_____

8. Sein Vater hat sie davor gewarnt.

_____

9. Die Jungen sollen nicht fluchen.

_____

10. Meine Großmutter wird es schnell vergessen.

_____

11. Ihr müsst im Wartesaal warten.

_____

12. Ich soll nicht vergessen.

_____

13. Jemand steht an der Tür und weint.

_____

14. Während der Krise waren sie hoffnungslos.

_____

15. Du darfst nicht lachen.

_____

Exercise 15

Change the subject of each sentence to **jemand** and then to **niemand**. For example:

Peter steht an der Tür.   _Jemand steht an der Tür._   _Niemand steht an der Tür._

1. Seine Schwester hat das Geld gefunden.

_____

_____

2. Ist mein Bruder da?

_____

_____

3. Die Lehrerinnen haben etwas zu sagen.

_____

_____

4. Der alte Herr hat den roten Sportwagen gekauft.

_____

_____

5. Ich werde dir helfen.

_____

_____

6. Frau Schneider hat das Geld verloren.

_____

_____

7. Heute kommen unsere Verwandten zu Besuch.

_____

_____

8. Meine Freunde warten an der Ecke.

_____

_____

4

Nominative Case

The nominative case identifies the subject of a sentence or a predicate nominative. The subject is the noun or pronoun that is carrying out the action of the verb in the sentence. For example:

Johann küsst Ingrid.	*Johann kisses Ingrid.*	The subject is **Johann**.
Wir finden das Geld.	*We find the money.*	The subject is **wir**.

A predicate nominative is the noun that follows a verb like **sein** (*to be*) or **werden** (*to become*). There is a method for determining whether a word is being used as a predicate nominative. If the positions of the subject of the sentence and the presumed predicate nominative of the sentence can be switched and still make sense, the noun that follows **sein** or **werden** is undoubtedly a predicate nominative. For example:

In dieser Schule ist ein Lehrer auch ein Studienberater.   *In this school, a teacher is also a counselor.*

or

In dieser Schule ist ein Studienberater auch ein Lehrer.   *In this school, a counselor is also a teacher.*

The nominative forms for the masculine, feminine, neuter, and plural are illustrated below with the definite article (**der, die, das**), indefinite article (**ein, eine**), and **kein**.

masculine	feminine	neuter	plural
der Junge	die Katze	das Pferd	die Kinder *(boy, cat, horse, children)*
ein Junge	eine Katze	ein Pferd	Kinder*
kein Junge	keine Katze	kein Pferd	keine Kinder

*The indefinite article does not exist in the plural. Using the plural noun alone derives the indefinite meaning.

Subject of the sentence and verbs

When a nominative noun or pronoun is the subject of a sentence, it determines what kind of conjugational ending the verb needs. All nouns require either a singular or plural third-person verb ending, depending upon whether the noun is singular or plural. Third-person pronouns have the same verb endings as nouns. First- and second-person pronouns require their own conjugational endings. Some examples with the verbs **kennen** and **sein** in the present tense follow.

singular nouns

der Mann kennt	der Mann ist	*the man knows, the man is*
die Frau kennt	die Frau ist	*the woman knows, the woman is*

plural nouns

die Kinder kennen	die Kinder sind	*the children know, the children are*
die Leute kennen	die Leute sind	*the people know, the people are*

singular pronouns

first person	ich kenne	ich bin	*I know, I am*
second person	du kennst	du bist	*you know, you are*
third person	er kennt	er ist	*he knows, he is*
third person	sie kennt	sie ist	*she knows, she is*
third person	es kennt	es ist	*it knows, it is*

plural pronouns

first person	wir kennen	wir sind	*we know, we are*
second person	ihr kennt	ihr seid	*you know, you are*
second person	Sie kennen	Sie sind	*you know, you are*
third person	sie kennen	sie sind	*they know, they are*

As verbs change, the endings required for the nouns and pronouns stay, for the most part, the same.

der Mann kennt, der Mann singt, der Mann hat (*sings, has*)
die Leute kennen, die Leute warten, die Leute tun (*wait, do*)
ich kenne, ich halte, ich komme (*hold, come*)
du kennst, du willst, du machst (*want, make*)

er kennt, er sagt, er spricht (*says, speaks*)

sie kennt, sie trägt, sie versteht (*carries, understands*)

es kennt, es bleibt, es riecht (*remains, smells*)

wir kennen, wir hören, wir trinken (*hear, drink*)

ihr kennt, ihr lacht, ihr geht (*laugh, go*)

Sie kennen, Sie senden, Sie kaufen (*send, buy*)

sie kennen, sie weinen, sie laufen (*cry, run*)

Questions

When asking a question that can be answered with either **ja** or **nein** (*yes* or *no*), the subject of the sentence (the nominative) becomes the second element in the sentence. The conjugated verb precedes the subject.

Ist **dein Vater** wieder gesund?	*Is your father well again?*
Ja, mein Vater ist wieder gesund.	*Yes, my father is well again.*
Wohnen **Sie** in Berlin?	*Do you live in Berlin?*
Nein, ich wohne in München.	*No, I live in Munich.*

If the question begins with an interrogative word, the verb will again precede the subject.

Wann kommt **der nächste Zug**?	*When does the next train arrive?*
Wie lange dauert **der Film**?	*How long does the movie last?*

However, if the subject is the interrogative word **wer** or **was**, it will stand in front of the conjugated verb.

Wer hat diese Blumen gekauft?	*Who bought these flowers?*
Was ist passiert?	*What has happened?*

The conjugated verb will also precede the subject when some element other than the subject begins the sentence. For example:

Heute fahren **wir** nach Goslar.	*We're driving to Goslar today.*
Als Martin in Amerika wohnte, sprach **er** kein Englisch.	*When Martin lived in America, he didn't speak any English.*

Exercise 16

In the blank provided, write **S** if the word or phrase in bold print is the subject of the sentence. Write **P** if the word or phrase in bold print is the predicate nominative. Write **N** if the word or phrase is neither the subject nor the predicate nominative. For example:

    _S_ **Die Männer** spielen Karten.

1. _____ Meine Eltern kaufen **ein neues Haus**.

2. _____ Wann haben **Sie** diesen Roman gelesen?

3. _____ **Meine Verwandten** wohnen jetzt in Bremen.

4. _____ Seine Schwester will **Ärztin** werden.

5. _____ Er ist **kein Genie**.

6. _____ Dürfen **die Gäste** jetzt ein Stück Kuchen haben?

7. _____ Diese Mädchen sind alle **Tänzerinnen**.

8. _____ **Sie** spricht nicht nur Deutsch, sondern auch Italienisch.

9. _____ Ich brauche **es** für ein Experiment.

10. _____ Wo hast **du** diese Münzen gefunden?

Exercise 17

Rewrite the following sentences as questions that could be answered **ja** or **nein**. For example:

    Mein Bruder spielte Tennis.   _Spielte dein Bruder Tennis?_

1. Meine Eltern haben sehr lange darauf gewartet.

_____

2. Onkel Franz war in Dänemark.

_____

3. Ich habe mit meinem Professor gesprochen.

_____

4. Die junge Krankenschwester ist eine Bekannte von ihm.

_____

5. Hamburg liegt an der Elbe.

_____

6. Die Brüder helfen einander.

_____

7. Das neue Gebäude in der Hauptstraße ist ein Museum.

_____

8. Die Brücke ist ziemlich weit von hier.

_____

9. Das versteht er nicht.

_____

10. Gestern waren sie noch in Paris.

_____

Exercise 18

Write the pronoun that appropriately replaces the noun or phrase in bold print. For example:

        Die Kinder bleiben zu Hause. _Sie_

1. **Der Weihnachtsmann** wird uns bald besuchen. _____

2. **Hamburg und Bremen** sind Häfen. _____

3. **Richard Wagner** wurde 1883 in Bayreuth begraben. _____

4. **Die Gäste** erinnern sich nicht daran. _____

5. Wo hat **dein Vater** so einen alten Wagen gekauft? _____

6. Wird **die ganze Mannschaft** dorthin fahren? _____

7. **Kein Mensch** versteht seine neue Theorie. _____

8. **Die Einwohner des Dorfes** versuchten zu fliehen. _____

9. Kann **das kleine Mädchen** schon lesen und schreiben? _____

10. **Der Brief** ist von einem Freund in Asien. _____

11. **Felix und ich** werden Handball spielen. _____

12. Ist **deine Tante** noch im Krankenhaus? _____

13. **Der Fernseher** ist kaputt. _____

14. Wegen des Urlaubs haben **die Studenten** viel versäumt. _____

15. **Das Mädchen** kennt ihn nicht. _____

Exercise 19

Determine the gender of each of the following nouns. Then fill in the blank with the pronoun **er** if the noun is masculine, with **sie** if it is feminine, with **es** if it is neuter, and **sie pl.** if it is plural.

1. _____ Haus
2. _____ Leute
3. _____ Schule
4. _____ Schülerin
5. _____ Lampen
6. _____ Stuhl
7. _____ Auto
8. _____ Kindergarten
9. _____ Papier
10. _____ Brille
11. _____ Tisch
12. _____ Länder
13. _____ Übung
14. _____ Wohnzimmer
15. _____ Mädchen
16. _____ Büchlein
17. _____ Spiegel
18. _____ Löwe
19. _____ Uhr
20. _____ Flugzeuge

Exercise 20

Write each noun in the nominative case with its definite article, indefinite article, and **kein**. For example:

Haus   *das Haus, ein Haus, kein Haus*

1. Kinder _____
2. Buch _____

3. Mensch _____

4. Tische _____

5. Dame _____

6. Schule _____

7. Wecker _____

8. Fluss _____

9. Männer _____

10. Theater _____

11. Übungen _____

12. Straße _____

13. Arm _____

14. Stuhl _____

15. Stück _____

Accusative Case

The accusative case requires a declensional change with masculine nouns and most pronouns. Compare the differences between the nominative case and the accusative case with a masculine noun, a feminine noun, a neuter noun, and a plural noun with a definite article (**der, die, das**), an indefinite article (**ein, eine**), and **kein**.

nominative

masculine	feminine	neuter	plural	
der Hund	die Katze	das Buch	die Bilder	*(dog, cat, book, pictures)*
ein Hund	eine Katze	ein Buch	Bilder	
kein Hund	keine Katze	kein Buch	keine Bilder	

accusative

masculine	feminine	neuter	plural
den Hund	die Katze	das Buch	die Bilder
einen Hund	eine Katze	ein Buch	Bilder
keinen Hund	keine Katze	kein Buch	keine Bilder

Most pronouns make a change from the nominative case to the accusative case.

nominative	accusative	
ich	mich	*I, me*
du	dich	*you, you*
er	ihn	*he, him*
sie s.	sie s.	*she, her*
es	es	*it, it*
wir	uns	*we, us*
ihr	euch	*you, you (plural informal)*
Sie	Sie	*you, you (singular or plural formal)*
sie pl.	sie pl.	*they, them*

niemand	niemand/niemanden	*no one*
jemand	jemand/jemanden	*someone*

The accusative case in German has three primary functions:

1. It identifies the direct object in a sentence.
2. It identifies the object of an accusative preposition.
3. It identifies certain time expressions.

Direct objects

Direct objects in English and German are identical. In English, you can ask *whom* or *what* of the verb in the sentence. The answer will be the direct object. It works the same way in German.

Mein Vater besucht einen Freund.	*My father visits a friend.*
(*Whom does my father visit?*)	The direct object is **einen Freund**.
Er lernt Deutsch.	*He is learning German.*
(*What is he learning?*)	The direct object is **Deutsch**.

Let's look at a variety of sample sentences that contain accusative pronouns.

Kennst du **mich** nicht?	*Don't you know me?*
Niemand kann **dich** verstehen.	*No one can understand you.*
Der Lehrer tadelt **ihn**.	*The teacher criticizes him.*
Herr Bauer hat **sie** gegrüsst.	*Mr. Bauer said hello to her.*
Meine Schwester hängt **es** an die Wand.	*My sister hangs it on the wall.*
Unsere Eltern lieben **uns** sehr.	*Our parents love us a lot.*
Eure Mutter hat **euch** gut erzogen.	*Your mother has raised you well.*
Professor Schmidt wird **Sie** jetzt prüfen.	*Professor Schmidt will quiz you now.*
Wer hat **sie** gekauft?	*Who bought them?*

Accusative prepositions

Also use the accusative case with noun or pronoun objects of accusative prepositions. The accusative prepositions are:

bis	*till, until, as far as*
durch	*through, across*
entlang	*along(side), down* (*the middle*)
für	*for*
gegen	*against*
ohne	*without*
um	*around, at* (*time on a clock*)
wider	*against, contrary to* (usually poetical)

The preposition **bis** is never followed by an article or other determiner. Therefore, it tends to be used with proper nouns. In all other instances, **bis** combines with other prepositions. For example, with proper nouns:

Wir fahren nur **bis** Goslar.	*We're only traveling as far as Goslar.*
Ich bleibe **bis** nächsten Freitag.	*I'm staying until next Friday.*

Compare with **bis** combined with other prepositions:

Sie spazieren **bis zum** Stadtpark.	*They're strolling as far as the city park.*
Ich ging mit ihr **bis an** das Ende der Straße.	*I went with her up to the end of the street.*
Der Weg führte **bis ins** Tal.	*The lane led as far as the valley.*

The preposition **entlang** is also a special case. It always follows the object in the accusative prepositional phrase.

Die Feiernden gingen die Straße **entlang**.	*The revelers went down the street.*
Dieser Weg führt den Bach **entlang**.	*This path goes along the brook.*

Entlang is sometimes combined with the preposition **an**. For example:

Dieser Weg führt **am** Fluss **entlang**.	*This path goes along the river.*

Let's look at some sample sentences with the other accusative prepositions.

Ein Mann schwimmt **durch** den Fluss.	*A man is swimming across the river.*
Ich habe ein Geschenk **für** dich.	*I have a gift for you.*

Der Junge versucht **gegen** den Strom zu schwimmen.	*The boy is trying to swim against the current.*
Ich kann nicht **ohne** sie leben.	*I can't live without her.*
Die Ernte ist **wider** alles Erwarten gut gewesen.	*The harvest was good contrary to all expectations.*
Die Planeten bewegen sich **um** die Sonne.	*The planets move around the sun.*

When a pronoun that refers to an inanimate object is used in a prepositional phrase, a *prepositional adverb* is formed in place of the preposition followed by the pronoun. For example:

prepositional adverbs

(für) + ihn	=	dafür	*for it*
(durch) + sie	=	dadurch	*through it*
(um) + es	=	darum	*around it*

If the preposition begins with a vowel, the letter **r** is added to the prefix, for example, **da-**: **da<u>r</u>um**.

Expressions of time

Adverbial phrases that express time and tell *when* something occurs at a particular point in time appear in the accusative case.

| Ich habe sie **letzte Woche** besucht. | *I visited them last week.* |
| Er wird **nächsten Sonntag** vorbeikommen. | *He'll drop by next Sunday.* |

If the adverbial phrase describes a longer period of time, the accusative case is used again, but the word **lang** is often placed at the end of the adverbial phrase. The English translation of such a phrase often begins with *for*.

| Wir blieben **einen Monat (lang)** in der Schweiz. | *We stayed in Switzerland for a month.* |
| Der Kranke muss **die ganze Woche (lang)** im Bett liegen. | *The patient has to stay in bed the whole week.* |

Wer and *was*

The interrogative pronouns **wer** and **was** become **wen** and **was** in the accusative case. Both can be used as direct objects, but only **wen** can follow a preposition as you will see later. Let's look at some examples with direct objects.

direct objects

Wen siehst du da?	*Whom do you see there?*
Was haben Sie gefunden?	*What did you find?*

As pointed out earlier, **wer** and **was** are affected by prepositions. Take special note of the pronoun **was**, which forms a *prepositional adverb*.

accusative prepositions

Für wen ist dieser Brief?	*For whom is this letter?*
Gegen wen haben sie gekämpft?	*Against whom did they fight?*

prepositional adverbs

(für) + was	=	**wofür?**	*for what?*
(durch) + was	=	**wodurch?**	*through what?*

If the preposition begins with a vowel, the letter **r** is added to the prefix, for example, **wo-: worum** (*around what*).

Exercise 21

In the blank provided, write the letter **S** if the word or phrase in bold print is the subject of the sentence. Write the letters **DO** in the blank if the word or phrase in bold print is the direct object. For example:

    ___*DO*___ Ich kaufe **einen Mantel**.

1. ___S___ Wo wohnen **Ihre Großeltern**?
2. ___S___ Morgen fährt **die ganze Familie** nach Wien.
3. ___DO___ Haben Sie **Herrn Schneider** schon kennen gelernt?
4. ___DO___ Ich lese gern **diese Zeitung**.
5. ___DO___ Martin liebt **sie** nicht.

6. _DO_ **Wen** haben Monika und Werner besucht?

7. _S_ In der Armee hat **er** Deutsch und Italienisch gelernt.

8. _DO_ Wann hast du **diese Blumen** bekommen?

9. _____ Der Ausländer versteht **jedes Wort**.

10. _____ Ich habe **dich** gestern in der Bibliothek gesehen.

Exercise 22

Rewrite each of the following sentences as a question, appropriately changing the word or phrase in bold print to either **wer**, **wen**, or **was**. For example:

Er ist ein Freund von Benno. *Wer ist ein Freund von Benno?*

1. **Die Touristen** durchziehen die Stadt.

_____

2. Das Kind schreibt **einen langen Brief.**

_____

3. Die junge Mutter legte **das Baby** aufs Bett.

_____

4. Man baut **ein großes Haus** in der Schillerstraße.

_____

5. Ich trinke gern **Limonade.**

_____

6. **Der Kellner** bringt uns Würstchen und Kartoffeln.

_____

7. **Eine Dichterin** hat ein paar neue Gedichte geschrieben.

_____

8. Die Gäste möchten **Fleisch und Gemüse** essen.

_____

9. Ich habe drei alte Briefmarken für **dich.**

_____

10. Herr Schäfer bäckt **Kuchen und Brot.**

_____

11. **Der Junge** hat ein Stein ins Fenster geworfen.

_____

12. Seine Tochter fängt **den Ball** mit einer Hand.

_____

13. Früher stand **ein kleiner Laden** an dieser Ecke.

_____

14. Die Studenten wollen **ein Glas Bier** trinken.

_____

15. Ihr Vater hat gegen **den Bürgermeister** gesprochen.

_____

Exercise 23

Rewrite each sentence, replacing the pronouns in bold print with any appropriate noun. For example:

    Sie hat **ihn** gefunden.   *Sie hat **den Hund** gefunden.*

1. Haben Sie **sie** verloren?

_____

2. Meine Tante stellte **ihn** auf den Tisch.

_____

3. Ich muss **sie** unterschreiben.

_____

4. Die Läufer erreichen **es**.

_____

5. Sie hat **es** in der Bibliothek gelesen.

_____

6. Kennst du **sie** nicht?

_____

7. Onkel Peter wird **uns** bald besuchen.

_____

8. Das Hochwasser hat **sie** zerstört.

_____

9. Ich verstehe **ihn** überhaupt nicht.

_____

10. Die Kinder wollen **sie** trinken.

_____

11. Herr Bauer wird **es** braten.

_____

12. Haben Sie **sie** angerufen?

_____

13. Ich möchte **ihn** vorstellen.

_____

14. Mein Bruder hat **ihn** noch nicht gekauft.

_____

15. Die jungen Eltern lieben **es** sehr.

_____

Exercise 24

Rewrite each prepositional phrase, changing the noun to a pronoun. Watch for prepositional adverbs. For example:

       ohne den Mann   *ohne ihn*

1. für meine Mutter _____

2. gegen den Rechtsanwalt _____

3. gegen die Wand _____

4. um die Ecke _____

5. durch einen Tunnel _____

6. ohne seine Geschwister _____

7. um das Kind _____

8. für seine Briefe _____

9. ohne Martin _____

10. durch das Fenster _____

Exercise 25

Complete the following accusative prepositional phrases with any appropriate word or phrase. For example:

Ich habe ein Geschenk für *deine Tochter.*

1. Wir fahren gerade durch _____ .

2. Wie viel Uhr ist es? Um _____ muss ich nach Hause gehen.

3. Können Sie bis _____ bleiben?

4. Ich habe wirklich nichts gegen _____ .

5. Erik spielt Klavier für _____ .

6. Warum ist dein Freund ohne _____ gekommen?

7. Ein Vogel flog durch _____ .

8. Der arme Mann sorgt und arbeitet für _____ .

9. Wir gehen _____ entlang.

10. Alle kämpfen gegen _____ .

Exercise 26

Fill in the blank with the time expression in parentheses. For example:

(der ganze Tag) Ich war *den ganzen Tag* zu Hause.

1. (eine Woche lang) Bleibst du _____ in Paris?

2. (letzter Montag) Sie kam _____ vorbei.

3. (zwei Tage) Er ist jede Woche _____ in der Hauptstadt.

4. (dieses Jahr) Wir bleiben _____ in Bremen.

5. (ein Augenblick) Ich begegnete ihr _____ zuvor.

6. (nächster Samstag) Wir fahren _____ nach Ulm.

7. (ein Monat lang) Er arbeitete _____ in einer Fabrik.

8. (ein paar Monate) Waren Sie _____ in Italien?

9. (der ganze Abend) Benno hat _____ auf dem Sofa geschlafen.

10. (letzte Woche) Wir haben ihn _____ gesehen.

6

Dative Case

Both nouns and pronouns make changes when they are in the dative case. Let's look at the dative case of some example nouns with the definite article (**der, die, das**), the indefinite article (**ein, eine**), and **kein**.

masculine	feminine	neuter	plural
dem Hund	der Tante	dem Haus	den Häusern
einem Hund	einer Tante	einem Haus	Häusern
keinem Hund	keiner Tante	keinem Haus	keinen Häusern

Notice that nouns in the dative plural must have an **-n** ending: **mit die Kinder** becomes **mit den Kinder̲n**.

The personal pronouns change from nominative to dative as follows:

nominative	dative
ich	mir
du	dir
er	ihm
sie	ihr
es	ihm
wir	uns
ihr	euch
Sie	Ihnen
sie	ihnen
wer	wem
jemand	jemand/jemandem
niemand	niemand/niemandem

The dative case is used in four specific ways:

1. It identifies the indirect object of a sentence.
2. It identifies the object of a dative verb.
3. It identifies the object of a dative preposition.
4. It identifies the object of an impersonal expression.

Indirect objects

Indirect objects function similarly in both English and German. To identify the indirect object in an English sentence, ask *to whom* or *for whom* of the verb. The answer will be the indirect object. It works the same way in German.

Johann gibt seinem Freund 10 Euro.	*Johann gives his friend 10 euros.*
Wem gibt Johann 10 Euro?	The indirect object is **seinem Freund**.
Ich kaufte meiner Mutter Blumen.	*I bought my mother flowers.*
Wem kaufte ich Blumen?	The indirect object is **meiner Mutter**.

Consider the following difference in the use of indirect objects in English and German. English tends to use a preposition (*to* or *for*) when forming the question about the indirect object. German asks the question with the dative pronoun **wem**. For example:

Wem gibst du das Geld?	*To whom are you giving the money?*
Wem hat er den Kuchen gekauft?	*For whom did he buy the cake?*

Dative verbs

There are many dative verbs. Here are some of the most commonly used ones.

begegnen	*meet, encounter*
danken	*thank*
dienen	*serve*
drohen	*threaten*
folgen	*follow*
gefallen	*please, like*
gehören	*belong to*
glauben	*believe*
helfen	*help*
raten	*advise*
schaden	*harm*
vertrauen	*trust*

Let's look at some example sentences with dative verbs.

Ich begegnete **einem alten Freund** in Bonn.	*I met an old friend in Bonn.*
Karin hat **mir** dafür gedankt.	*Karin thanked me for it.*
Ein fremder Mann folgt **uns**.	*A strange man is following us.*
Sie kann **den Jungen** nicht glauben.	*She can't believe the boys.*
Der Alkohol schadet **der Gesundheit**.	*Alcohol harms your health.*

Notice that in the English translations of these German sentences, the object of the verb is a direct object. But in the German sentences, each object is in the dative case.

Dative prepositions

The dative prepositions require their objects in prepositional phrases to be in the dative case. Here are the dative prepositions.

aus	*out, from*
außer	*except (for)*
bei	*by, at*
gegenüber	*opposite, across from*
mit	*with*
nach	*after*
seit	*since*
von	*from, of*
zu	*to*

Take note that **gegenüber** *does not precede pronouns.* It follows pronouns. But it can either precede or follow nouns. If a noun refers to a person, there is a tendency to place **gegenüber** after the noun. Let's look at some examples.

Wer sitzt ihm **gegenüber**?	*Who's sitting across from him?*
Die Kirche ist **gegenüber** dem Park.	*The church is across from the park.*
Wir sitzen dem Professor **gegenüber**.	*We sit opposite the professor.*

The dative prepositions act as signals that the nouns or pronouns that follow them must be in the dative case. Here are some examples with dative prepositions:

Die Kinder kommen **aus** der Schule.	*The children are coming out of the school.*
Niemand kennt sie **außer** meinem Bruder.	*No one knows him except my brother.*
Mein Onkel wird **bei** uns wohnen.	*My uncle is going to live at our house.*

Ich habe **mit** ihm Schach gespielt.	*I played chess with him.*
Nach dem Konzert gingen sie nach Hause.	*After the concert they went home.*
Ich wohne **seit** zwei Jahren in Leipzig.	*I've lived in Leipzig for two years.*
Er ist gerade **vom** Bahnhof gekommen.	*He just came from the train station.*
Welche Straße führt **zur** Universität?	*Which street leads to the university?*

Prepositional adverbs

If the object of a preposition is an inanimate object, a prepositional adverb is formed. For example:

preposition	prepositional adverb	question
(mit) + ihm =	damit	womit?
(zu) + ihr =	dazu	wozu?
(aus) + ihnen =	daraus	woraus?

If the preposition begins with a vowel, add the letter **r** between the prefix and the preposition: **aus** becomes **da<u>r</u>aus** and **wo<u>r</u>aus**.

Impersonal expressions

Numerous German expressions often use **es** as their subject. They are called *impersonal expressions*, because they do not identify a specific person or object as their subject. The impersonal *it* is the doer of the action. Often these expressions require a dative object. For example:

es fällt mir ein	*it occurs to me*
es gefällt dem Mann	*the man likes it*
es geht der Frau gut	*the woman feels well*
es gelingt mir	*I succeed, I manage (to do something)*
es genügt dem Studenten	*the student is satisfied (with something)*
es glückt dir	*you prosper, you succeed*
es kommt mir vor	*it appears to me*
es passt ihr gut	*it fits her well*
es scheint ihm	*it seems to him*
es schmeckt mir gut	*it tastes good to me*
es steht ihr gut	*she looks good in it*

The impersonal expressions are not used exclusively with the pronoun **es**. Almost any singular or plural noun that makes sense in the sentence can be used as the subject of these verbs. For example:

Diese Handschuhe gefallen dem Mann.   *The man likes these gloves.*
Das Kleid passt ihr gut.   *The dress fits her well.*

Exercise 27

Rewrite each of the following words or phrases in the accusative case and in the dative case.

nominative	accusative	dative
1. der Lehrer	_____	_____
2. kein Mann	_____	_____
3. die Leute	_____	_____
4. seine Mutter	_____	_____
5. dein Wagen	_____	_____
6. das Heft	_____	_____
7. ein Zimmer	_____	_____
8. Tische	_____	_____
9. keine Tasse	_____	_____
10. keine Tassen	_____	_____
11. mein Bruder	_____	_____
12. ein Schrank	_____	_____
13. ein Schiff	_____	_____
14. ihre Geschwister	_____	_____
15. die Gäste	_____	_____

Exercise 28

Rewrite the following sentences, replacing the word or phrase in bold print with the word or phrase in parentheses. For example:

> Er gibt **dem Kind** den Ball.
> (der Hund)   *Er gibt **dem Hund** den Ball.*

1. Was hast du **deinem Freund** geschickt?

(dein Bruder) _____

(deine Tante) _____

(meine Eltern) _____

(das Mädchen) _____

(deine Freundin) _____

2. Ich möchte mit **Herrn Schneider** sprechen.

(meine Lehrerin) _____

(die Schüler) _____

(ihr) _____

(sie pl.) _____

(du) _____

3. Niemand kann **uns** helfen.

(ich) _____

(er) _____

(die Frau) _____

(die Touristen) _____

(der Verbrecher) _____

Exercise 29

Circle the letter of the preposition that best completes each sentence.

1. Ich habe einen Brief _____ Erik bekommen.

a. zu

b. von

c. mit

d. um

2. _____ einem Mann wurden alle gerettet.

a. Für

b. Bei

c. Außer

d. Nach

3. Im Bus steht man vielen Menschen _____ .

a. gegenüber

b. seit

c. bis

d. von

4. Sie ist _____ vier Wochen in München.

a. zu

b. durch

c. zur

d. seit

5. Sie fragen _____ dem Weg in die Berge.

a. nach

b. von

c. mit

d. gegen

6. Was liegt auf dem Boden _____ der Tür?

a. bei

b. um

c. seit

d. außer

7. Ist dein Ring _____ Gold?

a. ohne

b. aus

c. außer

d. gegenüber

8. _____ wem sind sie spazieren gegangen?

a. Durch

b. Von

c. Wider

d. Mit

9. Gudrun wird _____ ihren Verwandten wohnen.

a. nach

b. bei

c. seit

d. außer

10. Er zieht die Uhr _____ seiner Tasche.

a. aus

b. zu

c. mit

d. gegen

Exercise 30

Circle the letter of the word or phrase that best completes each sentence.

1. Hast du mit _____ gesprochen?

   a. Herr Bauer

   b. die Ärztin

   c. ihnen

   d. Sie

2. Ich fahre aufs Land zu _____ .

   a. den Freund

   b. das Kind

   c. die Kinder

   d. meinem Bruder

3. Die Sportler kommen aus _____ .

   a. der Übung

   b. das Restaurant

   c. eine Stadt

   d. ihren Keller

4. Niemand hat sie außer _____ gesehen.

   a. ihrer Tante

   b. mich

   c. deinen Bruder

   d. ihn

5. Bei _____ hat er gewohnt?

   a. seine Verwandten

   b. sie s.

   c. Leute

   d. wem

6. Er hat seine Mutter seit _____ nicht gesehen.

a. zwei Jahren

b. eine Woche

c. morgen

d. letzten Freitag

7. Ich glaube _____ nicht.

a. dir

b. meinen Freund

c. meine Freundin

d. Sie

8. Sie kamen nach _____ .

a. die Kinder

b. dem Frühstück

c. einen Teller

d. ihn

9. Wird einer von _____ mitkommen?

a. den Lehrer

b. mir

c. Freunde

d. euch

10. Das wird _____ helfen.

a. dich

b. keinem Menschen

c. meine Frau

d. einen Jungen

Exercise 31

Change the dative pronoun or prepositional adverb in each sentence to any appropriate noun. For example:

Sie glaubt mir nicht.   *Sie glaubt **meinem Freund** nicht.*

1. Es gehört nicht dir.

_____

2. Sein Bruder hat mit ihr getanzt.

_____

3. Was hat sie ihm gegeben?

_____

4. In der Straßenbahn sitzt er mir gegenüber.

_____

5. Herr Schneider kommt davon.

_____

6. Morgen fahren wir zu ihnen.

_____

7. Ihre Ohrringe waren daraus.

_____

8. Danach gingen wir sofort ins Kino.

_____

9. Haben Sie lange bei ihm gewohnt?

_____

10. Der Anzug passt dir gar nicht.

_____

11. Ich habe ihr dafür gedankt.

_____

12. Wer hat Ihnen die Blumen geschenkt?

_____

13. Alle sprechen von uns.

_____

14. Die Würstchen schmecken mir nicht.

_____

15. Tante Gerda hat ihr eine Ansichtskarte geschickt.

_____

Exercise 32

Fill in the blanks with any appropriate word or phrase. Be careful! Some of the missing words and phrases require the accusative case, and others require the dative case. For example:

Ich kaufe _meinem Sohn_ ein neues Hemd. (dative case, indirect object)

1. Wem wirst du _____ geben?

2. Ich wohne lieber bei _____ .

3. Der Rundfunk teilt _____ die Nachrichten mit.

4. Erik hat seinem Onkel für _____ gedankt.

5. Brauchst du _____ nicht?

6. Ich werde nie gegen _____ sprechen.

7. Benno arbeitet seit _____ in Amerika.

8. Die Reiseleiterin hat es _____ gezeigt.

9. Kannst du _____ damit helfen?

10. Die Jungen wollen mit _____ tanzen.

11. Wir haben ein Paket von _____ bekommen.

12. Der Diener bringt _____ eine Tasse Tee.

13. Warum soll ich _____ glauben?

14. Die Frau gibt _____ eine Münze.

15. _____ machst du am Wochenende?

7

Genitive Case

The genitive case has two primary functions: (1) to link nouns to show possession and (2) to identify the object of genitive prepositions. Let's look at the genitive case of some example nouns with the definite article (**der, die, das**), the indefinite article (**ein, eine**), and **kein**.

masculine	feminine	neuter	plural
des Mannes	der Frau	des Kindes	der Lampen
eines Mannes	einer Frau	eines Kindes	N/A
keines Mannes	keiner Frau	keines Kindes	keiner Lampen

Notice that masculine and neuter nouns require the addition of the ending -(e)s. You can also see that the plural genitive does not have an indefinite form.

Names show possession by adding **-s** to them. For example:

Martins Familie   *Martin's family*
Deutschlands Grenzen   *Germany's borders*

Pronouns do not have a genitive declension. Instead, they form *possessive adjectives*.

pronoun	possessive adjective	
ich	mein	*my*
du	dein	*your* (singular, informal)
er	sein	*his*
sie s.	ihr	*her*
es	sein	*its*
wir	unser	*our*
ihr	euer	*your* (plural, informal)
sie pl.	ihr	*their*
Sie	Ihr	*your* (formal)
wer	wessen	*whose*

The possessive adjective **euer** requires a minor spelling change when an ending is added, for example: **eure, eurer, euren, eurem,** and **eures**. Possessive adjectives will be taken up in detail in Chapter 9.

Possession

English has two ways of showing possession. One way is to add an apostrophe and an *s* to a noun: *the boy*'s *wagon, women*'s *rights*, and so on. Another way is to use the preposition *of*: *the color* of *her hair, the speed* of *light*, and so on.

German uses the genitive case to indicate a possessive. The genitive can be translated into English as either apostrophe + *s* or *of*, depending on what sounds appropriate. For example:

der Vater der Braut	*the bride's father*, or *the father of the bride*
die Gesundheit des Kindes	*the child's health*, or *the health of the child*

It is also possible to form a possessive in German with the dative preposition **von**. This is similar to using the preposition *of* to form the possessive in English. The use of **von** is more common in the everyday spoken language, and the genitive declension tends to be used in the written language. Compare the following phrases:

written language	**everyday spoken language**	
die Kinder meiner Schwester	die Kinder von meiner Schwester	*my sister's children*
viele der Studenten	viele von den Studenten	*many of the students*

The preposition **von** is required in both writing and speech if (1) a noun stands alone without a definite or indefinite article or any other declined word; (2) the noun follows **etwas, nichts,** or **viel**; or (3) a pronoun is used in place of a noun. For example:

noun with an article (use genitive)	der Geruch der frischen Luft	*the smell of the fresh air*
noun standing alone	der Geruch von Essig	*the smell of vinegar*
etwas, nichts, viel (use *von*)	etwas von dem Bier	*some of the beer*
	nichts von dem Schatz	*nothing of the treasure*
	viel von der Arbeit	*much of the work*
pronouns	jeder von euch	*each of you*
	eine Bekannte von ihm	*an acquaintance of his*

Genitive prepositions

There are four primary genitive prepositions:

statt (anstatt)	*instead of*
trotz	*in spite of, despite*
während	*during*
wegen	*because of, on account of*

The objects of these four prepositions will be in the genitive case. For example:

Statt meines Bruders kam meine Schwester zu Besuch.	*Instead of my brother, my sister came for a visit.*
Trotz des Gewitters gingen die Wanderer weiter.	*In spite of the storm, the hikers continued on.*
Während des Sommers machten wir viele Ausflüge.	*During the summer, we took many excursions.*
Wegen ihrer Krankheit hat die Schülerin viel versäumt.	*Because of her illness, the pupil missed a lot.*

Exercise 33

Rewrite each word or phrase in the accusative, dative, and genitive cases.

	accusative	dative	genitive
1. der Professor			
2. die Lehrerin			
3. das Gebäude			
4. Bücher			
5. meine Kinder			
6. kein Brot			
7. eine Tür			
8. die Leute			
9. kein Krieg			
10. der Verbrecher			

Exercise 34

Write the possessive adjective forms of the following pronouns.

1. ich _____

2. du _____

3. er _____

4. sie s. _____

5. es _____

6. wir _____

7. ihr _____

8. sie pl. _____

9. Sie _____

10. wer _____

Exercise 35

Rewrite each sentence, changing the word or phrase in parentheses into a possessive formed by the genitive case. Place the possessive in the blank provided. For example:

(der Mann)   <u>Der Hut *des Mannes* ist sehr alt.</u>

1. (das Radio)   Die Lautsprecher _____ sind kaputt.

2. (meine Kusine)   Das Kleid _____ passt ihr nicht.

3. (die Kinder)   Das Spielzeug _____ ist überall auf dem Boden.

4. (meine Brüder)   Das Schlafzimmer _____ war zu klein.

5. (das Mädchen)   Die Stimme _____ ist süß.

6. (die Ärztin)   Der Sohn _____ wurde Rechtsanwalt.

7. (mein Gast)   Die Handschuhe _____ sind unter dem Bett.

8. (eine Freundin)   Das ist die Unterschrift _____ von mir.

9. (der Dichter)   Hast du die Briefe _____ gelesen?

10. (das Museum)   Der Eingang _____ ist frisch gestrichen.

Exercise 36

Circle the letter of the preposition that best completes each sentence.

1. _____ des Regens blieben wir nicht zu Hause.

a. Anstatt

b. Trotz

c. Während

d. Wegen

2. _____ einer Prüfung geht sie nicht ins Kino.

a. Anstatt

b. Trotz

c. Während

d. Wegen

3. Ich war _____ des Krieges in der Schweiz.

a. anstatt

b. trotz

c. während

d. wegen

4. _____ des schönen Wetters will er nicht im Garten spielen.

a. Anstatt

b. Trotz

c. Während

d. Wegen

5. _____ meines Onkels musste meine Tante arbeiten.

a. Anstatt

b. Trotz

c. Während

d. Wegen

6. _____ einer Erkältung konnte er nicht zur Schule gehen.

a. Anstatt

b. Trotz

c. Während

d. Wegen

7. _____ eines Hundes kaufte ich eine Katze.

a. Anstatt

b. Trotz

c. Während

d. Wegen

8. _____ des Tages arbeitet Erik in einer Fabrik.

a. Anstatt

b. Trotz

c. Während

d. Wegen

9. Die Studentin hat _____ ihres Urlaubs viel versäumt.

a. anstatt

b. trotz

c. während

d. wegen

10. _____ eines Gewitters ist niemand draußen.

a. Anstatt

b. Trotz

c. Während

d. Wegen

Exercise 37

Rewrite each sentence by replacing the word or phrase in bold print with the one in parentheses.

1. Seine Beschreibung **der Probleme** war ausführlich.

(seine Afrikareise) _____

(die Idee) _____

(das Verbrechen) _____

(der Urlaub) _____

(die Krisen) _____

(der Unfall) _____

2. Die neue Wohnung **meines Bruders** ist in einem Vorort.

(meine Eltern) _____

(eine Freundin) _____

(der Arzt) _____

(meine Verwandten) _____

(ein Freund) _____

(die Pflegerin) _____

3. Hast du die Reden **des Direktors** gehört?

(die Schauspielerin) _____

(die Politiker) _____

(der Bürgermeister) _____

(mein Chef) _____

(die Manager) _____

(meine Tochter) _____

8

Accusative-Dative Prepositions

A special category of prepositions takes either the accusative or the dative case. Take a look at these prepositions.

an	*at*
auf	*on, onto*
hinter	*behind*
in	*in, into*
neben	*next to*
über	*over*
unter	*under*
vor	*in front of, before*
zwischen	*between*

Use the dative case when the prepositional phrase shows *location*. Use the accusative case when the prepositional phrase shows *movement* from one place to another. This involves a verb of motion, for example: **gehen, fahren, fliegen**, and so on. Let's look at some examples where the prepositions take the dative case.

dative case

Die Kinder stehen am Fenster.	*The children are standing by the window.*
Er verbirgt sich hinter einem Baum.	*He's hiding behind a tree.*
Die Katze schläft unter dem Tisch.	*The cat is sleeping under the table.*
Gudrun sitzt zwischen ihren Eltern.	*Gudrun is sitting between her parents.*

These phrases tell *where* someone or something is, and the dative case is, therefore, used with these prepositions.

Let's look at some examples where these prepositions take the accusative case. In each example, a verb shows movement from one place to another: **stellt, läuft, fliegen**, and **legte**. When such verbs are followed by an accusative-dative preposition, the accusative case is used.

accusative case

Sie stellt eine Lampe hinter die Gardine.	*She places a lamp behind the curtains.*
Der Junge läuft in die Küche.	*The boy runs into the kitchen.*
Die Vögel fliegen über den Fluss hinüber.	*The birds fly across the river.*
Er legte Zeitungspapier unter den Tisch.	*He laid newspaper under the table.*

In each of the following examples, the verb of the sentence is not a verb of motion: **warten, denke, verliebte,** and **sprechen.** Normally this would mean that the accusative-dative prepositions should take the dative case. However, the dative case would indicate *location*, which is not what the prepositional phrases in these examples indicate. Therefore, the accusative case is required instead.

Auf wen warten Sie?	*For whom are you waiting?*
Ich denke oft an meine Familie.	*I often think about my family.*
Martin verliebte sich in sie.	*Martin fell in love with her.*
Alle sprechen über den Unfall.	*Everyone's talking about the accident.*

A list of commonly used verbs that are accompanied by accusative-dative prepositions follows. The case required by the preposition is indicated by the letter **A** for *accusative* or **D** for *dative*. Take note that some of the verbs that actually *do not indicate location* still require the dative case.

achten auf	A	*pay attention to*
sich beklagen über	A	*complain about*
denken an	A	*think about*
sich erinnern an	A	*remember, remind of*
erkennen an	D	*recognize by*
sich freuen auf	A	*look forward to*
sich freuen über	A	*be glad about*
glauben an	A	*believe in*
hoffen auf	A	*put faith in, hope for*
sich irren in	A	*be wrong about*
leiden an	D	*suffer from*
reden über	A	*talk about*
schreiben an	A	*write to*
schreiben über	A	*write about*
schützen vor	D	*protect from*
sprechen über	A	*speak about*
sterben an	D	*die from*
teilnehmen an	D	*take part in*
sich verlassen auf	A	*rely on*

sich verlieben in	A	*fall in love with*
verzichten auf	A	*do without*
warnen vor	D	*warn against*
warten auf	A	*wait for*

In questions that inquire into motion or location, use **wohin** to ask *to what place* someone or something *is going* and use **wo** to ask *where* someone or something *is located*. For example:

| **accusative** | in die Schule | Wohin? | *into the school* | *Where to? (To what place?)* |
| **dative** | in der Schule | Wo? | *in the school* | *Where?* |

Notice that this use of **wohin** and **wo** corresponds to the use of the accusative-dative prepositions. This difference of meaning in location and motion caused by the use of the dative or the accusative case occurs with both nouns and pronouns. Also remember that if a pronoun refers to an inanimate object, a prepositional adverb is used instead of a prepositional phrase. For example:

daneben	*next to it*
darin	*in it*
worauf	*on what*
wovor	*in front of what*

Exercise 38

Rewrite each sentence by replacing the word or phrase in bold print with the ones in parentheses. For example:

(der Lehrer) Er steht neben **einem Freund**. <u>Er steht neben *dem Lehrer*.</u>

1. Ein altes Porträt hing über **dem Bett**.

(der Schrank) _____

(eine Lampe) _____

(das Sofa) _____

(die Stühle) _____

2. Ihre Katze schläft gern auf **dem Bett**.

(der Tisch) _____

(ein Kissen) _____

(die Couch) _____

(das Fensterbrett) _____

3. Der neue Wagen steht hinter **dem Haus.**

(die Garage) _____

(die Bäume) _____

(ein Gebäude) _____

(der Supermarkt) _____

4. Ist die Milch in **dem Keller?**

(der Kühlschrank) _____

(die Küche) _____

(eine Flasche) _____

(das Esszimmer) _____

5. Hier sind wir unter unseren **Freunden.**

(Schulkameraden) _____

(Verwandte) _____

(Geschwister) _____

(Nachbarn) _____

Exercise 39

Rewrite each sentence by replacing the word or phrase in bold print with the ones in parentheses. For example:

(der Lehrer)   Er wartet auf **einen Freund.**   Er wartet auf *den Lehrer*.

1. Wir fahren vor **das Restaurant.**

(das Kino) _____

(die Schule) _____

(ein Laden) _____

(das Museum) _____

2. Denkst du niemals an **deinen Bruder?**

(Kinder) _____

(Freundin) _____

(Eltern) _____

(Sohn) _____

3. Eine kleine Maus kroch unter **das Bett**.

(der Tisch) _____

(das Kissen) _____

(der Ofen) _____

(die Decke) _____

4. Er hat sich neben **eine Bekannte** gesetzt.

(sein Freund) _____

(meine Schwester) _____

(unser Rechtsanwalt) _____

(seine Kinder) _____

5. Ich stelle mein Fahrrad hinter **das Haus**.

(ein Baum) _____

(die Garage) _____

(die Türen) _____

(das Tor) _____

Exercise 40

Rewrite each of the following prepositional phrases, changing the noun to a pronoun. Then rewrite the phrase as a question. Use prepositional adverbs where appropriate. For example:

am Fenster	*daran*	*woran*
an einen Freund	*an ihn*	*an wen*

1. an der Tür _____ _____

2. auf den Mann _____ _____

3. in die Freundin _____ _____

4. an der Wand _____ _____

5. vor das Kino   _____   _____

6. neben der Frau   _____   _____

7. auf Herrn Bauer   _____   _____

8. hinter die Kinder   _____   _____

9. aufs Land   _____   _____

10. in der Stadt   _____   _____

11. zwischen mich und meinen Mann   _____   _____

12. unter unsere Gäste   _____   _____

13. über den See   _____   _____

14. über dem See   _____   _____

15. unter dem Schreibtisch   _____   _____

Exercise 41

Circle the letter of the word or phrase that best completes each sentence.

1. Sie schreibt einen Brief _____ die Eltern.

a. auf

b. an

c. in

d. vor

2. Die Katzen springen _____ den Schrank.

a. auf

b. am

c. von

d. zwischen

3. Jemand steht _____ Tür.

a. ans

b. an der

c. in den

d. im

4. Erik wartete _____ dem Kino.

a. im

b. über

c. unter

d. vor

5. Frau Klein sitzt _____ Mann.

a. neben ihrem

b. neben ihren

c. zwischen ihrem

d. zwischen ihren

6. Sie ist _____ einer Woche angekommen.

a. in

b. neben

c. vor

d. zwischen

7. Wer hängte dieses Poster _____ mein Bett?

a. an

b. am

c. im

d. über

8. Das Kind schläft _____ seinen Eltern.

a. an die

b. in die

c. neben den

d. zwischen

9. Der alte Hund kriecht _____ Tisch.

a. unter den

b. vor die

c. neben

d. im

10. Ein Fremder steht _____ der Mauer.

   a. ans

   b. in

   c. hinter

   d. zwischen

11. Sie kommen _____ Wohnzimmer.

   a. in

   b. ins

   c. vor

   d. neben dem

12. Mein Vater hängt ein Bild _____ Tisch.

   a. am

   b. vor dem

   c. über den

   d. hinter

13. Gestern waren wir _____ der Stadt.

   a. auf

   b. hinter

   c. in

   d. neben

14. Gudrun stand _____ dem Spiegel.

   a. auf

   b. in

   c. im

   d. vor

15. Der Frosch springt _____ Felsen.

   a. auf den

   b. auf dem

   c. hinter der

   d. ins

Exercise 42

Complete each sentence with any appropriate word or phrase.

1. Die Wanderer wollen auf _____ steigen.

2. Die Zeitungen waren unter _____ .

3. Neben _____ sitzt Professor Bingen?

4. Warum stehst du so lange vor _____ ?

5. Wir mussten wieder auf _____ warten.

6. Der Kranke leidet an _____ .

7. Sie wird die Blumen auf _____ stellen.

8. Ich habe das alte Buch hinter _____ gefunden.

9. Vor _____ wohnten wir noch in Hamburg.

10. Die Jungen reden über _____ .

11. Ich freue mich schon auf _____ .

12. Das weinende Mädchen ist in _____ gelaufen.

13. Karl wird eine Postkarte an _____ schreiben.

14. Was machst du in _____ ?

15. Ein großer Wagen steht vor _____ .

16. Der Hund sitzt an _____ und wartet auf seinen Herrn.

17. Wir essen nur selten in _____ .

18. Das schlafende Baby liegt auf _____ .

19. Sie hat oft an _____ gedacht.

20. Der Junge stellte sich zwischen _____ und lächelte.

Exercise 43

Using the prepositions in parentheses, write two sentences—one with an accusative prepositional phrase and one with a dative prepositional phrase.

1. (auf)

accusative: _____

dative: _____

2. (unter)

accusative: _____

dative: _____

3. (vor)

accusative: _____

dative: _____

4. (hinter)

accusative: _____

dative: _____

5. (zwischen)

accusative: _____

dative: _____

9

Der Words and *Ein* Words

Nouns are generally preceded by *determiners*. Some determiners are the definite and indefinite articles such as <u>der</u> Mantel and <u>eine</u> Brücke. Another category is the interrogative words such as <u>welche</u> Schule or <u>wie viele</u> Leute. The largest categories are the **der** words and the **ein** words.

Der words

The **der** words function like the definite articles in that they identify the gender and number of nouns. One of the **der** words is **dieser** (*this*). Let's look at it in all the cases.

	masculine	feminine	neuter	plural
nominative	dieser Freund	diese Lampe	dieses Haus	diese Tische
accusative	diesen Freund	diese Lampe	dieses Haus	diese Tische
dative	diesem Freund	dieser Lampe	diesem Haus	diesen Tischen
genitive	dieses Freundes	dieser Lampe	dieses Hauses	dieser Tische

Other **der** words decline in the same way. Take note that some of them modify only plural nouns.

modify plural nouns	modify plural or singular nouns
alle (*all*)	jeder (*each, every*)
beide (*both*)	jener (*that*)
	welcher (*which*)
	mancher (*some, many a*)

A few other determiners are used only in the plural. Their declension with adjectives will be illustrated in detail in Chapter 10.

einige	*some*
mehrere	*several*
sämtliche	*all*

viele	*many*
wenige	*few*

Solcher is a special case. It is used mostly in the plural and is declined like **dieser**.

Solche Bücher sind sehr interessant.	*Such books (Books like that) are very interesting.*

When used with a singular noun, **solcher** is preceded by **ein** and is declined like an adjective. Adjective declensions will be taken up thoroughly in Chapter 10.

Ein solches Hemd würde ich nie tragen.	*I'd never wear such a shirt (a shirt like that).*

Solcher is also used in its undeclined form (**solch**) as a replacement for **so**. For example:

so eine Wohnung	*such an apartment*
solch eine Wohnung	*such an apartment*

so ein Flugzeug	*such an airplane*
solch ein Flugzeug	*such an airplane*

Ein words

The **ein** words function like the indefinite articles and include the possessive adjectives as well as **kein**. Let's look at **kein** in all the cases.

	masculine	**feminine**	**neuter**	**plural**
nominative	kein Freund	keine Lampe	kein Haus	keine Tische
accusative	keinen Freund	keine Lampe	kein Haus	keine Tische
dative	keinem Freund	keiner Lampe	keinem Haus	keinen Tischen
genitive	keines Freundes	keiner Lampe	keines Hauses	keiner Tische

The other **ein** words are declined in the same way, and all of them, except for **ein** itself, can be used with either singular or plural nouns.

mein	*my*
dein	*your* (singular, informal)

sein	*his, its*
ihr	*her*
unser	*our*
euer	*your* (plural, informal)
Ihr	*your* (singular or plural formal)
ihr	*their*

The effect of **der** words and **ein** words on adjective endings will be taken up in Chapter 10.

Some masculine nouns require an **-n** or **-en** ending when declined. This occurs with both **der** words and **ein** words. Some high-frequency nouns that do this are **der Herr, der Junge, der Mensch,** and **der Tourist** (*gentleman, boy, human, tourist*). For example:

nominative	der Herr	der Mensch
accusative	den Herrn	den Menschen
dative	dem Herrn	dem Menschen
genitive	des Herrn	des Menschen

Exercise 44

Write the nominative, accusative, dative, and genitive forms of the words in parentheses. For example:

| | **nominative** | **accusative** | **dative** | **genitive** |
| (dieser/Haus) | *dieses Haus* | *dieses Haus* | *diesem Haus* | *dieses Hauses* |

1. (kein/Blume) _____ _____ _____ _____

2. (mein/Kinder) _____ _____ _____ _____

3. (jener/Freunde) _____ _____ _____ _____

4. (welcher/Zug) _____ _____ _____ _____

5. (unser/Arzt) _____ _____ _____ _____

6. (einige/Tassen) _____ _____ _____ _____

7. (viele/Leute) _____ _____ _____ _____

8. (jeder/Stück) _____ _____ _____ _____

9. (dein/Kusine) _____ _____ _____ _____

10. (beide/Länder) _____ _____ _____ _____

Exercise 45

Fill in the blanks with **dieser** and **jener** respectively. Follow the example.

Er wohnt nicht in *diesem* Hause, sondern in *jenem*.

1. Sie wohnen nicht in _____ Straße, sondern in

   _____ .

2. Sie stand nicht an _____ Tür, sondern an _____ .

3. Ich kaufte nicht _____ Bild, sondern _____ .

4. Die Kinder gehen nicht zu _____ Schule, sondern zu

   _____ .

5. Wir verkaufen nicht _____ VW, sondern _____ .

6. Sie fahren nicht mit _____ Bus, sondern mit _____ .

7. Martin wird nicht an _____ Ecke stehen, sondern an

   _____ .

8. Ich warte nicht auf _____ Zug, sondern auf _____ .

9. Er spricht nicht über _____ Probleme, sondern über

   _____ .

10. Sie haben nicht _____ Mann verhaftet, sondern

    _____ .

Exercise 46

Rewrite each sentence, replacing the word in bold print with the determiners in parentheses.

1. Ich habe **deinen** Professor noch nicht kennen gelernt.

(dieser) _____

(sein) _____

(Ihr) _____

(jener) _____

(euer) _____

2. Meine Schwester will **seine** Romane lesen.

(dieser) _____

(viele) _____

(kein) _____

(mein) _____

(beide) _____

3. Sie liebt **jene** Menschen nicht.

(solch) _____

(dieser) _____

(viele) _____

(beide) _____

(mehrere) _____

4. Ich sorge mich um **diese** Kinder.

(alle) _____

(beide) _____

(euer) _____

(mein) _____

(kein) _____

5. Warum hast du **sein** Haus gekauft?

(dieser) _____

(ihr) _____

(jener) _____

(kein) _____

(solch ein) _____

Exercise 47

Rewrite each sentence, replacing the word in bold print with the noun in parentheses, making any necessary changes to the **der** or **ein** word.

1. Jeder **Schüler** muss vorsichtig sein.

(Schülerin) _____

(Tourist) _____

(Soldat) _____

(Gast) _____

(Mädchen) _____

(Krankenschwester) _____

(Kind) _____

(Mensch) _____

2. Vor solch einem **Mann** muss man sich hüten.

(Rechtsanwalt) _____

(Frau) _____

(Mensch) _____

(Dieb) _____

(Lehrerin) _____

(Kind) _____

(Gefahr) _____

(Unglück) _____

Exercise 48

Write an original sentence with each of the following **der** words and **ein** words.

 1. (dieser) _____

 2. (jener) _____

 3. (jeder) _____

 4. (welcher) _____

 5. (alle) _____

 6. (beide) _____

 7. (mehrere) _____

 8. (viele) _____

 9. (dein) _____

10. (solch ein) _____

11. (kein) _____

12. (mein) _____

13. (ihr) _____

14. (unser) _____

15. (euer) _____

Review 1

Exercise 49

Identify the gender of the following nouns by supplying the missing definite article (**der**, **die**, or **das**).

1. _____ Mantel
2. _____ Lehrer
3. _____ Prüfung
4. _____ Gesetz
5. _____ Speise
6. _____ Album
7. _____ Gesundheit
8. _____ Gold
9. _____ Tochter
10. _____ Eigentum
11. _____ Fundament
12. _____ Universität
13. _____ Eleganz
14. _____ Brunnen
15. _____ Position

Exercise 50

Rewrite the following plural nouns as singular nouns. Provide the appropriate definite article.

1. die Schulen _____
2. die Flüsse _____
3. die Häuser _____
4. die Übungen _____
5. die Kinder _____
6. die Bäume _____

7. die Wagen _____

8. die Lehrerinnen _____

9. die Zeitschriften _____

10. die Könige _____

Exercise 51

Rewrite the following singular nouns as plural nouns.

1. der Vogel _____

2. das Heft _____

3. der Sohn _____

4. die Schülerin _____

5. das Wort _____

6. der Gärtner _____

7. die Landkarte _____

8. das Kind _____

9. die Hausarbeit _____

10. der Laden _____

11. der Käfig _____

12. das Singen _____

13. die Richterin _____

14. das Gespräch _____

15. die Einheit _____

Exercise 52

Rewrite each sentence, changing the noun or phrase in bold print to the appropriate pronoun. For example:

Der Mann hat uns geholfen. *Er hat uns geholfen.*

1. **Unser Onkel** wohnt jetzt in Frankreich.

_____

2. Wo sind **die Stühle?**

_____

3. **Der Wissenschaftler** will eine Afrikareise machen.

_____

4. Ist **das Mädchen** eine Bekannte von dir?

_____

5. **Dieser Roman** ist sehr interessant.

_____

Exercise 53

Replace the pronoun in bold print with any appropriate noun. For example:

      Sie tanzt gut.   _**Meine Mutter** tanzt gut._

1. **Er** ist alt aber fährt gut.

_____

2. Ist **sie** eine Freundin von dir?

_____

3. **Sie** spielen gern Fußball.

_____

4. Liegt **er** auf dem Tisch?

_____

5. Ist **es** in der Küche?

_____

Exercise 54

Change the subject of each sentence to the pronoun **man**. For example:

      Du sollst nicht schreien. _Man soll nicht schreien._

1. Wir können nicht jedem gefallen.

_____

2. Warum musst du so lange warten?

_____

3. Bei Grün dürfen wir über die Straße gehen.

_____

4. Ihre Eltern haben sie davor gewarnt.

_____

5. Die Kinder sollen nicht fluchen.

_____

Exercise 55

Change the subject of each sentence to **jemand** and then to **niemand**. For example:

Peter steht an der Tür.   _Jemand steht an der Tür. Niemand steht an der Tür._

1. Die Gäste haben etwas zu sagen.

_____

_____

2. Wir werden euch helfen.

_____

_____

Exercise 56

In the blank provided, write **S** if the word or phrase in bold print is the subject of the sentence. Write **P** if the word or phrase in bold print is the predicate nominative. Write **N** if the word or phrase is neither the subject nor the predicate nominative. For example:

_S_ **Die Männer** spielen Karten.

1. _____ Meine Eltern kaufen **einen neuen Wagen**.
2. _____ Wann hast **du** diesen Roman gelesen?
3. _____ **Seine Eltern** wohnen jetzt in Heidelberg.
4. _____ Ich brauche **es** für ein Experiment.
5. _____ Alle sprechen von **der Krise** in Afrika.
6. _____ Der Lehrer ist auch **Wissenschaftler**.

Exercise 57

Rewrite each of the following sentences as a question, appropriately changing the word or phrase in bold print to either **wer, wen,** or **was.** For example:

Er ist ein Freund von Benno.   *Wer ist ein Freund von Benno?*

1. **Der Tourist** durchzieht die Stadt.

   _____

2. Die Männer trinken gern **Bier.**

   _____

3. **Ein Dichter** wird ein neues Gedicht schreiben.

   _____

4. Die Jungen möchten **Würstchen** essen.

   _____

5. Ich habe ein Geschenk für **sie.**

   _____

6. Herr Schäfer bäckt **Kuchen und Brot.**

   _____

7. **Die Jungen** haben ein Stein ins Fenster geworfen.

   _____

8. Ihr Vater hat gegen **ihn** gesprochen.

   _____

9. **Der Bus** kommt in fünf Minuten.

   _____

10. Ich hänge **das Bild** über das Bett.

    _____

Exercise 58

Rewrite each prepositional phrase, changing the noun to a pronoun. Use prepositional adverbs where appropriate. For example:

ohne den Mann *ohne ihn*
um die Stadt   *darum*

1. für meine Tante _____

2. gegen den Dieb _____

3. gegen die Tür _____

4. um die Ecke _____

5. wider den Bürgermeister _____

6. ohne seine Brüder _____

7. um das Kind _____

8. für seinen Brief _____

9. ohne die Jungen _____

10. durch den Tunnel _____

Exercise 59

Rewrite each of the following words or phrases first in the accusative case and then in the dative case.

	accusative	dative
1. die Lehrerin	_____	_____
2. keine Männer	_____	_____
3. die Zeitung	_____	_____
4. seine Tante	_____	_____
5. dein Wagen	_____	_____
6. das Auto	_____	_____
7. ein Zimmer	_____	_____
8. Bücher	_____	_____
9. keine Frage	_____	_____
10. ich	_____	_____
11. du	_____	_____

12. er _____ _____

13. sie s. _____ _____

14. es _____ _____

15. wir _____ _____

Exercise 60

Rewrite the following sentence, replacing the word or phrase in bold print with the one in parentheses. For example:

Er gibt **dem Kind** den Ball.   (der Hund)   Er gibt *dem Hund* den Ball.

Was hast du **deinem Freund** gezeigt?

1. (sein Bruder) _____

2. (deine Schwester) _____

3. (meine Verwandten) _____

4. (das Kind) _____

5. (deine Freundin) _____

Exercise 61

Rewrite each word or phrase in the accusative, dative, and genitive cases.

	accusative	dative	genitive
1. der Ausländer	_____	_____	_____
2. die Ärztin	_____	_____	_____
3. das Gebäude	_____	_____	_____
4. keine Gesetze	_____	_____	_____
5. wer	_____	_____	_____

Exercise 62

Rewrite each sentence, changing the word or phrase in parentheses into a possessive formed by the genitive case. Place the possessive in the blank provided. For example:

(der Mann)   Der Pullover *des Mannes* ist weiß.

1. (meine Kusine)   Der Rock _____ passt ihr nicht.

2. (mein Bruder)   Das Schlafzimmer _____ war zu klein.

3. (das Mädchen)   Die Stimme _____ ist laut.

4. (die Kellnerin)   Der Sohn _____ wurde Rechtsanwalt.

5. (unser Gast)   Der Wagen _____ ist rot.

Exercise 63

Circle the letter of the preposition that best completes each sentence.

1. _____ des Regens blieben wir nicht zu Hause.

a. Anstatt

b. Trotz

c. Während

d. Wegen

2. Im Bus steht man vielen Menschen _____ .

a. gegenüber

b. seit

c. bis

d. von

3. _____ einem Mann wurden alle gerettet.

a. Für

b. Bei

c. Außer

d. An

4. Ich war _____ des Krieges in der Schweiz.

a. anstatt

b. trotz

c. während

d. wegen

5. Gudrun wird _____ ihren Verwandten wohnen.

a. nach

b. bei

c. seit

d. außer

6. Er zieht die Uhr _____ seiner Tasche.

a. gegen

b. zu

c. mit

d. aus

Exercise 64

Rewrite each sentence, replacing the word or phrase in bold print with the ones in parentheses. For example:

    (der Lehrer)   Er steht neben **einem Freund**.   Er steht neben *dem Lehrer*.

1. Ein altes Porträt hing über **dem Bett**.

(der Schrank) _____

(eine Lampe) _____

(das Sofa) _____

(die Tische) _____

2. Erik hat einen Brief an **seine Mutter** geschrieben.

(eine Freundin) _____

(sein Vater) _____

(sein Bruder) _____

(seine Geschwister) _____

3. Ich habe **deinen** Professor noch nicht kennen gelernt.

(dieser) _____

(Ihr) _____

(jener) _____

(euer) _____

Adjectives

10

A predicate adjective follows a verb such as **sein** (*to be*) or **werden** (*to become*) and modifies the subject of the sentence. No ending is required on predicate adjectives.

| Meine Tante ist ziemlich **alt**. | *My aunt is rather* old. |
| Ein Freund von mir wurde **reich**. | *A friend of mine became* rich. |

Except for in the use of predicate adjectives, English and German differ greatly in how adjectives are used. German requires specific adjective endings for adjectives that directly modify nouns.

Adjectives in the nominative case should be looked at carefully because the noun's *gender* plays a key role in the choice of adjective endings. When a **der** word precedes the adjective, the **der** word indicates the noun's gender. Adjectives that follow **der** words have an -**e** ending. When an **ein** word precedes the adjective, the adjective identifies the noun's gender. Let's look at some examples in the nominative case.

adjectives in the nominative case with *der* words

masculine	feminine	neuter
der neue Mantel	die neue Decke	das neue Heft
dieser alte Wagen	jene alte Jacke	welches alte Buch

adjectives in the nominative case with *ein* words

masculine	feminine	neuter
ein neuer Mantel	eine neue Decke	ein neues Heft
kein alter Wagen	seine alte Jacke	ihr altes Buch

Feminine and neuter adjectives, whether with **der** words or **ein** words, are identical in both the nominative and accusative cases.

All other adjectives that follow either **der** words or **ein** words will have an -**en** ending:

1. in the masculine accusative
2. throughout the dative and genitive with all genders
3. throughout the plural in all the cases

For example:

	masculine	feminine	neuter	plural
nominative				seine **neuen** Schuhe
accusative	diesen **alten** Schlips			seine **neuen** Schuhe
dative	diesem **alten** Schlips	ihrer **besten** Bluse	meinem **kleinen** Auto	seinen **neuen** Schuhen
genitive	dieses **alten** Schlipses	ihrer **besten** Bluse	meines **kleinen** Autos	seiner **neuen** Schuhe

When a declined adjective is *not preceded* by either a **der** word or an **ein** word, the **der** word endings *become the adjective endings*. For example:

	masculine	feminine	neuter	plural
nominative	rote**r** Wein	kalt**e** Milch	gute**s** Wetter	krank**e** Menschen
accusative	rote**n** Wein	kalt**e** Milch	gute**s** Wetter	krank**e** Menschen
dative	rote**m** Wein	kalte**r** Milch	gute**m** Wetter	kranke**n** Menschen
genitive	rote**n** Weines	kalte**r** Milch	gute**n** Wetters	kranke**r** Menschen

A few determiners require a special adjective declension. These determiners are used exclusively with plural nouns.

einige	*some*
mehrere	*several*
sämtliche	*all*
viele	*many*
wenige	*few*

Notice how the declension of the adjectives that follow these determiners differs from the ones illustrated with **der** words and **ein** words. The adjective endings are like those used with adjectives that are not preceded by either **der** words or **ein** words.

	einige	*viele*
nominative	einig**e** jung**e** Leute	viel**e** interessant**e** Bücher
accusative	einig**e** jung**e** Leute	viel**e** interessant**e** Bücher
dative	einig**en** jung**en** Leuten	viel**en** interessant**en** Büchern
genitive	einig**er** jung**er** Leute	viel**er** interessant**er** Bücher

With these determiners, both the determiners and adjectives always have the same endings.

Many adjectives can be used as adverbs. Adverbs in both German and English function in a similar way and are used quite easily. They can modify verbs: **Er schreibt <u>gut</u>.** (*He writes well.*) And they can modify adjectives or other adverbs: **Er schreibt <u>sehr</u> gut.** (*He writes very well.*) Unlike adjectives, German adverbs never require an ending.

Exercise 65

Fill in the blanks with the missing endings for the cases indicated. Be careful! Not all of the blanks need an ending.

nominative case

1. ein nett_er_ Herr   dies____ kleine Katze____   unsere neu____ Freundin

2. meine gut____ Tasse   jen____ schnell____ Wagen   welche alt____ Männer

3. heiß____ Kaffee____   die schön____ Blume   alle deutsch____ Autos

4. das klein____ Dorf   mein____ neu____ Hefte   einige gut____ Weine

5. jed____ kluge Student   ihr erst____ Gedicht   kalt____ Suppe

accusative case

6. den letzt____ Zug   dies____ kurz____ Bleistift   ein____ langen Weg

7. sein____ besten Freund   unsere reich____ Freunde____   mein____ Kinder

8. warm____ Tee____   ein____ stolz____ Mann   eure arm____ Nachbarn

9. jen____ schwarze Hemd   jed____ nett____ Dame   deine neu____ Lehrerin

10. ein____ groß____ Haus   warm____ Milch____   ihre braun____ Hunde

dative case

11. diesem klein____ Jungen   unser____ alt____ Fahrrad   seinen neu____ Schuhen

12. weiß____ Wein____   vielen alt____ Zeitungen   beide gut____ Kinder____

13. ein____ schlecht____ Tag   dein____ jung____ Schwester   krank____ Leute____

14. dies____ scharfen Messer   jed____ neu____ Studentin   kalt____ Bier

15. einer eng____ Straße____   jen____ klein____ Zimmer   meiner dumm____
                                                                   Bekannten

genitive case

16. ein____ groß____ Problem____   dies____ jung____ Frau____

17. viel____ alt____ Menschen____   jed____ arm____ Kind____

18. kalt____ Bier____   wenig____ neu____ Schüler____

19. unser____ best____ Läufer____   kein____ deutsch____ Zeitung____

20. welch____ stolz____ Professor____   dein____ neu____ Auto____

Exercise 66

Rewrite each sentence, replacing the determiner or adjective in bold print with the ones in parentheses. Make any necessary changes to the adjective endings.

1. **Dieser** Mann war einmal Richter.

(jener) _____

(mein) _____

(ihr) _____

(welcher) _____

2. Mein **bester** Freund wohnt jetzt in Japan.

(gut) _____

(alt) _____

(neu) _____

(amerikanisch) _____

3. Ist **deine** neue Freundin Krankenschwester geworden?

(sein) _____

(dieser) _____

(euer) _____

(jener) _____

4. **Viele** junge Leute spielen gern Tennis.

(dieser) _____

(alle) _____

(kein) _____

(einige) _____

5. Trinkt ihr **kalten** Kaffee?

(heiß) _____

(warm) _____

(türkisch) _____

(stark) _____

6. Hast du **sein** neues Auto gesehen?

(ihr) _____

(jener) _____

(ein) _____

(dieser) _____

Exercise 67

Rewrite each sentence, replacing the noun in bold print with the ones in parentheses. Make any necessary changes to the adjectives.

1. Wie oft besuchen Sie ein deutsches **Museum**?

(Freund) _____

(Verwandter) _____

(Freundin) _____

(Kunstausstellung) _____

2. Ich habe keine neuen **Bücher**.

(Teller) _____

(Jacke) _____

(Auto) _____

(Mantel) _____

3. Sie wollen mit diesem armen **Mann** sprechen.

(Frau) _____

(Kind) _____

(Leute) _____

(Männer) _____

4. Ich denke oft an meinen ausgewanderten **Freund**.

(Schwester) _____

(Geschwister) _____

(Onkel) _____

(Bruder) _____

5. Er trinkt nicht gern kalten **Kaffee**.

(Tee) _____

(Milch) _____

(Bier) _____

(Wasser) _____

6. Das ist das neue Haus einer alten **Lehrerin** von mir.

(Freundin) _____

(Freund) _____

(Rechtsanwalt) _____

(Lehrer) _____

Exercise 68

Fill in each blank with any appropriate **der** word or **ein** word.

1. _____ einen Mann will ich nicht einladen.

2. Karl möchte _____ hübsche Mädchen kennen lernen.

3. _____ alte Menschen leben im Altersheim.

4. _____ gesunden Kinder dürfen wieder zur Schule gehen.

5. Morgen reisen _____ Touristen in die Schweiz.

6. Ich habe _____ einzige Münze bei mir.

7. _____ eleganten Damen sind Schauspielerinnen.

8. _____ ausländische Gäste kommen aus Schweden.

9. Wegen _____ langen Tages ging Martin sofort ins Bett.

10. Die Eltern _____ fleißigen Schülerin sind erfreut.

11. _____ eifrige Kaufmann muss viel reisen.

12. Frau Huber kaufte _____ schicken Mantel.

13. _____ neue Studenten gehen ins Lokal.

14. Leibniz hat _____ berühmte Akademie begründet.

15. Ein Fußgänger hat _____ verlorene Tasche gefunden.

Exercise 69

Fill in each blank with any appropriate adjective. Pay attention to the gender, number, and case.

1. Mein Sohn hat ein _____ Gedicht auswendig gelernt.

2. Der Lehrer wird diesen _____ Schüler fragen.

3. Welchem Bruder gleicht jener _____ Mann?

4. Sie erinnert sich gern an einige _____ Freunde.

5. Die Frau kann diesem _____ Handwerker vertrauen.

6. Trinkst du _____ Bier?

7. In diesem Zimmer sind zu viele _____ Lampen.

8. Sind eure _____ Übungen schwer?

9. Die Touristen reisen durch mehrere _____ Städte.

10. Dieses Dorf hat wenige _____ Straßen.

11. Meine Großmutter hat einen _____ Garten.

12. Diese zwei _____ Bäume tragen viele _____ Birnen.

13. Der Park ist auch ein Opfer des _____ Krieges gewesen.

14. Das _____ Kind stellt tausend _____ Fragen.

15. Über der Tür des _____ Ladens hängt ein Schild.

11

Contractions

Just as English uses contractions to combine two words together, German does the same thing but with different parts of speech. German combines prepositions with definite articles.

Contractions occur when masculine and neuter definite articles in the dative case combine with five prepositions. Notice also that there is only one feminine definite article in the dative case. It forms a contraction with **zu**.

an dem	**am**
in dem	**im**
bei dem	**beim**
von dem	**vom**
zu dem	**zum**
zu der	**zur**

Neuter definite articles in the accusative case also can form contractions with certain prepositions. In German, an apostrophe is never needed in a contraction.

an das	**ans**
auf das	**aufs**
für das	**fürs**
in das	**ins**
um das	**ums**

Although it is perfectly correct to use prepositions and definite articles in their full form, German sounds smoother and more normal with the use of contractions.

correct	Sie spielen **in dem** Garten.	*They play in the garden.*
more normal	Sie spielen **im** Garten.	

Exercise 70

Rewrite each prepositional phrase, changing the preposition and definite article into a contraction. For example:

      in dem Garten   *im Garten*

1. an dem Fenster _____

2. um das Haus _____

3. zu dem Klavier _____

4. bei dem Schwimmen _____

5. an das Tor _____

6. zu der Ausstellung _____

7. in dem Keller _____

8. von dem Professor _____

9. auf das Buch _____

10. für das Kind _____

11. in das Haus _____

Exercise 71

Fill in the blank with the missing definite article. Change the preposition in parentheses and the definite article into a contraction wherever possible. For example:

      Die Kinder spielen (in) *im* Garten.

or

      Sie laufen (in) *in den* Garten.

1. Die Krankenschwester schreibt einen Brief (für) _____ Kranken.

2. Wer hat den Ball (an) _____ Fenster geworfen?

3. Die große Mauer geht (um) _____ Gefängnis.

4. Andrea hat das Geld (in) _____ Tasche.

5. Sie fing an zu weinen (bei) _____ Packen des Koffers.

6. Die Studentin wurde (von) _____ Eltern gelobt.

7. Diese Straße führt (zu) _____ Universität.

8. Sechs Stühle standen (an) _____ Tisch.

9. Meine Mutter geht morgen (zu) _____ Arzt.

10. Jemand steht (an) _____ Tür.

11. Die Katze springt (auf) _____ Sofa.

12. Er steckte den Schlüssel (in) _____ Schloss.

13. Er dankt ihnen (für) _____ Geschenk zum Geburtstag.

14. Die Planeten bewegen sich (um) _____ Sonne.

15. Was liegt (bei) _____ Tür?

16. Die Jungen kommen gleich (von) _____ Sportplatz.

17. Der Bürgermeister spricht (zu) _____ Bürgern.

18. Früher hing ein Gemälde (an) _____ Wand.

19. Wie lange müssen wir (auf) _____ Bus warten?

20. Viele Tannen wachsen (in) _____ Walde.

21. Ich unterschreibe die Quittung (für) _____ alten Mann.

22. Der alte Hund schläft (bei) _____ Tür.

23. Der Ausflug hängt (von) _____ Wetter ab.

24. Führt diese Straße (zu) _____ Kirche?

12

Questions and Interrogatives

Just as English questions do, German questions fall into two major categories. There are questions that can by answered by **ja** or **nein** (*yes* or *no*); other questions begin with an interrogative word such as **wer** (*who*) and can have a variety of answers.

Yes and *no* questions

German questions that are answered with either **ja** or **nein** place the present or past tense verb, the modal auxiliary, or any other auxiliary before the subject of the sentence. The result is a question. For example:

present	Spielst du Schach?	*Do you play chess?*
past	Waren Sie schon in Berlin?	*Were you already in Berlin?*
modal	Könnt ihr mich verstehen?	*Can you understand me?*
present perfect	Hat Martin das Fenster zerbrochen?	*Did Martin break the window?*
future	Werden wir bald essen?	*Will we eat soon?*

No matter what tense the German verb is in, the first element in a **ja** or **nein** question will be a conjugated verb.

Interrogative words

Words that ask for information other than *yes* or *no* are interrogatives. They ask questions about time, place, or manner or ask for identification of someone or something. The German interrogative words are **wer, was, wann, wo, warum,** and **wie.** The rule used with questions answered with **ja** or **nein** prevails here, too: The verb precedes the subject of the sentence. And *the interrogative word precedes the verb.* For example:

Wen haben sie besucht?	*Whom did they visit?*
Mit **wem** spricht dein Sohn?	*With whom is your son speaking?*

Wessen Sportwagen ist das?	*Whose sports car is that?*
Was lernen die Kinder?	*What are the children learning?*
Wann kommt der Zug nach Bremen?	*When does the train to Bremen arrive?*
Wo liegt Hamburg?	*Where is Hamburg located?*
Warum bleibst du noch im Bett?	*Why are you still in bed?*
Wie fahren die Touristen nach Wien?	*How are the tourists getting to Vienna?*
Wie alt ist dein Bruder?	*How old is your brother?*

Be aware that a question beginning with **warum** (*why*) is answered with a statement that uses **weil** or **denn** (*because*). For example:

Warum willst du nicht Fußball spielen?	*Why don't you want to play soccer?*
Ich will nicht Fußball spielen, **denn** ich bin sehr müde.	*I don't want to play soccer, because I'm very tired.*

When the interrogative word is the subject of the sentence, as can be the case with **wer** or **was**, the interrogative word begins the sentence and is followed by the verb. Remember that the interrogative **wer** has three other forms: **wen** in the accusative, **wem** in the dative, and **wessen**, which replaces a possessive pronoun. For example:

nominative	**Wer** spielt Ziehharmonika?	*Who plays the accordion?*
accusative	**Wen** hast du gesehen?	*Whom did you see?*
dative	**Von wem** bekam sie das Geschenk?	*From whom did she receive the gift?*
possessive	**Wessen** Wagen ist das?	*Whose car is that?*

If a preposition is used with an interrogative word, it should precede the interrogative, unlike the flexibility of a preposition's position with an English interrogative.

Von wem hat er gesprochen?	*About whom did he speak?* or *Who did he speak about?*

Be aware that several new interrogatives are formed by combining certain words with **wie**. For example:

wie alt	*how old*
wie groß	*how big*
wie hoch	*how high*
wie lange	*how long*
wie oft	*how often*
wie spät	*how late*
wie viel	*how much*

Let's look at a couple examples with **wie**.

Wie alt ist dein Bruder?	*How old is your brother?*
Wie oft kommst du nach Freiburg?	*How often do you come to Freiburg?*

Various interrogatives are formed by using **wo-** as the prefix for certain prepositions and adverbs. They are prepositional adverbs. For example:

wobei	*at what*
wogegen	*against what*
wohin	*where (to)*
womit	*with what*
worin	*in what*
wozu	*to what*

Let's look at some example sentences.

Wohin fahren die Touristen?	*Where are the tourists traveling to?*
Womit schreibt man einen Brief?	*What does a person write a letter with?*

Other questions that seek distinguishing information begin with **welcher** (*which, what*). In such questions, **welcher** must be declined according to gender, number, and case. For example:

nominative	**Welches** Haus ist das Neue?	*Which house is the new one?*
accusative	**Welchen** Mann wird die Polizei verhaften?	*Which man will the police arrest?*
dative	**Mit welchem** Zug sollen wir fahren?	*By what train should we travel?*
genitive	Der Sohn **welcher** Frau ist Arzt geworden?	*Which woman's son became a physician?*

Exercise 72

Rewrite each sentence as a question that could be answered with **ja** or **nein**. For example:

Er spricht kein Deutsch. *Spricht er kein Deutsch?*

1. Er hat den Ofen noch nicht geheizt.

_____

2. Sie kämpfen gegen ihre Feinde.

_____

3. Der Student trinkt ein Glas Bier.

_____

4. Deutschland ist arm an Silber und Gold.

_____

5. Der Professor war nicht zufrieden.

_____

6. Der Zustand des Kranken wird von Tag zu Tag besser.

_____

7. Niemand kennt den geretteten Mann.

_____

8. Sein Bruder ist ebenso alt wie meine Schwester.

_____

9. Es gibt viele große Geschäfte mit sehenswerten Schaufenstern.

_____

10. Die Oberhemden liegen auf dem Boden.

_____

Exercise 73

Answer the following questions with any **ja** or **nein** statement.

1. Bleiben Sie noch ein paar Tage in Bonn?

_____

2. Ist die rote Tinte besser dafür?

_____

3. Kann sie Geige spielen?

_____

4. Ist der Hund über den Zaun gesprungen?

_____

5. Singen die Wanderer Volkslieder?

_____

6. Waren die Hunde ihrem Herrn treu?

_____

7. Hat der Schriftsteller ein neues Buch geschrieben?

_____

8. Werdet ihr eine Wohnung in München suchen?

_____

9. War die lange Trockenheit dem Wachstum der Bäume schädlich?

_____

10. Sind die hohen Preise den Kunden nicht angenehm gewesen?

_____

Exercise 74

Change each sentence to a question with either **wer** or **was** in place of the subject. For example:

Der Mann wartet auf ihn.   _Wer wartet auf ihn?_

1. Die Sache ist ihm äußert peinlich.

_____

2. Onkel Peter hat uns oft angerufen.

_____

3. Der Junge hat in Mathematik eine gute Note bekommen.

_____

4. Ich gebe abends Englischunterricht.

_____

5. Diese Studentinnen studieren an der Universität Hamburg.

_____

6. Das Flugzeug muss sofort landen.

_____

7. Physik und Chemie zählen zu den Naturwissenschaften.

_____

8. Die Touristen müssen jetzt mehr Geld ausgeben.

_____

9. Die Koffer sind zu schwer.

_____

10. Wir haben unsere Ferien in Italien verbracht.

_____

Exercise 75

Rewrite the following sentences as questions. Use the information in bold print to tell you which interrogative to use: **wer**, **wen**, **wem**, or **wessen**. For example:

Er besuchte **einen Freund**.   *Wen besuchte er?*

1. **Seine** Tante ist Physikerin.

_____

2. **Ich** bin ein Freund des neuen Bürgermeisters.

_____

3. Wir können **ihm** nicht glauben.

_____

4. Der Hauptmann möchte mit **der Krankenschwester** sprechen.

_____

5. **Ihre** Geschwister sind in der Schule.

_____

6. Martin versucht **Angela** zu küssen.

_____

7. Wir haben wieder auf **unsere Freunde** gewartet.

_____

8. **Der alte Dichter** hat seine Mappe verloren.

_____

9. Der Bäcker gibt **uns** zwei Plätzchen.

_____

10. **Der Schaffner** bittet um ihre Fahrkarten.

_____

Exercise 76

Rewrite the following sentences as questions. Use the information in bold print to tell you which interrogative to use: **wer** (in any case), **was, wann, wo, wohin, warum**, and **wie** (with various modifiers). For example:

Der Bus kommt **um 10 Uhr.**   *Wann kommt der Bus?* or *Um wie viel Uhr kommt der Bus?*

1. Der Eintritt **für Kinder unter fünf Jahren** ist kostenlos.

   _____

2. Wir können **den Gipfel des Berges** sehen.

   _____

3. Ich möchte eine Ansichtskarte **an meine Großmutter** schicken.

   _____

4. **Der Tenor** hat eine gute Stimme.

   _____

5. Du hast **ihren** alten Wagen gekauft.

   _____

6. **Heute** gehen wir italienisch essen.

   _____

7. Wir bleiben zu Hause, **weil das Wetter schlecht ist.**

   _____

8. Sie haben ein Häuschen **in den Bergen.**

   _____

9. Mein Bruder fährt mit der Straßenbahn **in die Stadt.**

   _____

10. Die Polizei hat **die Lage** unter Kontrolle gehabt.

    _____

11. Hamburg hat **mehr als 1,6 Millionen** Einwohner.

    _____

12. Die Kaufleute fahren **zweimal die Woche** nach Bremen.

    _____

13. Dieser treulose Mensch hat **sein Wort** gebrochen.

    _____

14. Die Blätter fallen **zur Erde** und vertrocknen.

---

15. **Eine Flasche Milch** ist in der Wärme verdorben.

---

16. Seine Nachbarn helfen **dem alten Herrn**.

---

17. Der neue Lehrer steht **an der Wandtafel**.

---

18. Er sagt nichts, **denn er spricht kein Deutsch**.

---

19. Der Hund will **seinen Herrn** warnen.

---

20. Die Reisenden sehen **den Zug** in den Bahnhof kommen.

---

21. Frau Schneider redet **über ihren ältesten Sohn**.

---

22. **Meine** Verwandten wohnen seit zwanzig Jahren in Heidelberg.

---

23. **Gold** ist ein teures Metall.

---

24. **Durch Zentralheizung** erhält man ein warmes Haus.

---

25. Seine Schwester ist jetzt **zwanzig Jahre alt**.

13

Present Tense

The English present tense is more complex than the German present tense. English has three forms to consider:

habitual	I speak German.
incomplete or progressive	I am speaking German.
emphatic	I do speak German.

German has only one present-tense form, which is similar to the English habitual form, but it can be translated into all three English forms:

Ich spreche Deutsch.   *I speak German. I am speaking German. I do speak German.*

Regular verbs

German regular verbs are those that do not make a change in the stem of the verb when conjugated. The stem of the verb is the infinitive minus the -en ending. For example:

heben	**heb-**
fragen	**frag-**

Let's look at a few regular verbs in the present-tense conjugation. Notice that the third-person singular (**er, sie, es** = *he, she, it*) is illustrated here by the pronoun **er**. The third-person plural **sie** (*they*) and **Sie** (*you* formal) are illustrated by the pronoun **sie**. When singular **sie** cannot be differentiated from plural **sie**, they will be identified as **sie s.** and **sie pl.** respectively.

	heben (lift)	*fragen* (ask)	*stellen* (put)	*brauchen* (need)
ich	hebe	frage	stelle	brauche
du	hebst	fragst	stellst	brauchst
er	hebt	fragt	stellt	braucht

wir	heben	fragen	stellen	brauchen
ihr	hebt	fragt	stellt	braucht
sie	heben	fragen	stellen	brauchen

All regular verbs follow the preceding pattern. However, there are some spelling rules to consider.

1. If a verb stem ends in -s, -ss, -ß, -z, or -tz, the second-person singular (du) present-tense ending reverts to a -t. The full ending -st is not used. For example:

du reist (*travel*)
du hasst (*hate*)
du schließt (*close*)
du heizt (*heat*)
du putzt (*polish*)

2. If a verb stem ends in -t or -d, an -e is added before the conjugational ending in the second-person singular and plural (du, ihr) and in the third-person singular (er, sie, es). For example:

	arbeiten (work)	*enden* (end)
ich	arbeite	ende
du	arbeitest	endest
er	arbeitet	endet
wir	arbeiten	enden
ihr	arbeitet	endet
sie	arbeiten	enden

3. If the verb stem ends in -eln or -ern, the written and spoken versions of the present-tense conjugation of the first-person singular (ich) often differ. Let's look at two examples.

written version

	lächeln (smile)	*hämmern* (hammer)
ich	lächele	hämmere
du	lächelst	hämmerst
er	lächelt	hämmert
wir	lächeln	hämmern
ihr	lächelt	hämmert
sie	lächeln	hämmern

spoken version

	lächeln (smile)	*hämmern* (hammer)
ich	lächle	hämmre
du	lächelst	hämmerst
er	lächelt	hämmert
wir	lächeln	hämmern
ihr	lächelt	hämmert
sie	lächeln	hämmern

The list of regular verbs is very large. Here are just a few of the most commonly used regular verbs:

hören	*hear*
kaufen	*buy*
klatschen	*clap*
lachen	*laugh*
legen	*lay*
machen	*make, do*
öffnen	*open*
setzen	*set*
suchen	*look for*
warten	*wait*

Irregular verbs

German irregular verbs in the present tense are of two types: (1) those that make a vowel change in the stem of the infinitive and (2) those that add an umlaut to the vowel in the stem of the infinitive. First let's look at some verbs that make a vowel change in the stem of the infinitive. That vowel change is always from -e- to -i- or -ie- and occurs only in the second- and third-person singular.

	geben (give)	*befehlen* (order)
ich	gebe	befehle
du	gibst	befiehlst
er	gibt	befiehlt
wir	geben	befehlen

ihr	gebt	befehlt
sie	geben	befehlen

Here are just a few of the irregular verbs that change the vowel -e- in the present-tense conjugation to -i- or -ie-.

brechen (i)	*break*
essen (i)	*eat*
helfen (i)	*help*
lesen (ie)	*read*
nehmen (i)	*take*
sehen (ie)	*see*
sprechen (i)	*speak*
stehlen (ie)	*steal*
sterben (i)	*die*
treffen (i)	*meet*

Verbs that add an umlaut to the vowel (**a** or **o**) of the stem of an infinitive make this change only in the second- and third-person singular.

	halten (hold)	*stoßen* (punch, kick)
ich	halte	stoße
du	**hältst**	**stößt**
er	**hält**	**stößt**
wir	halten	stoßen
ihr	haltet	stoßt
sie	halten	stoßen

Here are just a few of the irregular verbs that add an umlaut to a vowel in the present-tense conjugation.

backen (ä)	*bake*
einladen (ä)	*invite*
fahren (ä)	*travel*
fallen (ä)	*fall*
fangen (ä)	*catch*
laufen (ä)	*run*
schlafen (ä)	*sleep*
schlagen (ä)	*hit*
tragen (ä)	*wear, carry*
waschen (ä)	*wash*

The verb **stoßen** is the only verb that adds an umlaut to the vowel **o** in the irregular present tense. In all other cases, it is the vowel **a** that takes an umlaut in the irregular present tense.

Three important irregular verbs are **haben, sein,** and **werden.** Besides their own basic meaning, these three verbs are also used to form other tenses and must be understood well. Here is their conjugation in the present tense.

	haben (have)	*sein* (be)	*werden* (become)
ich	habe	bin	werde
du	hast	bist	wirst
er	hat	ist	wird
wir	haben	sind	werden
ihr	habt	seid	werdet
sie	haben	sind	werden

Modal auxiliaries

The modal auxiliaries are verbs that are conjugated in a special way in the present tense, and they are frequently used in combination with another verb in the form of an infinitive. The present-tense conjugation of a modal auxiliary has one stem form in the singular and another stem form in the plural. This also occurs with the verb **wissen.** Let's look at the present tense of the modal auxiliaries and **wissen.**

	dürfen (may)	*können* (can)	*mögen* (like, may)	*müssen* (must)
ich	darf	kann	mag	muss
du	darfst	kannst	magst	musst
er	darf	kann	mag	muss
wir	dürfen	können	mögen	müssen
ihr	dürft	könnt	mögt	müsst
sie	dürfen	können	mögen	müssen

	sollen (should)	*wollen* (want)	*wissen* (know)
ich	soll	will	weiß
du	sollst	willst	weißt
er	soll	will	weiß
wir	sollen	wollen	wissen
ihr	sollt	wollt	wisst
sie	sollen	wollen	wissen

The complete conjugation of modal auxiliaries in all the tenses is taken up in Chapter 21.

When the subject of a sentence is a noun, singular nouns will use the third-person singular conjugation of a verb, and plural nouns will use the third-person plural conjugation of a verb. For example:

Er spricht Deutsch.   *He speaks German.*
Das Kind spricht Deutsch.   *The child speaks German.*

Sie lernen schnell.   *They learn fast.*
Diese Mädchen lernen schnell.   *These girls learn fast.*

When the subject of the sentence is **wer, was,** or **man,** the verb is likewise conjugated in the third-person singular.

Wer ist das?   *Who's that?*
Was liegt unter dem Tisch?   *What's lying under the table?*
Man soll fleißig arbeiten.   *One should work diligently.*

Exercise 77

Rewrite each sentence in the present tense with the subjects provided in parentheses.

1. Ich gebe meinem Freund ein paar Euro.

(du) _____

(Martin) _____

(meine Eltern) _____

(sie s.) _____

(ihr) _____

2. Wir warten auf Gudrun und Angela.

(er) _____

(sie pl.) _____

(der Kellner) _____

(unsere Freunde) _____

3. Man muss vorsichtig sein.

(wir) _____

(Frau Bauer) _____

(die Kinder) _____

(du) _____

4. Ist sie noch in Köln?

(ihr) _____

(sie pl.) _____

(Herr Schmidt) _____

(du) _____

5. Ich habe heute keine Zeit.

(sie s.) _____

(Andrea) _____

(du) _____

(ihr) _____

6. Er will eine alte Freundin besuchen.

(wir) _____

(sie s.) _____

(Karl und Benno) _____

(wer) _____

7. Wir wissen nicht, wo er wohnt.

(mein Vater) _____

(seine Eltern) _____

(du) _____

(sie pl.) _____

Exercise 78

Circle the letter of the verb that best completes each sentence.

1. Was _____ der Lehrer?

a. sagen

b. fragt

c. wollt

d. kannst

2. Die Schülerin _____ schnell antworten.

a. kann

b. sollt

c. habt

d. stellt

3. Die Männer _____ in einer Fabrik.

a. können

b. sollt

c. lernst

d. arbeiten

4. Was _____ du nach der Schule?

a. machst

b. will

c. wollen

d. hat

5. Seine Schwester _____ kein Buch.

a. hat

b. soll

c. musst

d. lesen

6. _____ ihr gern Fußball oder Tennis?

a. Spielt

b. Könnt

c. Seid

d. Werdet

7. Es _____ immer früher dunkel.

a. wird

b. will

c. bist

d. hört

8. Wer _____ eine Brille?

a. suchst

b. trägt

c. glaubt

d. helfen

9. Wir _____ jeden Tag neue Wörter.

a. braucht

b. lernen

c. müssen

d. besuchst

10. Der Richter _____ zu laut.

a. kommt

b. verstehst

c. spricht

d. hat

11. Der neue Lehrer _____ vor dem Katheder.

a. will

b. wollt

c. bin

d. steht

12. Die Frau _____ ein Blatt Papier.

a. nimmt

b. wollt

c. ist

d. siehst

13. _____ du fleißig oder faul?

a. Sein

b. Bist

c. Kannst

d. Sollst

14. Ich _____ noch in der Hauptstraße.

a. wartet

b. komme

c. habe

d. wohne

15. Der Bus _____ schneller als die Straßenbahn.

a. fährt

b. gehen

c. fahrt

d. gehe

Exercise 79

Fill in the blank with an appropriate pronoun: **ich, du, er, sie s., es, wir, ihr, sie pl., Sie, wer,** or **was.** Some sentences have more than one answer.

1. Auf dem Platz sehen _____ viele grüne Bäume.

2. _____ bin noch sehr krank.

3. Kannst _____ verstehen, was sie sagt?

4. Dort ist das Geschäft. Ist _____ jetzt offen?

5. _____ macht immer viele Fehler.

6. Im Garten spielen _____ mit dem Hund.

7. _____ sollt versuchen seine Fragen zu beantworten.

8. Haben _____ Ihre Brille verloren, Herr Schneider?

9. _____ nimmt die Kreide und schreibt.

10. Auf der Straße sieht _____ viele Autos und Fahrräder.

11. Was wollt _____ heute tun?

12. _____ trägt immer eine bunte Bluse.

13. Warum sprecht _____ nicht mit Frau Schäfer?

14. _____ hat rote Haare? Karl oder Martin?

15. _____ ist wirklich ein sehr kluger Junge.

16. _____ ist besser? Ein Film oder ein Schauspiel?

17. _____ gibt ihrer Schwester ein schönes Kleid.

18. Brauchen _____ noch etwas, Professor Schmidt?

19. _____ sind zu schwer. Der Gepäckträger muss die Koffer tragen.

20. Was suchst _____ im Schrank, Peter?

21. _____ bringen mir ein Glas Wein und ein Butterbrot.

22. _____ mag kein Sauerkraut.

23. Weißt _____ , wo Frau Kamps wohnt?

24. _____ wird wieder sehr heiß.

25. Was seht _____ unter dem Bett?

14

Past Tense

Just like the English present tense, the past tense has three forms:

habitual	I spoke German.
incomplete or progressive	I was speaking German.
emphatic	I did speak German.

Like the German present tense, the German past tense has only one form that is translated into any of the three forms in English:

Ich sprach Deutsch.	*I spoke German. I was speaking German. I did speak German.*

The German past tense is used primarily as a written form, although it exists in the spoken language. The present perfect tense, which will be taken up in Chapter 15, is more commonly used in the spoken language to express a past-tense idea.

Regular verbs

The past-tense conjugation of regular verbs consists of the stem of the infinitive attached to the suffix **-te** with the appropriate conjugational ending. Notice that the third-person singular (**er, sie, es** = *he, she, it*) is illustrated here by the pronoun **er**. The third-person plural **sie** (*they*) and **Sie** (*you* formal) are illustrated by the pronoun **sie**. When singular **sie** cannot be differentiated from plural **sie**, they will be identified as **sie s.** and **sie pl.** respectively. Let's look at some example verbs.

	kaufen (buy)	*reisen* (travel)	*bestellen* (order)
ich	kaufte	reiste	bestellte
du	kauftest	reistest	bestelltest
er	kaufte	reiste	bestellte
wir	kauften	reisten	bestellten
ihr	kauftet	reistet	bestelltet
sie	kauften	reisten	bestellten

If a verb stem ends in -t or -d, an -e is added before the conjugational ending. For example:

	arbeiten (work)	*enden* (end)
ich	arbeitete	endete
du	arbeitetest	endetest
er	arbeitete	endete
wir	arbeiteten	endeten
ihr	arbeitetet	endetet
sie	arbeiteten	endeten

Irregular verbs

German irregular verbs do what many English irregular verbs do: they form the past tense not by a suffix but *by a vowel or stem change*. Look at how the German and English infinitives change to the irregular past tense:

German irregular past		**English irregular past**	
kommen	**kam**	*come*	*came*
singen	**sang**	*sing*	*sang*
sprechen	**sprach**	*speak*	*spoke*

When you know the irregular past-tense stem, you are ready to place the appropriate conjugational endings on the stem. The irregular past tense of most verbs does not require the -te suffix. For example:

	springen (jump)	*rufen* (call)	*fliegen* (fly)
ich	sprang	rief	flog
du	sprangst	riefst	flogst
er	sprang	rief	flog
wir	sprangen	riefen	flogen
ihr	sprangt	rieft	flogt
sie	sprangen	riefen	flogen

Notice that the first- and third-person singular (**ich, er, sie, es**) do not require an ending in the irregular past tense.

The following is a list of commonly used irregular verbs with their past-tense formations:

infinitive	past tense	
bleiben	blieb	*stayed*
essen	aß	*ate*
fahren	fuhr	*traveled*
fallen	fiel	*fell*
geben	gab	*gave*
gehen	ging	*went*
helfen	half	*helped*
laufen	lief	*ran*
lesen	las	*read*
nehmen	nahm	*took*
schlafen	schlief	*slept*
schlagen	schlug	*hit*
schreiben	schrieb	*wrote*
stehen	stand	*stood*
tragen	trug	*wore, carried*

It is important to look specifically at **haben, sein,** and **werden,** because they play an important role in the formation of other tenses as well as have a function when they stand alone. Their irregular past-tense conjugations are:

	haben (have)	*sein* (be)	*werden* (become)
ich	hatte	war	wurde
du	hattest	warst	wurdest
er	hatte	war	wurde
wir	hatten	waren	wurden
ihr	hattet	wart	wurdet
sie	hatten	waren	wurden

Some irregular verbs require the suffix **-te.** They not only make a vowel change in the stem, but they also require a suffix with the appropriate conjugational endings. For example:

	senden (send)	*nennen* (name)	*rennen* (run)
ich	sandte	nannte	rannte
du	sandtest	nanntest	ranntest
er	sandte	nannte	rannte
wir	sandten	nannten	rannten
ihr	sandtet	nanntet	ranntet
sie	sandten	nannten	rannten

Other irregular verbs that follow this pattern are:

brennen (brannte)	*burn*
bringen (brachte)	*bring*
denken (dachte)	*think*
kennen (kannte)	*know, be acquainted*
wenden (wandte)	*turn*
wissen (wusste)	*know*

Modal auxiliaries

The modal auxiliaries look, for the most part, as if they are formed like regular verbs. But they do not have an umlaut in the past tense, even if the infinitive has an umlaut. Let's look at their conjugations in the past tense.

	dürfen (may)	*können* (can)	*mögen* (like, may)
ich	durfte	konnte	mochte
du	durftest	konntest	mochtest
er	durfte	konnte	mochte
wir	durften	konnten	mochten
ihr	durftet	konntet	mochtet
sie	durften	konnten	mochten

	müssen (must)	*sollen* (should)	*wollen* (want)
ich	musste	sollte	wollte
du	musstest	solltest	wolltest
er	musste	sollte	wollte
wir	mussten	sollten	wollten
ihr	musstet	solltet	wolltet
sie	mussten	sollten	wollten

As with all verb conjugations, the third-person singular conjugation is used with all singular noun subjects of sentences, as well as with **wer, was,** and **man.** The third-person plural conjugation is used with all plural noun subjects.

Exercise 80

Rewrite each sentence in the past tense with the new subjects provided in parentheses.

1. Die Kinder gingen langsam nach Hause.

(ich) _____

(ihr) _____

(der Arzt) _____

(du) _____

2. Mein Mann war vier Wochen in den USA.

(er) _____

(sie pl.) _____

(wer) _____

(ihre Verwandten) _____

3. Warum kamst du nicht mit?

(sie s.) _____

(ihr) _____

(Ihr Bruder) _____

(Sie) _____

4. Am Freitag starb der alte Herr.

(sie s.) _____

(die Soldaten) _____

(sie pl.) _____

(Frau Bauer) _____

5. Eine schwarze Katze lief ins Wohnzimmer.

(ich) _____

(du) _____

(wer) _____

(die Hunde) _____

6. Ich musste einer Freundin damit helfen.

(du) _____

(Felix und Gudrun) _____

(Andrea) _____

(ihr) _____

7. Er kannte den Gast nicht.

(wer) _____

(Sie) _____

(Doktor Braun) _____

(meine Eltern) _____

Exercise 81

Circle the letter of the word or phrase that best completes each sentence.

1. Es _____ meine Pflicht.

a. konnte

b. war

c. hattet

d. brannte

2. _____ stahl seine Brieftasche?

a. Mochte

b. Wer

c. Waren

d. Verkaufte

3. Der Professor _____ seine Handschuhe.

a. musste

b. mussten

c. vergaß

d. vergessen

4. _____ gingen nach dem Konzert zum Stadtpark.

a. Was

b. Wurden

c. Kam

d. Alle

5. Um wie viel Uhr _____ der Zug ab?

a. kamt

b. fuhr

c. führt

d. kamen

6. _____ blieb auf der Party.

a. Niemand

b. Was

c. Warst

d. Du

7. Das Kind _____ mit einem Stück Kreide.

a. schlieft

b. standen

c. schrieb

d. stiegst

8. Ich _____ ihn kaum verstehen.

a. ließ

b. konnte

c. hatte

d. solltet

9. _____ wurde wieder sehr kalt.

a. Wir

b. Ihr

c. Du

d. Es

10. Wer _____ dir die schönen Blumen?

   a. fragte

   b. mochte

   c. brachte

   d. wusste

11. Anstatt eines Arztes _____ er Rechtsanwalt.

   a. wollte

   b. wurde

   c. sollte

   d. musste

12. Das Kind _____ zwischen seinen Eltern.

   a. saß

   b. muss

   c. musste

   d. setztet

13. _____ lag auf dem Fußboden?

   a. Wen

   b. Wann

   c. Wo

   d. Was

14. Sie _____ ihren neuen Nachbarn damit.

   a. halfen

   b. sahen

   c. zeigten

   d. brachen

15. Was _____ der Mann über dieses Problem?

   a. wer

   b. wollte

   c. legte

   d. sagte

Exercise 82

Rewrite the following present-tense sentences in the past tense.

1. Viele Krankheiten quälen die Menschen.

_____

2. Essen Sie nur Obst und Gemüse?

_____

3. Sie gibt dem Kellner das Trinkgeld.

_____

4. Man hat das Recht zu schweigen.

_____

5. Es wird wieder regnerisch.

_____

6. Wir finden ein paar Euro auf der Straße.

_____

7. Sie klagen vor Gericht gegen ihren Mieter.

_____

8. Kannst du diesen Fluss nennen?

_____

9. Felix bringt seiner Freundin einen Blumenstrauß.

_____

10. Wir sitzen am Strand und beobachten die großen Wellen.

_____

11. Die anderen Kinder lachen über ihn.

_____

12. Die Sterne leuchten.

_____

13. Es blitzt und donnert.

_____

14. Er lächelt und macht mir ein Kompliment.

_____

15. Herr Bauer bittet sie um diesen Tanz.

_____

16. Wer befiehlt der Armee anzugreifen?

_____

17. Wir sammeln Briefmarken und Ansichtskarten.

_____

18. Mein Schlafzimmer ist sehr klein und dunkel.

_____

19. Der Student hat eine kleine Zweizimmerwohnung unter dem Dach.

_____

20. Fahrt ihr nach Hannover?

_____

21. Mein Onkel kommt aus Basel.

_____

22. Die Eltern lieben ihre Kinder über alles.

_____

23. Diese Jungen treiben viel Sport.

_____

24. Ich denke oft an meine alten Freunde in Deutschland.

_____

15

Present Perfect
and Past Perfect Tenses

The English present perfect and past perfect tenses have both a habitual form and a progressive form in their conjugation.

habitual	They have worked here.
	They had worked here.
incomplete or progressive	They have been working here.
	They had been working here.

German has only one form for both meanings.

Sie haben hier gearbeitet.	*They have worked here. They have been working here.*
Sie hatten hier gearbeitet.	*They had worked here. They had been working here.*

If the action of the verb began in the past and ended in the present, it is in the present perfect tense. If the action began in the past and ended in the past, the verb is in the past perfect tense.

Regular verbs

The German present perfect tense of regular verbs is formed from a conjugation of either **haben** or **sein** plus a past participle. The auxiliary **haben** is used with transitive verbs, and the auxiliary **sein** is used with intransitive verbs, verbs of motion, or verbs that show a change of state or condition. The past participle consists of the prefix **ge-** plus the stem of the infinitive and the ending **-t**; for example, the infinitive **kaufen** (*buy*) becomes **ge-** + **kauf** + **-t**, written as **gekauft**. Let's look at another regular transitive verb, **suchen**, conjugated fully in the present perfect and past perfect tenses.

	present perfect	past perfect
ich	habe gesucht	hatte gesucht (*have looked for, had looked for*)
du	hast gesucht	hattest gesucht

er	hat gesucht	hatte gesucht
wir	haben gesucht	hatten gesucht
ihr	habt gesucht	hattet gesucht
sie	haben gesucht	hatten gesucht

If the verb requires the auxiliary **sein**, the formation of the participle remains the same. The only difference is the conjugation of the verb **sein**. But remember that the English translation of **sein** in the present perfect and past perfect tenses is still **have** or **had**. Let's look at a verb of motion, **reisen**, conjugated fully in the present perfect and past perfect tenses.

	present perfect	**past perfect**
ich	bin gereist	war gereist (*have traveled, had traveled*)
du	bist gereist	warst gereist
er	ist gereist	war gereist
wir	sind gereist	waren gereist
ihr	seid gereist	wart gereist
sie	sind gereist	waren gereist

A large category of regular verbs have infinitives that end in **-ieren**. Often these words come to German from foreign sources. They are conjugated like other regular verbs in the present and past tenses. But when verbs ending in **-ieren** become past participles in the present perfect or past perfect tenses, they do not have the prefix **ge-**. Let's look at examples with the verbs **studieren** and **marschieren**.

	studieren (study)	*marschieren* (march)
ich	habe/hatte studiert	bin/war marschiert
du	hast/hattest studiert	bist/warst marschiert
er	hat/hatte studiert	ist/war marschiert
wir	haben/hatten studiert	sind/waren marschiert
ihr	habt/hattet studiert	seid/wart marschiert
sie	haben/hatten studiert	sind/waren marschiert

Irregular verbs

The perfect tenses of irregular verbs require either **haben** or **sein** as the auxiliary, conjugated in the same way as with regular verbs. The difference is in the participle. Irregular participles are a combination of the prefix **ge-** plus an irregular stem and in most cases, the ending **-en**; for example, the verb

sprechen (*speak*) becomes **ge-** + **sproch** + **-en**, written as **gesprochen**. Let's look at another irregular transitive verb, **finden**, conjugated fully in the present perfect and past perfect tenses.

	present perfect	past perfect
ich	habe gefunden	hatte gefunden (*have found, had found*)
du	hast gefunden	hattest gefunden
er	hat gefunden	hatte gefunden
wir	haben gefunden	hatten gefunden
ihr	habt gefunden	hattet gefunden
sie	haben gefunden	hatten gefunden

If the verb requires the auxiliary **sein**, the formation of the participle remains the same. The only difference is the conjugation of the verb **sein**. Let's look at a verb of motion, **gehen**, conjugated fully in the present perfect and past perfect tenses.

	present perfect	past perfect
ich	bin gegangen	war gegangen (*have gone, had gone*)
du	bist gegangen	warst gegangen
er	ist gegangen	war gegangen
wir	sind gegangen	waren gegangen
ihr	seid gegangen	wart gegangen
sie	sind gegangen	waren gegangen

Let's look at **haben, sein,** and **werden** in the present perfect and past perfect tenses.

	haben (**have**)	*sein* (**be**)	*werden* (**become**)
ich	habe/hatte gehabt	bin/war gewesen	bin/war geworden
du	hast/hattest gehabt	bist/warst gewesen	bist/warst geworden
er	hat/hatte gehabt	ist/war gewesen	ist/war geworden
wir	haben/hatten gehabt	sind/waren gewesen	sind/waren geworden
ihr	habt/hattet gehabt	seid/wart gewesen	seid/wart geworden
sie	haben/hatten gehabt	sind/waren gewesen	sind/waren geworden

Some irregular verbs change the vowel in the stem of the participle but have a **-t** ending like a regular verb. For example:

	senden (**send**)	*nennen* (**name**)	*rennen* (**run**)
ich	habe gesandt	habe genannt	bin gerannt
du	hast gesandt	hast genannt	bist gerannt

er	hat gesandt	hat genannt	ist gerannt
wir	haben gesandt	haben genannt	sind gerannt
ihr	habt gesandt	habt genannt	seid gerannt
sie	haben gesandt	haben genannt	sind gerannt

Other irregular verbs that follow this pattern are:

brennen	gebrannt	*burn*
bringen	gebracht	*bring*
denken	gedacht	*think*
kennen	gekannt	*know, be acquainted*
wenden	gewandt	*turn*
wissen	gewusst	*know*

Modal auxiliaries

The modal auxiliaries all use **haben** as their auxiliary in the present perfect and past perfect tenses. Also, they form their participles from the stem of the infinitive *without an umlaut* and unlike most other irregular verbs, end their participles in **-t**. For example:

dürfen	gedurft
können	gekonnt
mögen	gemocht
müssen	gemusst
sollen	gesollt
wollen	gewollt

Used in sentences a modal in the present perfect tense looks like the following:

| Er hat Englisch gekonnt. | *He knew English.* |
| Wer hat das gewollt? | *Who wanted that?* |

Just like the modal-auxiliary participles, the participles of all regular and irregular verbs stand at the end of the sentence.

| Ich habe ihm ein Fahrrad **gekauft**. | *I bought him a bike.* |
| Sind sie in die Schweiz **gefahren**? | *Did they travel to Switzerland?* |

The present perfect tense is the preferred tense for making statements in the spoken language about things that have occurred in the past. The simple past tense is used more often in the written language.

| **written language** | Er kam nach Hause. | *He came home.* |
| **spoken language** | Er ist nach Hause gekommen. | *He came home.* |

However, when stating that something has been occurring for a period of time or since a point in time, the *present tense* is used to convey this meaning, but the English translation is in the present perfect tense. For example:

Ich wohne seit zehn Jahren in Bonn.   *I have been living in Bonn for ten years.*
Er ist seit zwei Wochen sehr krank.   *He has been very sick for two weeks.*

Exercise 83

Rewrite each sentence in the present perfect tense and then in the past perfect tense, changing the subject of the sentence to the word or phrase in parentheses.

1. Liese hat mit dem Hund gespielt.

(ich) _____

_____

(ihr) _____

_____

(du) _____

_____

(die Jungen) _____

_____

2. Haben Sie genug Zeit gehabt?

(du) _____

_____

(sie pl.) _____

_____

(Karl) _____

_____

(Felix und Benno) _____

_____

3. Ihr Sohn ist wieder gesund geworden.

(ich) _____

_____

(wir) _____

_____

(ihr) _____

_____

(du) _____

_____

4. Wie hast du das gewusst?

(er) _____

_____

(sie pl.) _____

_____

(sie s.) _____

_____

(die Wissenschaftler) _____

_____

5. Meine Kusine hat es nie gekonnt.

(ich) _____

_____

(du) _____

_____

(wir) _____

_____

(ihr) _____

_____

Exercise 84

Rewrite each present-tense sentence in the simple past tense and then in the present perfect tense.

1. Wir sind schon fertig.

_____

_____

2. Glauben Sie, dass diese Idee gut ist?

_____

_____

3. Peter fängt den Ball nicht.

_____

_____

4. Ich kenne den neuen Studenten nicht.

_____

_____

5. Tante Gerda stellt die Vase aufs Klavier.

_____

_____

6. Er geht mit seiner Freundin auf eine Party.

_____

_____

7. Wir reden mit Herrn Müller.

_____

_____

8. Sie wirft ein Stein ins Fenster.

_____

_____

9. Alle kritisieren diese Politiker.

_____

_____

10. Wer schwimmt besser? Maria oder Tanja?

_____

_____

Exercise 85

Circle the letter of the word that best completes each sentence.

1. Vor einer Woche ist er _____.

a. geglaubt

b. wollte

c. gestorben

d. genommen

2. Wie lange _____ der Film gedauert?

a. habt

b. hat

c. hattet

d. ist

3. Wart _____ mit dem Zug gekommen?

a. sie

b. Sie

c. er

d. ihr

4. Meine Freunde _____ Pfleger geworden.

a. sind

b. seid

c. war

d. hatten

5. Ich _____ oft ins Theater gegangen.

a. waren

b. habe

c. bin

d. hatte

6. Hattet _____ direkt am Strand gewohnt?

a. ihr

b. du

c. er

d. Sie

7. Der Geschäftsmann _____ wieder ins Ausland gereist.

a. ist

b. wart

c. hat

d. hatte

8. Wir sind noch nicht im neuen Stadtpark _____.

a. gemacht

b. gewesen

c. waren

d. wart

9. Sie haben wirklich keine Zeit _____.

a. gedacht

b. geworden

c. gewesen

d. gehabt

10. Sie haben die neue Kirche _____.

a. fotografiert

b. gewesen

c. gefahren

d. verliert

11. Ich _____ Sauerkraut nie gemocht.

a. habe

b. hatten

c. bin

d. sein

12. _____ hatte diese Messer zum Schneiden gebraucht.

  a. Du

  b. Ihr

  c. Wir

  d. Er

13. Wo haben Sie die Bären _____ ?

  a. geholfen

  b. gebracht

  c. gebrochen

  d. gesehen

14. Jemand _____ in jenes Haus gerannt.

  a. wart

  b. hatte

  c. hat

  d. ist

15. Sie _____ sehr lange gewartet.

  a. war

  b. hatte

  c. habt

  d. ist

Exercise 86

The following sentences are in various tenses. Rewrite each one in the present tense.

1. Ich konnte ihnen gar nicht helfen.

_____

2. Sie haben am Fenster gesessen und Kaffee getrunken.

_____

3. Warum hatte er den Sessel ins Wohnzimmer gestellt?

_____

4. Das Mädchen war sehr müde.

_____

5. Waren Ihre Gäste mit der Straßenbahn gekommen?

_____

6. Peter spielte Klavier für sie.

_____

7. Ich lächelte aber sagte nichts.

_____

8. An wen hat sie diesen Brief geschrieben?

_____

9. Wir haben selten an jene schlechten Tage gedacht.

_____

10. Wer hat diesen Ausflug arrangiert?

_____

16

Future Tenses

Like other tenses in English, the future tense has more than one form:

habitual   I will go to school.
incomplete or progressive   I will be going to school.

Both forms are translated into German by a single future-tense conjugation, which consists of the present-tense conjugation of **werden** and an infinitive located at the end of the sentence. For example:

Ich werde zur Schule gehen.   *I'll go to school.*
Er wird seinen Onkel besuchen.   *He'll visit his uncle.*
Die Männer werden Karten spielen.   *The men will play cards.*

Another way to express the future tense in German is by a present-tense conjugation where the future tense is inferred or understood by the context or because of an adverb accompanying the verb. For example:

Was **macht** ihr morgen? Wir **fahren**   *What are you doing tomorrow?*
 in die Stadt.   *We're driving to the city.*
Fährt euer Vater auch mit?   *Will your father be going along?*
Ich **habe** nächste Woche eine Prüfung.   *I have a test next week.*

Take note that English often does something similar, as in the last example: *I have a test next week.* This sentence is in the present tense, but the meaning is the future tense.

Future perfect tense

The future perfect tense in German is used like its counterpart in English. It consists of the conjugation of **werden** followed by a past participle and either **haben** or **sein**, whichever auxiliary is appropriate for the verb in question. It is called "future" and "perfect," because it combines a form of **werden** with *a participle and its auxiliary*—for example, **werden** + **gesprochen** + **haben**. The auxiliary **haben** or **sein** will always be in the infinitive form.

Let's compare the future-tense conjugation with the future perfect tense.

	future	**future perfect**
ich	werde kommen	werde gekommen sein (*will come, will have come*)
du	wirst kommen	wirst gekommen sein
er	wird kommen	wird gekommen sein
wir	werden kommen	werden gekommen sein
ihr	werdet kommen	werdet gekommen sein
sie	werden kommen	werden gekommen sein

In essence, these two tenses are formed in the same way if you consider the participle and infinitive of the future perfect tense as a *participial infinitive* composed of those two elements. Therefore, the structure is **werden** + the *infinitive or participial infinitive*.

ich werde **sprechen**	*I will speak*
ich werde **gesprochen haben**	*I will have spoken*

The future perfect tense is used to tell that something will have occurred by a certain point in time in the future.

Sie werden bis morgen Abend angekommen sein.	*They'll have arrived by tomorrow evening.*

Exercise 87

Write the future-tense conjugation of each of the following verbs.

	lachen	*kennen*	*gehen*	*schreiben*
1. ich	_____	_____	_____	_____
2. du	_____	_____	_____	_____
3. er	_____	_____	_____	_____
4. wir	_____	_____	_____	_____
5. ihr	_____	_____	_____	_____
6. sie	_____	_____	_____	_____

Exercise 88

Change the following present-tense sentences to the future tense with **werden**. Then write a present-tense sentence that infers the future tense with the adverb **morgen**. For example:

> Sie spielen Fußball.
> *Sie werden Fußball spielen.*
> *Morgen spielen sie Fußball.*

1. Die Mädchen gehen auf eine Party.

   _____

   _____

2. Doktor Schneider arbeitet in einem großen Krankenhaus.

   _____

   _____

3. Ein Auslandsbrief kostet 1 Euro.

   _____

   _____

4. Der kleine Felix dankt seinen Großeltern dafür.

   _____

   _____

5. Martin kommt mit seiner Verlobten nach Hause.

   _____

   _____

Exercise 89

The following sentences are in various tenses. Change each one to the future tense with **werden**.

1. Er berichtete über die Lage in Afghanistan.

   _____

2. Wir informieren sie über die Gefahren dieser Industrie.

   _____

3. Haben Sie eine Nachricht von Ihrem Sohn erhalten?

   _____

4. Ich traf sie im Garten.

   _____

5. Wo hattest du den Schatz gefunden?

_____

6. Ich habe kein Wort gesagt.

_____

7. Die Jungen sind dorthin gewandert.

_____

8. Der Dieb hat mir den Mantel gestohlen.

_____

9. Hat er den Nagel in die Wand geschlagen?

_____

10. Sie riskierte ihr Leben.

_____

11. Wer hat für die alte Frau gesorgt?

_____

12. Katrina teilt ihr Spielzeug mit den anderen Kindern.

_____

13. Der reiche Mann wohnte in einem riesigen Haus.

_____

14. Hast du die Röcke selbst gemacht?

_____

15. Die Studenten sind nach Paris gefahren.

_____

Exercise 90

Each group of four sentences that follows should be in the present, past, present perfect, and future tenses. Only one of the tenses is provided. Fill in the blanks with the missing tenses of the sentence given.

1. present: Ihr Haus wird für sie zu klein.

past: _____

present perfect: _____

future: _____

2. present: _____

past: _____

present perfect: Die Haustür ist oft offen gewesen.

future: _____

3. present: _____

past: Diese Treppe führte in den Keller.

present perfect: _____

future: _____

4. present: _____

past: _____

present perfect: _____

future: Sie werden die ganze Wohnung renovieren.

5. present: _____

past: _____

present perfect: Sie hat die Ringe von ihrer Mutter geerbt.

future: _____

Exercise 91

Rewrite each of the future-tense sentences in the future perfect tense.

1. Er wird es sagen. _____

2. Sie wird mich fragen. _____

3. Ich werde nichts kaufen. _____

4. Wirst du mitkommen? _____

5. Werden Sie darüber lachen? _____

6. Die Frauen werden Karten spielen. _____

7. Werdet ihr dorthin fahren? _____

8. Tina wird weinen. _____

9. Sie wird zum Ziel laufen. _____

10. Ich werde das Geld borgen. _____

17

Imperatives

Imperatives are commands. German commands are given to the *second person*, and they have to conform to the second-person pronouns **du, ihr,** and **Sie.** For most verbs, the imperative for **du** comprises the stem of the infinitive plus an **-e** ending. In casual speech the **-e** ending is often dropped. The imperative for **ihr** is the same as its present-tense conjugation. This is also true for the imperative for **Sie,** except that the pronoun **Sie** always follows the imperative verb. Remember that **du** is used to address children, close friends, or family members. Use **ihr** when addressing more than one child, friend, or family member. Use **Sie** when addressing strangers, officials, or others you are on a formal basis with. Let's look at some example verbs.

du	*ihr*	*Sie*	
Kaufe! (Kauf)	Kauft!	Kaufen Sie!	*Buy!*
Lache! (Lach)	Lacht!	Lachen Sie!	*Laugh!*
Besuche! (Besuch)	Besucht!	Besuchen Sie!	*Visit!*

If the verb has an inseparable prefix, like the verb **besuchen** in the previous example, the verb is not affected in any way. But if the verb has a separable prefix, the prefix stands at the end of the phrase.

du	*ihr*	*Sie*	
Höre auf! (Hör)	Hört auf!	Hören Sie auf!	*Stop!*
Komme mit! (Komm)	Kommt mit!	Kommen Sie mit!	*Come along!*
Stehe auf! (Steh)	Steht auf!	Stehen Sie auf!	*Stand up!*

Irregular verbs are treated similarly, but those that make a vowel change in the present tense show that change in the imperative form for **du.** In addition, verbs that have a vowel change in the present tense do not have an **-e** ending in the imperative for **du.** The umlaut in the present tense of certain irregular verbs does not affect the imperative. For example:

du	*ihr*	*Sie*	
Gib!	Gebt!	Geben Sie!	*Give!*
Befiehl!	Befehlt!	Befehlen Sie!	*Order!*
Sprich aus!	Sprecht aus!	Sprechen Sie aus!	*Pronounce!*
Halte! (Halt)	Haltet!	Halten Sie!	*Hold!*

The omission of the final -e of the imperative form for **du** in casual speech cannot occur with certain verbs. Regular verbs that end in **-eln**, **-ern**, **-nen**, **-igen**, or **-men** cannot omit the final -e. Consider the following examples:

lächeln	Lächele!	*Smile!*
kümmern	Kümmere!	*Worry!*
öffnen	Öffne!	*Open!*
reinigen	Reinige!	*Clean!*
atmen	Atme!	*Breathe!*

The verbs **haben**, **sein**, and **werden** require special consideration.

du	*ihr*	*Sie*	
Habe!	Habt!	Haben Sie!	*Have!*
Sei!	Seid!	Seien Sie!	*Be!*
Werde!	Werdet!	Werden Sie!	*Become!*

Another form of imperative is one widely used on signs or by officials speaking to a group. This imperative is the infinitive of the verb, and like all German imperatives, it is followed by an exclamation point. For example, a sign on a wall:

Nicht rauchen!   *No smoking.*

The stationmaster speaking to a crowd on the platform as a train comes in:

Zurückbleiben!   *Stand back.*

Exercise 92

Write the three imperative forms for each of the following verbs.

	arbeiten	*singen*	*fahren*	*verkaufen*
1. du	_____	_____	_____	_____
2. ihr	_____	_____	_____	_____
3. Sie	_____	_____	_____	_____
	sein	*annehmen*	*zugeben*	*stören*
4. du	_____	_____	_____	_____
5. ihr	_____	_____	_____	_____
6. Sie	_____	_____	_____	_____

Exercise 93

Rewrite each of the following sentences as imperatives. Use the names and words in parentheses as signals to tell you whether the imperative should be for **du, ihr,** or **Sie.** For example:

> Er kauft einen neuen Hut.
> (mein Freund) *Kaufe einen neuen Hut!*

1. Wir singen in einem Chor.

(Kinder) _____

2. Alle sprechen über den Wildwestfilm.

(mein Bruder) _____

3. Der Lehrer erzählt von einer Reise nach China.

(Professor Bauer) _____

4. Sie brät die Würstchen in Öl.

(Vater) _____

5. Ich schneide das Brot für Butterbrote.

(Frau Benz) _____

6. Die Jungen essen Hähnchen mit Pommes frites.

(meine Schwester) _____

7. Karl nimmt eine Suppe vor dem Hauptgericht.

(Thomas und Liese) _____

8. Er zieht einen Braunen Gürtel an.

(Mutter) _____

9. Die Studenten bügeln die Hemden und Hosen.

(meine Tochter) _____

10. Jemand gräbt ein tiefes Loch.

(meine Geschwister) _____

11. Die Kinder sind artig.

(mein Sohn) _____

12. Ich ziehe den schmutzigen Pullover aus.

(meine Lehrerin) _____

13. Wir decken das Kind mit der Bettdecke gut zu.

(mein Onkel) _____

14. Sie werfen den harten Käse weg.

(der Rechtsanwalt) _____

15. Die Jungen sehen den komischen Mann an.

(mein Sohn) _____

Exercise 94

Change the following imperatives to the infinitive type that a person of authority often uses to address a group.

1. Bleiben Sie zurück!

_____

2. Steigt hier um!

_____

3. Mach das Gepäck auf!

_____

4. Bitte schweigen Sie!

_____

5. Sprecht nicht!

_____

18

Reflexive Pronouns

Unlike English, German does not use a suffix to form a reflexive (*myself, yourself, himself*, etc.). Instead, individual reflexive pronouns are used. But German has two forms of reflexive pronouns: accusative and dative.

Accusative reflexive pronouns

The accusative reflexive pronouns are so named because they occur where the accusative case is required in the sentence. The accusative case is used:

1. to identify direct objects
2. following accusative prepositions
3. following accusative-dative prepositions

The accusative reflexive pronoun is used when that pronoun and the subject of the sentence are the same person. A personal pronoun is used when that pronoun and the subject of the sentence are different persons. For example:

same person	I hated **myself** for doing that.
different person	I hated **her** for doing that.

German works similarly:

same person	Ich frage **mich** warum.	*I ask myself why.*
different person	Ich frage **sie** warum.	*I ask her why.*

Let's look at all the accusative reflexive pronouns and compare them with their personal-pronoun counterparts.

nominative	accusative personal	accusative reflexive	
ich	mich	mich	*myself*
du	dich	dich	*yourself*
er	ihn	sich	*himself*

sie	sie	sich	*herself*
es	es	sich	*itself*
wir	uns	uns	*ourselves*
ihr	euch	euch	*yourselves*
Sie	Sie	sich	*yourself, yourselves*
sie	sie	sich	*themselves*

If the subject of a sentence is **wer** or **was**, their accusative reflexive pronoun will be **sich**. This is also true of all singular or plural nouns.

In sentences, the reflexive pronouns occur after the conjugated verb or after a preposition. For example:

direct object	Ärgere **dich** nicht!	*Don't get angry.*
accusative preposition	Sie kaufte etwas **für sich**.	*She bought something for herself.*
accusative-dative preposition (accusative case)	Ich denke nur **an mich** selbst.	*I only think about myself.*

Dative reflexive pronouns

Dative reflexive pronouns function like the accusative reflexive pronouns, but they are used where the dative case is required:

1. to identify indirect objects
2. to identify objects of dative verbs
3. following dative prepositions
4. following accusative-dative prepositions

The dative reflexive pronoun is used when that pronoun and the subject of the sentence are the same person. A personal pronoun is used when that pronoun and the subject of the sentence are different persons. For example:

same person	Ich kaufte **mir** einen neuen Gürtel.	*I bought myself a new belt.*
different person	Ich kaufte **ihm** einen neuen Gürtel.	*I bought him a new belt.*

As you can see from the preceding example, the dative reflexive pronoun **mir** happens to be the same as the dative personal pronoun **mir**. This occurs with other pronouns as well. Let's look at all the dative reflexive pronouns and compare them with their personal-pronoun counterparts.

nominative	dative personal	dative reflexive	
ich	mir	mir	*myself*
du	dir	dir	*yourself*
er	ihm	sich	*himself*
sie	ihr	sich	*herself*
es	ihm	sich	*itself*
wir	uns	uns	*ourselves*
ihr	euch	euch	*yourselves*
Sie	Ihnen	sich	*yourself, yourselves*
sie	ihnen	sich	*themselves*

If the subject of a sentence is **wer** or **was**, the dative reflexive pronoun will be **sich**. This is also true of all singular or plural nouns.

In sentences, the reflexive pronouns occur after the conjugated verb or after a preposition. For example:

indirect object	Kauft ihr **euch** einen neuen Wagen?	*Are you buying yourselves a new car?*
dative verb	Sie trauen **sich** diese Arbeit zu.	*They entrust themselves with this job.*
dative preposition	Ich habe kein Geld **bei mir**.	*I don't have any money on me.*
accusative-dative preposition (dative case)	Ich verberge das Geschenk **hinter mir**.	*I hide the gift behind me.*

Reflexive verbs

German *reflexive verbs* are always used with reflexive pronouns to achieve their full meaning. It's like the English verb *enjoy oneself*. Without the reflexive pronoun or a direct object, the verb makes no sense. For example:

If someone asks, "Did you have fun at the party?"
you *cannot* reply, "Yes, I really enjoyed."

To achieve the complete meaning of the verb, the reflexive must be added:

"Yes, I really enjoyed *myself*."

This occurs with many German verbs. They are used together with reflexive pronouns to achieve their full meaning. Here are a few commonly used reflexive verbs:

sich befinden	*be located*
sich benehmen	*behave, conduct oneself*
sich erholen	*recover*
sich erinnern	*remember*
sich erkälten	*catch cold*
sich fragen	*wonder (ask oneself)*
sich interessieren	*be interested (interest oneself)*
sich irren	*be mistaken*
sich unterhalten	*converse*

Exercise 95

Rewrite each sentence, changing the accusative object in bold print to the appropriate reflexive pronoun.

1. Sie fragte **ihren Freund,** warum es so kalt ist.

_____

2. Ich erinnere **die Kinder** an die Schularbeit.

_____

3. Wir waschen **den Hund** im Keller.

_____

4. Warum willst du **Onkel Peter** so ärgern?

_____

5. Setze **die Vase** auf einen Stuhl!

_____

6. Legt **die Bücher** hin!

_____

7. Mutter will **ihren Sohn** vor einer Erkältung schützen.

_____

8. Wir brauchen das Geld für **unsere Eltern.**

_____

9. Siehst du **ihr Gesicht** im Spiegel?

_____

10. Felix und Karl denken nur an **ihre Familie.**

_____

Exercise 96

Rewrite each sentence, changing the dative object in bold print to the appropriate reflexive pronoun.

1. Wir suchen **ihnen** gute Plätze in der ersten Reihe.

_____

2. Wer hat **mir** ein Glas Wein bestellt?

_____

3. Wirst du **deinen Freunden** diese Arbeit zutrauen?

_____

4. Ich konnte **ihr** diese Dummheit nicht verzeihen.

_____

5. Der alte Mann verbirgt die Blumen hinter **der Krankenschwester.**

_____

6. Wie könnt ihr **diesen Menschen** helfen?

_____

7. Haben Sie **Ihrer Frau** einen Pelzmantel gekauft?

_____

8. Ich helfe **dem Bettler,** so gut ich kann.

_____

9. Warum musst du **uns** widersprechen?

_____

10. Wer kaufte **Angela** die Rosen?

_____

Exercise 97

Fill in the blank of each sentence twice: once with a noun and once with a reflexive pronoun. For example:

Er setzte *eine Lampe* ans Fenster.
Er setzte *sich* ans Fenster.

1. Wirst du _____ ein Fahrrad kaufen?

Wirst du _____ ein Fahrrad kaufen?

2. Wo kann ich _____ waschen?

Wo kann ich _____ waschen?

3. Onkel Martin hat _____ ein Telegramm geschickt.

Onkel Martin hat _____ ein Telegramm geschickt.

4. Der Vater muss _____ daran erinnern.

Der Vater muss _____ daran erinnern.

5. Trauen Sie _____ diese Arbeit zu?

Trauen Sie _____ diese Arbeit zu?

6. Die Kinder ärgerten _____ nicht.

Die Kinder ärgerten _____ nicht.

7. Ich will _____ vor der Grippe schützen.

Ich will _____ vor der Grippe schützen.

8. Widersprich _____ nicht!

Widersprich _____ nicht!

9. Sie half _____ , so gut sie konnte.

Sie half _____ , so gut sie konnte.

10. Herr Schneider hat ein Geschenk für _____ .

Herr Schneider hat ein Geschenk für _____ .

Review 2

Exercise 98

Fill in the blanks with the missing endings for the cases indicated. Be careful! Not all of the blanks require an ending.

nominative case

1. ein nett_____ Mann   dies_____ kleine Katze_____   unsere neu_____ Schule

2. eine gut_____ Tasse   jen_____ schnell_____ Wagen   welche alt_____ Leute

accusative case

3. den letzt_____ Platz   dies_____ kurz_____ Bleistift   ein_____ langen Stock

4. sein_____ besten Freunde   unseren reich_____ Freund   mein_____ Kinder

dative case

5. ein_____ schlecht_____ Tag   dein_____ jung_____ Schwester   krank_____ Leute_____

6. dies_____ scharfen Messer   jed_____ neu_____ Studentin   kalt_____ Bier

genitive case

7. ein_____ groß_____ Problem_____   dies_____ jung_____ Dame_____

8. viel_____ alt_____ Frauen_____   jen_____ arm_____ Kind_____

Exercise 99

Rewrite each sentence by replacing the word in bold print with the ones in parentheses. Make any necessary changes to the adjective endings.

1. **Diese** Frau war einmal Richterin.

(jener) _____

(mein) _____

(welcher) _____

2. Ist **dein** neuer Freund Reporter geworden?

(ihr) _____

(dieser) _____

(jener) _____

3. Er trinkt nicht gern kalten **Kaffee.**

(Tee) _____

(Milch) _____

(Bier) _____

Exercise 100

Fill in each blank with any appropriate adjective. Pay attention to the gender, number, and case.

1. Die Lehrerin wird diesen _____ Schüler fragen.

2. Sie erinnerte sich gern an einige _____ Verwandte.

3. Die Frau kann diesem _____ Politiker vertrauen.

4. Trinkst du _____ Wasser?

5. Meine Mutter hat einen _____ Garten.

Exercise 101

Rewrite each prepositional phrase, changing the preposition and definite article to a contraction. For example:

in dem Garten *im Garten*

1. um das Haus _____

2. zu dem Klavier _____

3. bei dem Schwimmen _____

4. an das Tor _____

5. zu der Ausstellung _____

6. von dem Professor _____

7. auf das Buch _____

Exercise 102

Rewrite each sentence as a question that could be answered with **ja** or **nein**. For example:

    Er spricht kein Deutsch. *Spricht er kein Deutsch?*

1. Dieses Land ist arm an Silber und Gold.

    _____

2. Frau Schneider war nicht zufrieden.

    _____

3. Niemand hat den geretteten Mann gekannt.

    _____

4. Seine Schwester ist ebenso alt wie mein Bruder.

    _____

5. Die Touristen möchten das Schloss fotografieren.

    _____

Exercise 103

Rewrite the following sentences as questions. Use the information in bold print to tell you which interrogative to use: **was, wer, wen, wem,** or **wessen**. For example:

    Er besuchte **einen Freund**.   *Wen besuchte er?*

1. **Meine** Tante ist Physikerin.

    _____

2. **Er** ist ein Freund des neuen Bürgermeisters.

    _____

3. Sie hat **eine Blume** für mich gekauft.

    _____

4. **Unser Garten** sieht jetzt sehr schön aus.

    _____

5. Der Bäcker gibt **ihm** eine Torte.

    _____

6. **Der Schaffner** bittet um ihre Fahrkarten.

    _____

7. Er sah **den Dieb** an der Ecke.

    _____

Exercise 104

Write the present- and past-tense conjugation of each of the following verbs with the pronouns provided.

	suchen	werden	fahren	lesen
1. du	_____	_____	_____	_____
2.	_____	_____	_____	_____
3. er	_____	_____	_____	_____
4.	_____	_____	_____	_____
5. wir	_____	_____	_____	_____
6.	_____	_____	_____	_____

Exercise 105

Rewrite each sentence in the present tense with the subjects provided in parentheses.

1. Man muss vorsichtig sein.

(ich) _____

(die Kinder) _____

(du) _____

2. Ist sie noch in Ulm?

(ihr) _____

(sie pl.) _____

(du) _____

3. Ich habe keine Zeit.

(sie s.) _____

(du) _____

(ihr) _____

Exercise 106

Rewrite each sentence in the past tense with the new subjects provided in parentheses.

1. Die Mädchen gingen langsam nach Hause.

(ich) _____

(der Lehrer) _____

(du) _____

2. Meine Kusine war vier Wochen in Madrid.

(sie pl.) _____

(wer) _____

(ihre Verwandten) _____

3. Warum kamst du nicht mit?

(sie s.) _____

(ihr) _____

(Sie) _____

4. Am Montag Abend starb er.

(die Soldaten) _____

(sie pl.) _____

(Frau Bauer) _____

Exercise 107

Circle the letter of the word that best completes each sentence.

1. _____ stahl seine Brieftasche?

a. Mochte

b. Wer

c. Waren

d. Verkaufte

2. Der Arzt _____ seine Mappe.

a. musste

b. mussten

c. vergaß

d. vergessen

3. _____ blieb auf der Bühne.

a. Niemand

b. Was

c. Warst

d. Du

4. _____ liegt unter dem Tisch?

a. Wen

b. Wann

c. Wo

d. Was

5. Vor einer Woche ist er _____ .

a. geglaubt

b. wollte

c. geboren

d. genommen

6. Wart _____ mit dem Zug gekommen?

a. sie

b. Sie

c. er

d. ihr

7. Die Professorin _____ wieder in die Schweiz gereist.

a. ist

b. wart

c. hat

d. hatte

8. Robert _____ sehr lange gewartet.

a. war

b. hatte

c. habt

d. ist

Exercise 108

Write the present perfect and past perfect conjugation of each of the following verbs.

	kennen	*sagen*	*laufen*	*schreiben*
1. ich				
2.				
3. er				
4.				
5. ihr				
6.				

Exercise 109

Rewrite each present-tense sentence in the simple past tense and then in the present perfect.

1. Die Jungen sind fertig.

_____

_____

2. Glaubst du, dass diese Idee gut ist?

_____

_____

3. Sein Bruder fängt den Ball nicht.

_____

_____

4. Sie geht mit ihren Freundinnen zur Party.

_____

_____

5. Alle kritisieren seine Politik.

_____

_____

Exercise 110

The following sentences are in various tenses. Rewrite each one in the present tense.

1. Er konnte ihr nicht helfen.

_____

2. Wir haben in der Küche gesessen und Kaffee getrunken.

_____

3. Warum hatten Sie diesen Tisch ins Wohnzimmer gestellt?

_____

4. Die Kinder waren sehr müde.

_____

5. An wen hat er die Ansichtskarte geschrieben?

_____

Exercise 111

Change the following present-tense sentences to the future tense with **werden**. Then write a present-tense sentence that infers the future tense with the adverb **morgen**. For example:

Sie spielen Fußball.
Sie werden Fußball spielen.
Morgen spielen sie Fußball.

1. Auslandsbriefe kosten 1 Euro.

_____

_____

2. Er kommt spät nach Hause.

_____

_____

3. Du bist gesund.

_____

_____

Exercise 112

Each group of four sentences that follows should be in the present, past, present perfect, and future tenses. Only one of the tenses is provided. Fill in the blanks with the missing tenses of the sentence given.

1. present: _____

   past: Diese Treppe führte in den Keller.

   present perfect: _____

   future: _____

2. present: _____

   past: _____

   present perfect: _____

   future: Sie werden Fußball spielen.

3. present: _____

   past: _____

   present perfect: _____

   future: Sie wird mit dem Zug kommen.

4. present: _____

   past: Ihre Tante nannte sie Geli.

   present perfect: _____

   future: _____

Exercise 113

Write the three forms of imperative for each of the following verbs.

	sein	*annehmen*	*ausgeben*	*werden*
1. du	_____	_____	_____	_____
2. ihr	_____	_____	_____	_____
3. Sie	_____	_____	_____	_____

Exercise 114

Rewrite each sentence, changing the object in bold print to the appropriate reflexive pronoun.

1. Sie fragte **ihre Mutter,** warum es so kalt ist.

   _____

2. Ich erinnere **meinen Sohn** an die Schularbeit.

   _____

3. Er wäscht **den Hund** im Keller.

   _____

4. Setze **die Blumen** auf diesen Stuhl!

   _____

5. Hat sie **Ihrer Mutter** einen Pelzmantel gekauft?

   _____

6. Warum musst du **uns** widersprechen?

   _____

7. Legt **die Bücher** hin!

   _____

8. Wer hat **mir** ein Glas Wein bestellt?

   _____

9. Wie kannst du **diesen Menschen** helfen?

   _____

10. Ich kaufte **ihm** eine neue Brille.

    _____

19

Prefixes

German uses prefixes far more than English does. Also, a single verb derives a variety of new meanings from the prefixes. For example:

schreiben	*write*
anschreiben	*write up*
beschreiben	*describe*
zuschreiben	*attribute to*

German has two categories of prefixes: inseparable prefixes and separable prefixes. But a few prefixes can be used in either category.

Inseparable prefixes

Prefixes are always attached to the front end of a verb, and inseparable prefixes are never removed from this position, no matter the tense or form of the verb. The inseparable prefixes are **be-, emp-, ent-, er-, ge-, miss-, ver-,** and **zer-**. The stress in a verb with an inseparable prefix is always on the stem of the verb (**bestéllen**). Attached to verbs, the inseparable prefixes look like this:

bekommen	*receive*
besuchen	*visit*
empfehlen	*recommend*
empfinden	*feel*
entlaufen	*run away*
entschließen	*decide*
erschlagen	*kill*
erwarten	*expect*
gefallen	*please*
gehören	*belong to*
missachten	*ignore*
misslingen	*be unsuccessful*

vergessen	*forget*	
verstehen	*understand*	
zerreißen	*tear to pieces*	
zerschmettern	*smash*	

Notice the position of the inseparable prefix on the following verbs in all the tenses.

	besuchen (visit)	*entlaufen* (run away)
present	er besucht	wir entlaufen
past	er besuchte	wir entliefen
present perfect	er hat besucht	wir sind entlaufen
past perfect	er hatte besucht	wir waren entlaufen
future	er wird besuchen	wir werden entlaufen
future perfect	er wird besucht haben	wir werden entlaufen sein

In the perfect tenses, a **ge-** prefix is not required for past participles with inseparable prefixes. The inseparable prefix replaces **ge-**. Also, the function of the inseparable prefix is not affected whether the verb is regular or irregular or whether it requires **haben** or **sein** as its auxiliary.

Separable prefixes

There are many separable prefixes. These are adverbs and prepositions used to alter the meaning of a verb. Some of the commonly used separable prefixes are **an, auf, aus, bei, ein, fort, mit, nach, vor, weg,** and **zu**. But there are many others. The stress in a verb with a separable prefix is always on the separable prefix (**vórstellen**). Attached to verbs, separable prefixes look like this:

ankommen	*arrive*
aufhören	*cease*
aussprechen	*pronounce*
beibringen	*teach*
fortfahren	*continue*
mitgehen	*go along*
nachahmen	*imitate*
vorstellen	*introduce*
weglaufen	*run away*
zunehmen	*increase*

When a verb with a separable prefix is conjugated, the separable prefix appears at the end of the sentence or clause in the present and past tenses and is separated from the past participle by the prefix **ge-** in the perfect tenses. In the future tense, the prefix remains on the infinitive. Notice the position of the separable prefix with the following example verbs in all the tenses.

	aufhören (cease)	*mitgehen* (go along)
present	er hört auf	wir gehen mit
past	er hörte auf	wir gingen mit
present perfect	er hat aufgehört	wir sind mitgegangen
past perfect	er hatte aufgehört	wir waren mitgegangen
future	er wird aufhören	wir werden mitgehen
future perfect	er wird aufgehört haben	wir werden mitgegangen sein

Prefixes that can be separable and inseparable

A few prefixes are used in either category—separable and inseparable. If the stress is on the prefix itself, the prefix is separable. When the stress is on the stem of the verb, it is a signal that the prefix is being used as an inseparable prefix. Let's look at some examples. Notice where the stress of the verb lies:

separable	**inseparable**
dúrchfallen *to fail*	durchdríngen *to penetrate*
hinter- N/A	hintergéhen *to deceive*
sich übersehen *to get fed up*	übertréiben *to exaggerate*
úmkommen *to die*	umármen *to embrace*
únterkommen *to find housing*	unterbréchen *to interrupt*
vólltanken *to fill up the gas tank*	vollzíehen *to carry out*
wíderrufen *to retract*	widerspíegeln *to reflect*
wíedergeben *to give back*	wiederhólen *to repeat*

Compare the differences in the conjugations with the same prefix, used in one example as a separable prefix and in the second example as an inseparable prefix. The subject of each sentence will be **er**.

	wíderrufen (retract)	*widerspíegeln* (reflect)
present	ruft wider	widerspiegelt
past	rief wider	widerspiegelte
present perfect	hat widergerufen	hat widerspiegelt

past perfect	hatte widergerufen	hatte widerspiegelt
future	wird widerrufen	wird widerspiegeln
future perfect	wird widergerufen haben	wird widerspiegelt haben

Prefixes on nouns

If a verb has a noun form, its prefix also accompanies the noun. If the prefix is separable, the stress is on the prefix of the noun. If the prefix is inseparable, the stress is on the stem of the noun. Prefixes on nouns always remain in one position. For example:

| behaúpten | die Beháuptung | *claim* |
| aússprechen | die Aússprache | *pronunciation* |

Exercise 115

Rewrite each sentence, changing the subject to the new ones provided in parentheses. Make all the other necessary changes.

1. Was befiehlt der General?

(Sie) _____

(er) _____

(sie s.) _____

(sie pl.) _____

(du) _____

2. Er erfand die ganze Geschichte.

(ich) _____

(wir) _____

(ihr) _____

(Sie) _____

(du) _____

3. Meine Tante ruft die Polizei an.

(die Gäste) _____

(ich) _____

(du) _____

(er) _____

(wir) _____

    4. Das Baby schlief gleich ein.

(sie s.) _____

(du) _____

(die Kinder) _____

(alle) _____

(niemand) _____

Exercise 116

Fill in the blank with the inseparable prefix that best completes each verb: **be-, emp-, ent-, er-, ge-, miss-, ver-,** or **zer-.**

    1. Der Gefangene ist _____ flohen.

    2. Ein verwunderter Soldat _____ blutete.

    3. Ich _____ warte seit vier Wochen diese Zeitschrift.

    4. Das Mädchen _____ rötete und fing an zu lächeln.

    5. Während des Krieges haben sie das Dorf _____ stört.

    6. Ich _____ spreche die Wahrheit zu erzählen.

    7. Wann haben Sie diesen Brief _____ kommen?

    8. Der Schüler hat seinen Aufsatz _____ gessen.

    9. Wir werden heute abend viele Gäste _____ fangen.

10. Wie sieht er aus? Können Sie ihn _____schreiben?

Exercise 117

Circle the letter of the separable prefix that best completes the verbs in the following sentences.

    1. Hoffentlich wirst du _____ kommen.

    a. auf

    b. bei

    c. mit

    d. vor

2. Der Ritter hat den Drachen _____ gebracht.

a. an

b. ein

c. um

d. zurück

3. Ich werde es ihnen sofort _____ teilen.

a. an

b. auf

c. ein

d. mit

4. Er gibt viel Geld _____ .

a. an

b. aus

c. nach

d. vor

5. Um wie viel Uhr kommt der Zug _____ ?

a. an

b. fort

c. um

d. weiter

6. An der Ecke müssen wir _____ steigen.

a. aus

b. mit

c. vor

d. voran

7. Bist du nicht durstig? Trink deine Milch _____ !

a. an

b. auf

c. aus

d. zu

8. Ist der Hund wieder _____ gelaufen?

a. auf

b. bei

c. hinter

d. weg

9. Er hat eine Lösung _____ geschlagen.

a. ab

b. aus

c. hin

d. vor

10. Das Kind ist im Schlafanzug _____ gelaufen.

a. an

b. auf

c. hinaus

d. zusammen

Exercise 118

Write one original sentence with each of the following verbs.

1. übersetzen _____

2. verlangen _____

3. zurückkommen _____

4. sich benehmen _____

5. gehorchen _____

6. zumachen _____

7. unterrichten _____

8. aussehen _____

9. erklären _____

10. vorbereiten _____

20

Numbers, Time, Days of the Week, and the Calendar

Numbers have functions that go beyond their application in arithmetic. They have other important roles as well.

Cardinal numbers

Cardinal numbers (Arabic numerals) are the ones usually learned early in foreign language, and they are the ones that are used in arithmetic expressions. Let's look at their spelling.

0 null	10 zehn
1 eins	11 elf
2 zwei	12 zwölf
3 drei	13 dreizehn
4 vier	14 vierzehn
5 fünf	15 fünfzehn
6 sechs	16 sechzehn
7 sieben	17 siebzehn
8 acht	18 achtzehn
9 neun	19 neunzehn
20 zwanzig	30 dreißig
21 einundzwanzig	40 vierzig
22 zweiundzwanzig	50 fünfzig
23 dreiundzwanzig	60 sechzig
24 vierundzwanzig	70 siebzig
25 fünfundzwanzig	80 achtzig
26 sechsundzwanzig	90 neunzig
27 siebenundzwanzig	100 hundert
28 achtundzwanzig	1000 tausend
29 neunundzwanzig	1 000 000 eine Million

From twenty through ninety, the second part of those numbers is added to the *front* of the number, as in the English nursery rhyme, "Four and twenty blackbirds baked in a pie . . ."

For numbers higher than a million, German differs from English. For example:

1 000 000 000	eine Milliarde	*one billion*
1 000 000 000 000	eine Billion	*one trillion*

Also notice that thousands are separated in German by spaces, where in English they are separated by commas: for example, German 1 000 000 = English 1,000,000. However, decimals are separated by commas in German: for example, German 15,75 = English 15.75. It is said as **fünfzehn Komma fünfundsiebzig**. Finally, long numbers are rarely written out in words. If they are, they are written as one word: for example, 1055 = **tausendfünfundfünfzig**.

The four major arithmetic forms are addition (**die Addition**), division (**das Teilen**), multiplication (**die Multiplikation**), and subtraction (**die Subtraktion**). Also, equations are expressed in the following two ways:

5 + 3 = ?	Wie viel ist fünf plus drei? *or* Wie viel ist fünf und drei?
5 + 3 = 8	Fünf plus drei ist acht. *or* Fünf und drei ist acht.

Division equations are expressed like this:

12 ÷ 3 = ?	Wie viel ist zwölf geteilt durch drei?
12 ÷ 3 = 4	Zwölf geteilt durch drei ist vier.

Multiplication equations are expressed like this:

10 × 3 = ?	Wie viel ist zehn mal drei?
10 × 3 = 30	Zehn mal drei ist dreißig.

Subtraction equations are expressed like this:

22 − 11 = ?	Wie viel ist zweiundzwanzig minus elf? *or* Wie viel ist zweiundzwanzig weniger elf?
22 − 11 = 11	Zweiundzwanzig minus elf ist elf. *or* Zweiundzwanzig weniger elf ist elf.

The currency of Germany as well as of most of Europe is **der Euro** (€). When stating the cost of something, the euros and cents are said separately and when written as numbers are separated by a comma.

Es kostet 8,50 €. (acht Euro fünfzig Cent)   *It costs 8 euros 50 cents.*

Es kostet 11,25 €. (elf Euro fünfundzwanzig Cent) *It costs 11 euros 25 cents.*

Ordinal numbers

When numbers become adjectives, they are called ordinal numbers. In English, the suffix *-th* is added to most numbers to make them ordinal numbers: for example, *fifth*, *tenth*, *twentieth*, and so on. German does something similar: it adds the suffix **-te** to numbers up to nineteen and the suffix **-ste** to numbers over nineteen. For example:

zweite	*second*
fünfte	*fifth*
elfte	*eleventh*
neunzehnte	*nineteenth*
zwanzigste	*twentieth*
vierundzwanzigste	*twenty-fourth*
hundertste	*hundredth*
tausendste	*thousandth*

Three German ordinal numbers have an irregular formation. They are:

erste	*first*
dritte	*third*
siebte	*seventh*

Since ordinal numbers are adjectives, they must conform to the gender, number, and case of the noun they modify. For example:

der vierte Satz	*the fourth sentence*
von seiner ersten Klasse	*from his first class*
mit ihrem zweiten Mann	*with her second husband*

Let's look at two examples in all the cases.

nominative	der zehnte Wagen *the tenth car*	meine erste Freundin *my first girlfriend*
accusative	den zehnten Wagen	meine erste Freundin

dative	dem zehnten Wagen	meiner ersten Freundin
genitive	des zehnten Wagens	meiner ersten Freundin

In the same way as adjectives, ordinal numbers decline differently with **der** words and **ein** words. For example:

dieses **zweite** Gedicht	*this second poem*
sein **zweites** Gedicht	*his second poem*

Fractions

Fractions are formed quite simply by adding the suffix **-el** to the stem of the ordinal number. For example:

ordinal number	stem	fraction	
dritte	dritt-	Drittel	*a third*
sechste	sechst-	Sechstel	*a sixth*
zehnte	zehnt-	Zehntel	*a tenth*

Notice that the words for the German fractions are capitalized. They have become *neuter nouns*.

When fractions are used to express measurement, the measurement (meter, centimeter, liter, etc.) is written together with the fraction: **ein Viertelmeter**. When the two parts—the fraction and the measurement—can be written as two words, the fraction is no longer capitalized: **ein viertel Meter** (*a quarter of a meter*).

A few fractions have a special formation that is used throughout the German-speaking world. They are:

½	ein halb	*one-half*
1½	anderthalb, eineinhalb	*one and a half*
2½	zweieinhalb	*two and a half*
4½	viereinhalb	*three and a half*
¾	drei viertel	*three-fourths, three quarters*

You must distinguish between **die Hälfte** and **halb,** both of which mean *half.* The former is a noun and is *not* an arithmetic fraction. The latter is an adjective and can be declined like any other adjective. For example:

Wir haben das Brot in zwei gleiche **Hälften** geteilt.	*We divided the bread in two equal halves.*
Ich werde nur ein **halbes** Brot kaufen.	*I'm going to buy only half a loaf of bread.*

Telling time

Cardinal and ordinal numbers are also used for telling time in German. Look at these commonly used expressions for telling time. Notice that German, like English, sometimes omits the *element of time*, because it is understood: for example, *It's ten minutes after three* or *It's ten after three*.

1:00	Es ist ein Uhr. (Es ist eins.)
2:00	Es ist zwei Uhr. (Es ist zwei.)
3:05	Es ist fünf Minuten nach drei. (Es ist fünf nach drei.)
4:10	Es ist zehn Minuten nach vier. (Es ist zehn nach vier.)
5:15	Es ist Viertel nach fünf.
6:20	Es ist zwanzig Minuten nach sechs. (Es ist zwanzig nach sechs.)
7:25	Es ist fünf vor halb acht.
8:30	Es ist halb neun.
9:35	Es ist fünf nach halb zehn.
10:40	Es ist zwanzig vor elf.
11:45	Es ist Viertel vor zwölf.
12:50	Es ist zehn Minuten vor eins. (Es ist zehn vor eins.)
1:55	Es ist fünf Minuten vor zwei. (Es ist fünf vor zwei.)

Germans do not use A.M. or P.M. to designate the hours before and after noon. Instead, the twenty-four-hour clock that is often used in the military replaces A.M. and P.M. For example:

3:15 A.M.	drei Uhr fünfzehn
6:30 A.M.	sechs Uhr dreißig
2:11 P.M.	vierzehn Uhr elf
10:40 P.M.	zweiundzwanzig Uhr vierzig
12:00 A.M. (*midnight*)	vierundzwanzig Uhr (Mitternacht)
12:38 A.M.	null Uhr achtunddreißig

Time is usually expressed after the preposition **um** when telling at what time something occurs.

Der Bus kommt **um** zehn Uhr zwanzig.	*The bus arrives at 10:20.*
Um wie viel Uhr steht ihr auf?	*What time do you get up?*

Days of the week

The seven days of the week in German are very similar to their English counterparts:

Sonntag	*Sunday*
Montag	*Monday*
Dienstag	*Tuesday*
Mittwoch	*Wednesday*
Donnerstag	*Thursday*
Freitag	*Friday*
Samstag *or* Sonnabend	*Saturday*

When you say that something occurs *on* a particular day, use the preposition **an** in the dative case. The days of the week are masculine, so when the preposition **an** combines with **dem**, it forms the contraction **am**.

Kommst du am Freitag an?	*Are you arriving on Friday?*
Nein, ich komme erst am Sonntag.	*No, I'm not arriving until Sunday.*

Months and Dates

The German months of the year are also very similar to English:

Januar	*January*
Februar	*February*
März	*March*
April	*April*
Mai	*May*
Juni	*June*
Juli	*July*
August	*August*
September	*September*
Oktober	*October*
November	*November*
Dezember	*December*

The preposition **in** with the dative case is used to express *in which month* something occurs. The months are masculine. Remember that the contraction **im** stands for **in dem**.

In welchem Monat bist du geboren?	*What month were you born in?*
Ich bin **im** Oktober geboren.	*I was born in October.*

All the months can appear in the same kind of prepositional phrase with **im: im Januar, im März, im Juli, im August**, and so forth.

When the days of the week or the months of the year are used with numbers to express dates, the ordinal numbers are used with the appropriate declension. Use the nominative case to tell the date of a day of the week. Because the word **Tag** is masculine, the ordinal number is also used with the masculine.

Montag ist der achte Mai.	*Monday is the eighth of May.*
Ist Mittwoch der Zwanzigste?	*Is Wednesday the twentieth?*
Freitag war der Einunddreißigste.	*Friday was the thirty-first.*

The dative case after the preposition **an** is required when expressing *on what date* something occurs. For example:

Am ersten Juni kommt er nach Hause.	*He's coming home on the first of June.*
Ihr Geburtstag ist am Achten.	*Her birthday is on the eighth.*
Der Film läuft erst am Siebzehnten.	*The movie starts running on the seventeenth.*

Ordinarily, Germans do not write out the dates as words. The *first of June* is written as **der 1. Juni** and *on the seventeenth* is written as **am 17.** Notice that a period follows the date and identifies it as an ordinal number.

When expressing years, use the phrase **im Jahre** before the year. However, it is also common to state a year by itself. For example:

Sie ist im Jahre 1988 geboren.	*She was born in 1988.*

or

Sie ist 1988 geboren.

Der Krieg endete im Jahre 1991.	*The war ended in 1991.*

or

Der Krieg endete 1991.

The preposition **in** alone is not used with years. Use **im Jahre** or no preposition at all.

When a day, month, and year are combined as one phrase, they are expressed in this manner:

Sie erklärten ihre Unabhängigkeit   *They declared their independence on the*
am 4. Juli 1776.   *Fourth of July, 1776.*

The date is said as **am vierten Juli**. The year is said as **siebzehnhundertsechsundsiebzig.**

Exercise 119

Rewrite the following equations, changing the Arabic numerals to words.

1. $6 + 4 = 10$ _____
2. $18 - 10 = ?$ _____
3. $4 \times 3 = 12$ _____
4. $15 \div 5 = ?$ _____
5. $23 - 13 = 10$ _____
6. $16 + 4 = ?$ _____
7. $21 \div 7 = 3$ _____
8. $31 \times 4 = ?$ _____
9. $9 + 8 = 17$ _____
10. $100 \div 10 = ?$ _____

Exercise 120

Write each number as an ordinal number. For example:

8   *achte*

1. 15 _____
2. 2 _____
3. 100 _____
4. 75 _____
5. 20 _____
6. 11 _____
7. 1 _____
8. 3 _____

9. 30 _____

10. 1000 _____

Exercise 121

Rewrite each sentence, changing the date to the ones provided in parentheses.

1. Ist heute der zehnte Dezember?

(1) _____

(2) _____

(3) _____

(31) _____

2. Meine Schwester ist am zehnten Juli geboren.

(5) _____

(20) _____

(23) _____

(29) _____

Exercise 122

Write the given times in words. For example:

    1:00   *ein Uhr*

1. 5:00 _____

2. 7:00 _____

3. 10:10 _____

4. 12:30 _____

5. 1:30 _____

6. 3:40 _____

7. 6:45 _____

8. 8:55 _____

9. 4:05 _____

10. 5:18 _____

11. 8:27 _____

12. 9:33 _____

13. 11:42 _____

14. 00.01 _____

15. 24.00 _____

Exercise 123

Rewrite the following sentences as questions that ask *what time* something occurs. For example:

Er steht um elf Uhr auf. *Um wie viel Uhr steht er auf?*

1. Die nächste Vorlesung beginnt um dreizehn Uhr.

   _____

2. Ich fahre um halb neun nach Hause.

   _____

3. Wir sind um einundzwanzig Uhr auf eine Party gegangen.

   _____

4. Der alte Herr starb um Mitternacht.

   _____

5. Frau Schneider ist um halb fünf eingeschlafen.

   _____

Exercise 124

Fill in each blank with the missing preposition or contraction. If no preposition is required, leave the line blank.

1. Ich musste _____ sechs Uhr aufstehen.

2. Ist dein Geburtstag _____ Sonnabend?

3. _____ welchem Jahre wurde Mozart geboren?

4. Sieben plus drei ist _____ zehn.

5. War gestern _____ der dritte März?

6. Die Revolution fing _____ 1776 an.

7. Ich möchte _____ Januar nach Italien reisen.

8. Die Zwillinge sind _____ 5. Oktober geboren.

9. Mein Onkel ist _____ Jahre 1989 nach Kanada ausgewandert.

10. Wie viel ist dreiunddreißig geteilt durch _____ elf?

Exercise 125

Circle the letter of the word or phrase that best completes each sentence.

1. Ist eure Abreise um achtzehn _____ ?

   a. am

   b. durch

   c. Uhr

   d. September

2. Der Kranke kam um _____ Uhr um.

   a. elf

   b. elften

   c. vierzehnte

   d. Viertel

3. Kolumbus hat im _____ 1492 die neue Welt entdeckt.

   a. Freitag

   b. Mitternacht

   c. Amerika

   d. Jahre

4. Ist ihr Geburtstag am _____ ?

   a. Dritten

   b. Milliarde

   c. Februar

   d. vierundzwanzig

5. Sechs minus sechs ist _____ .

   a. eins

   b. null

   c. weniger

   d. durch

6. Darf ich eine _____ der Torte haben?

a. Hälfte

b. drei viertel

c. Viertel

d. halb

7. Das Kind ist im _____ sehr krank geworden.

a. Mittwoch

b. Dezember

c. 2003

d. vierten

8. Der Zug kam um _____ eins.

a. drei viertel

b. zehn Minuten

c. Hälfte

d. sechs Stunden

9. Martin muss _____ Montag zu Hause bleiben.

a. in

b. an

c. im

d. am

10. Ich habe _____ in Bremen gewohnt.

a. um neun Uhr

b. 2001

c. der 2. Mai

d. Donnerstag

21

Modal Auxiliaries and Double Infinitives

You have already encountered the modal auxiliaries **dürfen**, **können**, **mögen**, **müssen**, **sollen**, and **wollen** in the present and past tenses. This group of verbs forms a unique conjugation in the perfect and future tenses called a *double infinitive*.

When the modal auxiliary is the only verb in a sentence, it forms a participle in the perfect tenses. For example, let's look at two modals, **können** and **wollen**.

	können	*wollen*
present	er kann	er will
past	er konnte	er wollte
present perfect	er hat **gekonnt**	er hat **gewollt**

But when another verb appears in the infinitive form in the sentence, the modal does not become a participle in the perfect tenses. Instead, it appears as an infinitive side-by-side with the other infinitive, thus forming a *double infinitive*. This structure also occurs in the future tense. Let's look at **können** and **wollen** once again, this time with another infinitive in the sentence. Notice the placement and formation of the double infinitive.

present	Er kann ihn einfach nicht verstehen.	*He simply can't understand him.*
past	Er konnte ihn einfach nicht verstehen.	*He simply couldn't understand him.*
present perfect	Er hat ihn einfach nicht **verstehen können.**	*He simply couldn't understand him.*
past perfect	Er hatte ihn einfach nicht **verstehen können.**	*He simply hadn't been able to understand him.*
future	Er wird ihn einfach nicht **verstehen können.**	*He simply won't be able to understand him.*
present	Er will es kaufen.	*He wants to buy it.*
past	Er wollte es kaufen.	*He wanted to buy it.*
present perfect	Er hat es **kaufen wollen.**	*He wanted to buy it.*

| past perfect | Er hatte es **kaufen wollen**. | *He had wanted to buy it.* |
| future | Er wird es **kaufen wollen**. | *He'll want to buy it.* |

In the perfect tenses, all modal auxiliaries use **haben** as their auxiliary. Even when the modal auxiliary is accompanied by a verb of motion, which uses **sein** as its auxiliary, **haben** remains the auxiliary in the perfect tenses, because the modal is conjugated, not the verb of motion. Compare the following pairs of sentences.

| Er **hat** es **gekauft**. | *He bought it.* |
| Er **hat** es **kaufen müssen**. | *He had to buy it.* |

| Ich **bin** nach Hause **gegangen**. | *I went home.* |
| Ich **habe** nach Hause **gehen sollen**. | *I was supposed to go home.* |

Another small group of verbs follow the double-infinitive pattern. They form a double infinitive in the perfect and future tenses just like modal auxiliaries. These verbs are **helfen, hören, lassen,** and **sehen** (*help, hear, get something done, see*). Compare them in the present tense and present perfect tense.

| Martin hilft dem Mann arbeiten. | *Martin helps the man work.* |
| Martin hat dem Mann **arbeiten helfen**. | *Martin helped the man work.* |

| Hörst du die Kinder singen? | *Do you hear the children singing?* |
| Hast du die Kinder **singen hören**? | *Did you hear the children singing?* |

| Sie lässt ihren Wagen reparieren. | *She gets her car repaired.* |
| Sie hat ihren Wagen **reparieren lassen**. | *She got her car repaired.* |

| Wir sehen sie spielen. | *We see them playing.* |
| Wir haben sie **spielen sehen**. | *We saw them playing.* |

Notice that this group of verbs also uses **haben** as its auxiliary in the perfect tenses. Also, because **helfen** is a dative verb, the object in a sentence with **helfen** is in the dative case. For example: **Martin hat <u>dem Mann</u> arbeiten helfen.**

As the subject changes in a perfect- or future-tense sentence with a double infinitive, only the auxiliary is affected. The double infinitive remains constant. For example:

Ich habe mit ihr tanzen wollen.	*I wanted to dance with her.*
Du hast mit ihr tanzen wollen.	*You wanted to dance with her.*
Er hat mit ihr tanzen wollen.	*He wanted to dance with her.*
Wir haben mit ihr tanzen wollen.	*We wanted to dance with her.*

Ihr habt mit ihr tanzen wollen.	*You wanted to dance with her.*
Sie haben mit ihr tanzen wollen.	*They wanted to dance with her.*
Ich werde ihn vom Bahnhof abholen müssen.	*I'll have to pick him up from the train station.*
Du wirst ihn vom Bahnhof abholen müssen.	*You'll have to pick him up from the train station.*
Er wird ihn vom Bahnhof abholen müssen.	*He'll have to pick him up from the train station.*
Wir werden ihn vom Bahnhof abholen müssen.	*We'll have to pick him up from the train station.*
Ihr werdet ihn vom Bahnhof abholen müssen.	*You'll have to pick him up from the train station.*
Sie werden ihn vom Bahnhof abholen müssen.	*They'll have to pick him up from the train station.*

Exercise 126

Rewrite each of the following sentences in the present and past tenses with the new subjects provided in parentheses. For example:

Ich will nichts.

(du)   *Du willst nichts.*   *Du wolltest nichts.*

1. Ich kann Deutsch und Spanisch.

(wir) _____

_____

(sie pl.) _____

_____

2. Sie muss schneller lernen.

(ihr) _____

_____

(du) _____

_____

3. Was hörst du?

(er) _____

_____

(Sie) _____

_____

4. Er lässt den neuen Wagen waschen.

(wir) _____

_____

(ich) _____

_____

5. Der Hund will die Kinder warnen.

(ihr) _____

_____

(sie s.) _____

_____

6. Das darf man nicht tun.

(du) _____

_____

(Sie) _____

_____

Exercise 127

Rewrite each sentence in the present tense with the modal provided in parentheses. For example:

> Er spricht Deutsch.
>
> (wollen)   *Er will Deutsch sprechen.*

1. Der Ausländer liest den Brief nicht.

(können) _Der Ausländer kann den Brief nicht lesen._

2. Raucht man hier?

(dürfen) _Darf man hier rauchen?_

3. Was trinken Sie zu Ihrem Essen?

(mögen) _Was mögen Sie zu Ihrem Essen trinken._

4. Sie erwarten ihren Freund an der Ecke.

(sollen) _Sie soll ihren Freund an der Ecke erwarten._

5. Wie lange arbeitet ihr jeden Tag?

(müssen) _Wie lange musstet ihr jeden Tag arbeiten?_____

6. Der Mann schneidet sich die Haare.

(lassen) _____

7. Was zeigt der Fremdenführer den Touristen?

(wollen) _____

8. Benutzt ihr die Volksbücherei?

(dürfen) _____

9. Was tun wir am Abend?

(können) _____

10. Sie tun jetzt Ihre Pflicht.

(sollen) _____

Exercise 128

Rewrite each sentence in the present perfect tense and the future tense.

1. Ich kann die Prüfung nicht bestehen.

_____

_____

2. Warum muss er sterben?

_____

_____

3. Wir sehen ihn im Garten arbeiten.

_____

_____

4. In diesem Abteil darf man nicht rauchen.

_____

_____

5. Er kann das norddeutsche Klima nicht vertragen.

_____

_____

6. Der alte Hund hört Schritte kommen.

_____

_____

7. Die Lehrerin kann die Fehler nicht finden.

_____

_____

8. Wir helfen ihnen die Bücher tragen.

_____

_____

9. Sie lässt die Schüler einen Aufsatz schreiben.

_____

_____

10. Darf die kranke Frau die Reise nicht machen?

_____

_____

Exercise 129

Rewrite the infinitive phrase in the present, past, present perfect, and future tenses with the subject provided in parentheses.

1. (ich) können gut Mundharmonika spielen.

present: _____

past: _____

present perfect: _____

future: _____

2. (wir) wollen in die Berge fahren.

present: _____

past: _____

present perfect: _____

future: _____

3. (die Kinder) dürfen nicht streiten.

present: _____

past: _____

present perfect: _____

future: _____

4. (sie s.) hören ihre Eltern in der Küche sprechen.

present: _____

past: _____

present perfect: _____

future: _____

5. (du) sollen dich besser benehmen.

present: _____

past: _____

present perfect: _____

future: _____

6. (er) müssen seine Verwandten in Berlin besuchen.

present: _____

past: _____

present perfect: _____

future: _____

7. (ihr) sehen die Flugzeuge über der Stadt fliegen?

present: _____

past: _____

present perfect: _____

future: _____

8. (er) lassen sich einen neuen Anzug machen.

present: _____

past: _____

present perfect: _____

future: _____

9. (sie pl.) helfen mir den alten Wagen reparieren.

present: _____

past: _____

present perfect: _____

future: _____

10. (wir) können seine Theorie nicht verstehen.

present: _____

past: _____

present perfect: _____

future: _____

Exercise 130

Circle the letter of the verb that best completes each sentence.

1. Ich _____ bis in die Nacht arbeiten.

a. könnt

b. musste

c. willst

d. wolltest

2. Dieser Mann _____ sehr krank sein.

a. gekonnt

b. muss

c. wollten

d. sollt

3. Sie _____ die Arbeit nicht in der kurzen Zeit schaffen.

a. kann

b. musstet

c. dürft

d. gedurft

4. Er hat einen Kurort aufsuchen _____ .

a. soll

b. sollt

c. darf

d. dürfen

5. Sie _____ nach ihrem Examen ins Ausland reisen.

a. wollt

b. sollt

c. hilft

d. will

6. Wer _____ so etwas machen wollen?

a. können

b. hat

c. sollt

d. ist

7. Hier wirst du sie Fußball spielen _____ .

a. sehen

b. hört

c. hörst

d. können

8. Sie _____ die alte Dame nach Hause begleiten.

a. sollen

b. haben

c. werdet

d. hat

9. Habt ihr das kranke Kind weinen _____ ?

a. sollen

b. dürfen

c. sein

d. hören

10. Haben sie auch Englisch _____ ?

   a. kann

   b. wollen

   c. wollten

   d. gekonnt

11. Niemand _____ zu ihrer Party kommen wollen.

   a. wird

   b. sollen

   c. habt

   d. mögen

12. Er will noch ein halbes Jahr _____ .

   a. dürfen

   b. kommen

   c. können

   d. warten

13. Ich habe den Männern schaufeln _____ .

   a. sehen

   b. lassen

   c. müssen

   d. helfen

14. Die taube Frau _____ kein Wort verstehen.

   a. konnte

   b. wollt

   c. müssen

   d. sollen

15. Man _____ nicht fluchen.

   a. könnt

   b. hat

   c. habt

   d. soll

22

Conjunctions

Short, individual sentences can sound uninteresting in both writing and speech. To make language more appealing and flow more smoothly, use conjunctions to combine sentences.

Coordinating conjunctions

The most commonly used coordinating conjunctions in German are **aber, oder, und, denn,** and **sondern** (*but, or, and, because, but rather*). A coordinating conjunction combines two independent clauses, each of which can stand alone and make sense. When a coordinating conjunction combines two independent clauses, normal word order takes place, which means that the verb is the second element in each of the two clauses. For example:

> Jochen **wohnt** in Bonn, aber seine Schwester **wohnt** in Wien.

> *Jochen lives in Bonn, but his sister lives in Vienna.*

Naturally, if the combined clauses are formed as a **ja** or **nein** question, the verbs in the sentences precede the subject. Compare the preceding example with the following example.

> **Fahrt** ihr mit dem Zug, oder **fliegt** ihr nach Paris?

> *Are you traveling by train, or are you flying to Paris?*

Questions are the only exception to the rule: with coordinating conjunctions, the verb is the second element in each of the combined clauses. Let's look at some example sentences with the remaining three conjunctions. Take note that the conjunction **und** is the only one of the five that does not require a comma separating the two independent clauses.

> Werner spielt Klavier und Tanja hört Radio.

> *Werner is playing the piano, and Tanja is listening to the radio.*

> Erik geht nicht ins Kino, denn er hat kein Geld.

> *Erik isn't going to the movies, because he doesn't have any money.*

> Sie wohnt nicht in Heidelberg, sondern sie wohnt in Darmstadt.

> *She doesn't live in Heidelberg, but rather she lives in Darmstadt.*

The conjunction **sondern** begins a clause that follows another clause with a *negative*. Look at the phrase in the preceding example again and notice **nicht in Heidelberg, sondern**. The negative word **nicht** is the signal that the second clause will start with **sondern**. Since the subjects and verbs in the two independent clauses of this example are identical, it is possible to shorten the sentence and omit the subject and verb from the second clause:

Sie wohnt nicht in Heidelberg, sondern in Darmstadt.

She doesn't live in Heidelberg, but rather in Darmstadt.

Subordinating conjunctions

The list of subordinating conjunctions is long. They differ from coordinating conjunctions in that the clauses that follow a subordinating conjunction do not make complete sense when standing alone. Let's look at a couple of examples in English first.

When I returned home, I found the front door locked.

In this sentence, *when* is a subordinating conjunction. When you separate the first clause from the second one, you find that the first clause doesn't make complete sense by itself: *When I returned home.* Let's look at another example.

They lived with relatives since the war ended.

In this example, *since* is a subordinating conjunction. When the subordinating clause stands alone, it does not make complete sense: *Since the war ended.*

In a German clause beginning with a subordinating conjunction, the verb stands at the end of the clause.

Ich weiß, dass Tina zu Hause **ist**.   *I know that Tina is at home.*

If the sentence begins with a subordinating clause, the verb precedes the subject in the second clause. Compare the following two sentences.

Ich **besuche** Tante Luise, wenn ich in Bremen **bin**.

I visit Aunt Luise, whenever I'm in Bremen.

Wenn ich in Bremen **bin**, **besuche** ich Tante Luise.

Whenever I'm in Bremen, I visit Aunt Luise.

Here is a list of commonly used subordinating conjunctions:

als ob (als wenn)	*as if* (See Chapter 26.)
als	*when* (used for statements in the past tense)
bevor	*before*
bis	*until, by the time*
da	*since*
damit	*so that*
dass	*that*
ehe	*before*
falls	*in case*
indem	*by*
nachdem	*after*
ob	*whether, if*
obwohl	*although*
seit(dem)	*since*
sobald	*as soon as*
sooft	*as often as*
soviel	*as far as*
während	*while*
weil	*because*
wenn	*when(ever)*
wie (used together with **so**)	*as*

Use **indem** where *by* + present participle is used in English.

Sie löste das Problem, indem sie ihm mehr Geld gab.	*She solved the problem by givng him more money.*

Also, both **da** and **seit(dem)** mean *since*. But **da** is used to show *a cause*.

Da er betrunken war, konnte er nicht fahren.	*Since he was drunk, he wasn't able to drive.*

Seit(dem) tells *from what moment in time* something occurred.

Seitdem er das Haus verkauft hat, wohnt er bei seinen Eltern.	*Since he sold his house, he's been living with his parents.*

Here are the conjunctions used in sentences. Take special note of the position of the conjugated verb in the subordinate clauses.

Sie schrie, als ob Erik sie schlüge.	*She screamed as if Erik were hitting her.*
Als ich in Kiel wohnte, ging ich oft segeln.	*When I lived in Kiel, I often went sailing.*
Bevor das Kind einschlief, lächelte es seinem Vater zu.	*Before the child fell asleep, he smiled at his father.*

Ich kann warten, bis du fertig bist.	I can wait until you're ready.
Da sie krank geworden war, musste sie zu Hause bleiben.	Since she had gotten sick, she had to stay at home.
Du musst schneller fahren, damit wir pünktlich ankommen.	You have to drive faster so that we arrive on time.
Ich wusste nicht, dass du das Examen bestanden hast.	I didn't know that you passed the exam.
Ehe er abfuhr, küsste er mich.	Before he departed, he kissed me.
Wir werden uns bei mir treffen, falls es regnet.	We'll meet at my house, in case it rains.
Er hat ihr geholfen, indem er ihr 50 Euro gab.	He helped her by giving her 50 euros.
Nachdem die Kinder nach Hause gekommen waren, wollten sie etwas zu essen haben.	After the children had come home, they wanted to have something to eat.
Niemand weiß, ob er noch in der Stadt wohnt.	No one knows whether he's still living in the city.
Obwohl er ein guter Mensch ist, kann ich ihm kein Geld leihen.	Although he's a good person, I can't lend him money.
Seitdem er bei seinem Vater eingezogen war, hat er nicht gearbeitet.	Since he moved in with his father, he hasn't worked.
Sobald der Junge das Geräusch hörte, lief er aus dem Haus hinaus.	As soon as the boy heard the noise, he ran out of the house.
Ich komme, sooft du es wünschst.	I'll come as often as you like.
Soviel wir wissen, ist Frau Gerber noch in Afrika.	As far as we know, Ms. Gerber is still in Africa.
Mein Urgroßvater ist gestorben, während wir in den USA waren.	My great-grandfather died while we were in the U.S.A.
Er ist um halb elf aufgestanden, weil sein Wecker kaputt ist.	He got up at ten-thirty, because his alarm clock is broken.
Wenn ich in Goslar bin, besuche ich meinen Schwager.	Whenever I'm in Goslar, I visit my brother-in-law.
Seine Rede war nicht so interessant, wie wir erwartet hatten.	His speech wasn't as interesting as we had expected.

Exercise 131

Fill in the blank with the coordinating conjunction that makes the most sense: **aber, oder, denn, und,** or **sondern**.

1. Der Vater rief laut, _____ die Kinder kamen nicht.

2. Ich bleibe lieber zu Hause, _____ es ist heute sehr kalt.

3. Sie spricht nicht nur Englisch, _____ sie beherrscht auch Deutsch.

4. Onkel Erhardt kommt morgen an _____ kann bis Freitag bei uns bleiben.

5. Gehst du zur Party, _____ hast du noch zu tun?

Exercise 132

Rewrite each sentence, beginning with the subordinating clause. For example:

Er besucht uns, wenn er nach Deutschland kommt.
Wenn er nach Deutschland kommt, besucht er uns.

1. Karl konnte nicht fahren, da er betrunken war.

_____

2. Sie müssen sich beeilen, damit sie pünktlich ankommen.

_____

3. Wir kommen morgen vorbei, falls wir Zeit haben.

_____

4. Karin trägt eine Brille, damit sie besser sieht.

_____

5. Erik sah seine Verlobte an der Ecke stehen, als er vom Bahnhof ankam.

_____

6. Die Jungen spielen gern Fußball, wenn es nicht regnet.

_____

7. Er wollte sich eine Weile hinlegen, nachdem er gegessen hatte.

_____

8. Viele Leute verreisen nach dem Süden, da das Klima dort besser ist.

_____

Exercise 133

Circle the letter of the conjunction that best completes each sentence.

1. Der Schüler wurde gelobt, _____ er so klug war.

a. denn

b. ob

c. seitdem

d. weil

2. Ich trage einen schweren Mantel, _____ ich nicht friere.

a. damit

b. obwohl

c. wenn

d. wie

3. Mein Bruder geht zum Arzt, _____ er krank ist.

a. als

b. oder

c. denn

d. weil

4. Er hat gewartet, _____ er konnte.

a. wie

b. solange

c. bevor

d. wenn

5. Wir warten hier, _____ der nächste Bus kommt.

a. bis

b. wenn

c. als

d. dass

6. Angela fragt, _____ wir den neuen Mieter kennen.

a. weil

b. ob

c. seitdem

d. dass

7. Ich bin froh, _____ du wieder gesund bist.

a. als ob

b. nachdem

c. oder

d. dass

8. Meine Mutter ist krank geworden, _____ ich in der Schweiz war.

   a. während

   b. weil

   c. wenn

   d. denn

9. _____ ich weiß, wohnt Herr Schneider wieder in Leipzig.

   a. Soviel

   b. Damit

   c. Wie

   d. Falls

10. _____ sie mich liebt, will sie mich nicht heiraten.

    a. Wenn

    b. Und

    c. Obwohl

    d. Indem

11. _____ sie ihren Sohn auf dem Bahnsteig sahen, fingen sie an zu weinen.

    a. Falls

    b. Als

    c. Wenn

    d. Bis

12. Ich weiß nicht, _____ ich das Problem lösen kann.

    a. wie

    b. ob

    c. dass

    d. weil

13. _____ er abfuhr, gab er ihr einen Ring.

    a. Falls

    b. Denn

    c. Ehe

    d. Seit

14. Erik ist im Januar geboren _____ Karl ist im März geboren.

 a. denn

 b. weil

 c. und

 d. bevor

15. Er liest nicht ein Buch, _____ eine Zeitung.

 a. während

 b. solange

 c. oder

 d. sondern

Exercise 134

Complete each sentence with any appropriate phrase.

 1. Ich wusste nicht, dass _____ .

 2. Können Sie mir sagen, ob _____ ?

 3. Sie sind nicht zum Park gegangen, sondern _____ .

 4. Ich bedauere es sehr, dass _____ .

 5. Sobald _____ , rief ich den Artz an.

 6. Wir bleiben in Kiel, bis _____ .

 7. Sie können kommen, sooft _____ .

 8. Während _____ , fing der Krieg an.

 9. Mein Vater ist wieder gesund, aber _____ .

10. Ich kann dich nicht hören, denn _____ .

11. Wissen Sie, ob _____ ?

12. Sie hat die Klingel abgestellt, damit _____ .

13. Beabsichtigt ihr ein Haus zu mieten oder _____ ?

14. Sie können in der Küche essen, weil _____ .

15. Wir heizen im Schlafzimmer, wenn _____ .

23

Relative Pronouns

Relative pronouns are used to combine two sentences together that have an identical noun or pronoun element in them. For example:

> *The man* is a friend of mine. You met *the man* in Chicago.
> The man whom you met in Chicago is a friend of mine.

There are three categories of relative pronouns in English: (1) *who* and *which*, which introduce a *nonrestrictive* relative clause that gives parenthetical information, (2) *that*, which introduces a *restrictive* relative clause that helps define the antecedent, and (3) an elliptical relative pronoun, which is understood but not spoken or written. All three types of English relative pronouns can be translated into one type in German: the German *definite article*.

German definite article

Like so many other elements in German, the relative pronouns always conform to the gender, number, and case of the nouns they refer to.

	masculine	feminine	neuter	plural
nominative	der	die	das	die
accusative	den	die	das	die
dative	dem	der	dem	denen
genitive	dessen	deren	dessen	deren

As you can see, the declension of the relative pronouns resembles the declension of the definite articles. The genitive and the plural dative are the only exceptions. The genitive relative pronoun, it must be remembered, is used to replace a possessive adjective (**mein, dein, unser,** etc.).

When two German sentences have the same noun or pronoun element in them, a relative pronoun can replace one of those elements and the two sentences can then be stated as one. Let's look at some examples:

Der neue Lehrer ist aus Darmstadt.	*The new teacher is from Darmstadt.*
Sie kennen schon **den neuen Lehrer**.	*They already know the new teacher.*

In the first example, **der neue Lehrer** is in the nominative case. In the second example, it's in the accusative case. If the first sentence is made into a relative clause, the relative pronoun that replaces **der neue Lehrer** must be the same gender, number, and case. Therefore, the relative pronoun is **der**.

Sie kennen schon den neuen Lehrer, **der aus Darmstadt ist**.	*They already know the new teacher who is from Darmstadt.*

If the second sentence is made the relative clause, then **den neuen Lehrer**, which is in the accusative case, must be replaced by **den**.

Der neue Lehrer, **den sie schon kennen**, ist aus Darmstadt.	*The new teacher, whom they already know, is from Darmstadt.*

Since relative clauses are considered subordinating clauses, the verb in the relative clause stands at the end of the clause.

Let's look at relative pronouns as they appear in all the cases, sometimes as subjects, direct or indirect objects, or objects of prepositions.

Felix tanzt mit der Frau, die Amerikanerin ist.	*Felix is dancing with the woman who is an American.* (relative pronoun = nominative subject)
Felix tanzt mit der Frau, die Gudrun eingeladen hat.	*Felix is dancing with the woman whom Gudrun invited.* (relative pronoun = accusative direct object)
Felix tanzt mit der Frau, für die Johannes sich interessiert.	*Felix is dancing with the woman whom Johannes is interested in.* (relative pronoun = object of accusative preposition)
Felix tanzt mit der Frau, der Johannes eine Blume gab.	*Felix is dancing with the woman, to whom Johannes gave a flower.* (relative pronoun = dative indirect object)
Felix tanzt mit der Frau, von der Maria gesprochen hat.	*Felix is dancing with the woman whom Maria spoke about.* (relative pronoun = object of dative preposition)
Felix tanzt mit der Frau, der Herr Schneider sehr imponierte.	*Felix is dancing with the woman whom Mr. Schneider really impressed.* (relative pronoun = object of dative verb)
Felix tanzt mit der Frau, deren Mutter Physikerin war.	*Felix is dancing with the woman whose mother was a physicist.* (relative pronoun = possessive adjective)

Welcher

The definite article used as a relative pronoun is sometimes replaced by **welcher**. Look at its declension in all the cases.

	masculine	feminine	neuter	plural
nominative	welcher	welche	welches	welche
accusative	welchen	welche	welches	welche
dative	welchem	welcher	welchem	welchen
genitive	dessen	deren	dessen	deren

Note that the genitive form consists of the possessive adjectives **dessen** and **deren**. **Welcher** does not replace these words. In sentences, **welcher** is used as follows:

Felix tanzt mit der Frau, welche Amerikanerin ist.
Felix tanzt mit der Frau, welche Gudrun eingeladen hat.
Felix tanzt mit der Frau, für welche Johannes sich interessiert.
Felix tanzt mit der Frau, welcher Johannes eine Blume gab.
Felix tanzt mit der Frau, von welcher Maria gesprochen hat.
Felix tanzt mit der Frau, welcher Herr Schneider sehr imponierte.
Felix tanzt mit der Frau, deren Mutter Physikerin war.

Was

In some cases **was** is used as a relative pronoun. This occurs after **alles, etwas, nichts, viel(es)**, and **das** when used as a demonstrative pronoun. For example:

Ich verstehe alles, was du sagst.	*I understand everything you're saying.*
Sag doch etwas, was ich glauben kann!	*Say something I can believe.*
Sie hat nichts, was sie verkaufen will.	*She has nothing she wants to sell.*
Er sagte vieles, was er jetzt bedauert.	*He said a lot that he now regrets.*
Sie liest viel von dem, was er in seiner Jugend geschrieben hat.	*She reads a lot of what he wrote in his youth.*

In addition, **was** becomes the relative pronoun when its antecedent is a neuter adjective used as a noun.

Ist das das Beste, was Sie haben?	*Is that the best you have?*
Das war das Letzte, was er zu sagen hatte.	*That was the last he had to say.*

A complete sentence can be the antecedent of the relative pronoun **was**. For example:

Sie ist Ärztin geworden, was ihre Eltern sehr erfreute.	*She became a physician, which pleased her parents very much.*

When a preposition is needed with the relative pronoun **was**, it forms a compound with **wo(r)-**, for example: (**von**) + **was** becomes **wovon** and (**auf**) + **was** becomes **worauf**. In sentences, they appear as follows:

Er hat etwas, **wofür** du dich interessieren wirst.	*He has something that you will be interested in.*
Sie verreisen nach dem Süden, **worauf** die Kinder sich schon freuen.	*They're traveling to the south, to which the children are looking very much forward.*

Wer

The pronoun **wer** is also used as a relative pronoun, but it tends to introduce a sentence rather than the second clause of a sentence. Unlike **was, wer** can be declined: **wen** (accusative), **wem** (dative), and the possessive-adjective form **wessen**. This relative pronoun is often combined with a form of **der**. Let's look at a couple of examples.

Wer einmal lügt, **dem** kann man niemals glauben.	*He who lies once can never be believed.*
Wem das Buch nicht gefällt, **der** soll es nicht lesen.	*He who doesn't like the book shouldn't read it.*

The translation of **wer** is often *he who* but can also be stated as *whoever*.

The case required for **wer** or **der** in such sentences depends upon the use of the pronouns in those sentences. In the first of the previous examples, **wer** is the subject of the sentence; therefore, it is in the nominative case. In the second example, **wem** is the object of the dative verb **gefallen** and therefore is in the dative case.

Exercise 135

Rewrite each sentence in groups of four, changing the antecedents in bold print to the new antecedents in parentheses. Make all the other necessary changes. Follow the example provided with the antecedent **der Junge**.

1. Er sieht **das Kind**, das in Amerika geboren ist.

Er sieht **das Kind**, das Gudrun fotografieren will.

Er sieht **das Kind**, mit dem Tanja spielt.

Er sieht **das Kind**, dessen Vater Zahnarzt ist.

(der Junge)

> *Er sieht den Jungen, der in Amerika geboren ist.*
> *Er sieht den Jungen, den Gudrun fotografieren will.*
> *Er sieht den Jungen, mit dem Tanja spielt.*
> *Er sieht den Jungen, dessen Vater Zahnarzt ist.*

(das Mädchen)

_____

_____

_____

_____

(die Kinder)

_____

_____

_____

_____

(die Schülerin)

_____

_____

_____

_____

2. Sie findet **den Brief**, den Martin geschrieben hat.

Sie findet **den Brief**, nach dem ihre Schwester fragte.

Sie findet **den Brief**, dessen Inhalt ein Geheimnis ist.

Sie findet **den Brief**, der unter dem Tisch gelegen hat.

(die Briefe)

_____

_____

_____

(das Telegramm)

_____

_____

_____

(die Postkarte)

_____

_____

_____

3. Liebst du **die Frau**, die schon verlobt ist?

Liebst du **die Frau**, von der deine Tante gesprochen hat?

Liebst du **die Frau**, gegen die Lilo etwas hat?

Liebst du **die Frau**, deren Bruder ein Dieb ist?

(das Mädchen)

_____

_____

_____

(der Mann)

_____

_____

_____

(der Student)

_____

_____

_____

_____

Exercise 136

Rewrite each sentence, changing the relative pronoun to the appropriate form of **welcher**.

1. Er sieht das Kind, das in Amerika geboren ist.

Er sieht das Kind, das Gudrun fotografieren will.

Er sieht das Kind, mit dem Tanja spielt.

Er sieht das Kind, dessen Vater Zahnarzt ist.

_____

_____

_____

_____

2. Sie findet den Brief, den Martin geschrieben hat.

Sie findet den Brief, nach dem ihre Schwester fragte.

Sie findet den Brief, dessen Inhalt ein Geheimnis ist.

Sie findet den Brief, der unter dem Tisch gelegen hat.

_____

_____

_____

_____

3. Sie haben einige Bücher, die sehr alt und teuer sind.

Sie haben einige Bücher, die sie verkaufen wollen.

Sie haben einige Bücher, in denen sie alte Ansichtskarten gefunden haben.

Sie haben einige Bücher, deren Verlag sich in Bonn befindet.

_____

_____

_____

_____

Exercise 137

Fill in the blanks with the appropriate form of the relative pronouns derived from definite articles.

1. Er hat ein Bild, _____ von einem Freund gemalt wurde.

2. Der junge Sänger, _____ die Zeitungen loben, ist nur einundzwanzig Jahre alt.

3. Das Dorf, in _____ ich einmal wohnte, wurde vom Erdbeben zerstört.

4. Sie kaufte ein Fernrohr, mit _____ sie die Sterne beobachten kann.

5. Wir brauchen einen Tisch, auf _____ diese Lampe stehen kann.

6. Der Kranke, von _____ mein Onkel erzählte, war einmal Pianist.

7. Die Handschuhe, _____ Farbe rot ist, passen dir nicht.

8. Im Esszimmer ist der Schrank, in _____ wir unsere Bücher aufbewahren.

9. Eine Witwe ist eine Frau, _____ Mann gestorben ist.

10. Kennst du die Künstlerin, über _____ der Reporter berichtet hat?

11. Die Mutter, _____ Kind sich gut entwickelt, freute sich sehr.

12. Die Hunde, _____ Tag und Nacht bellen, gehören unseren Nachbarn.

13. Der Onkel, bei _____ Karl wohnte, ist ein reicher Mann.

14. Wo sind eure Kinder, für _____ ich ein paar Geschenke habe?

15. Hier baut man einen neuen Tennisplatz, auf _____ wir eines Tages spielen werden.

Exercise 138

Fill in the blank with the appropriate form of **was** or **wer**.

1. Alles, _____ du sagst, ist Unsinn.

2. _____ die einen lieben, den hassen die anderen.

3. Ich will das Beste kaufen, _____ Sie haben.

4. _____ du nicht traust, bleibe ihm fern!

5. Meine Gäste reisen heute ab, _____ ich sehr bedauere.

6. Das ist aber das Schönste, _____ ich jemals gesehen habe!

7. Erzähle mir etwas, _____ ich nicht früher gehört habe.

8. Sie haben nichts, _____ wir kaufen wollen.

9. Die Schüler haben eine gute Prüfung gemacht, _____ den Lehrer sehr erfreut.

10. _____ ihn gesehen hat, der vergisst ihn nie.

11. Rede nichts, _____ andere Menschen nicht hören dürfen!

12. Es gibt vieles in der Welt, _____ man nicht versteht.

13. _____ neu ist, ist nicht immer gut.

14. Das war das Schlechteste, _____ ich jemals getrunken habe.

15. Die Kinder machen einen großen Lärm, _____ mich sehr ärgert.

Exercise 139

Circle the letter of the word that best completes each sentence.

1. Ich habe _____ , was dir gefallen wird.

a. der

b. den

c. etwas

d. jemand

2. Der Mann, _____ sie alles glaubte, hat sie betrogen.

a. den

b. wem

c. dem

d. welchen

3. Das ist doch _____ , was er sagen will.

a. wem

b. welcher

c. alles

d. nicht

4. Wir danken allen, _____ zur Party beigetragen haben.

a. was

b. wer

c. denen

d. die

5. Das sind die Sportler, _____ für die Olympischen Spiele trainieren.

a. die

b. der

c. das

d. welcher

6. Das ist Herr Weber, _____ ich das Buch ausgeliehen habe.

a. dessen

b. dem

c. wessen

d. wem

7. Wo sind die Mieter, über _____ viele Leute schimpfen?

a. die

b. was

c. wen

d. welches

8. Das ist alles, _____ er sich erinnern kann.

a. was

b. woran

c. das

d. dass

9. Der Junge, _____ Mutter gestorben ist, muss bei Verwandten wohnen.

a. der

b. welches

c. dessen

d. denen

10. Der Dichter wurde in der Stadt, _____ er berühmt gemacht hatte, begraben.

a. der

b. die

c. den

d. denen

24

Comparatives and Superlatives

The comparative of adjectives and adverbs shows a *comparison* between two persons or objects.

> *John is* taller *than Mary.*
> *Mary runs* faster *than John.*

The superlative describes the ultimate degree or quality of adjectives and adverbs.

> *John is the* tallest *man in town.*
> *Mary runs the* fastest *of anyone on the team.*

German uses comparatives and superlatives in the same way. But they are formed uniquely. Also remember that comparatives and superlatives can be adjectives. That means they can have adjective endings and must conform to the gender, number, and case of the nouns they modify.

Comparatives

The basic German form of comparative adjectives and adverbs is the attachment of the suffix **-er** to the adjective or adverb. For example:

positive	comparative	
klein	kleiner	*smaller*
reich	reicher	*richer*
schnell	schneller	*faster*

Some adjectives and adverbs add an umlaut to the vowel in the adjective or adverb when forming the comparative. The following is a list of some of the commonly used adjectives and adverbs that require an umlaut in the comparative form.

positive	comparative	
alt	älter	*older*
arm	ärmer	*poorer*
dumm	dümmer	*more stupid*
grob	gröber	*coarser*
hart	härter	*harder*
jung	jünger	*younger*
kalt	kälter	*colder*
klug	klüger	*smarter*
krank	kränker	*sicker*
kurz	kürzer	*shorter*
lang	länger	*longer*
schwach	schwächer	*weaker*
stark	stärker	*stronger*
warm	wärmer	*warmer*

Notice that these adjectives and adverbs are one-syllable words.

When a comparative is used as an adjective, it will have an adjective ending except when it is a predicate adjective.

Kennst du den älteren Jungen?	*Do you know the older boy?*
Mein Bruder ist viel stärker.	*My brother is a lot stronger.*

When it is an adverb, it will have no ending.

Tina kann schneller laufen.	*Tina can run faster.*

When an adjective or adverb ends in **-el**, **-en**, or **-er**, it drops the final -e- before adding the comparative suffix **-er**.

positive	comparative	
dunkel	dunkler	*darker*
teuer	teurer	*more expensive*
trocken	trockner	*drier*

A few comparatives have an irregular form. Fortunately, the list is short.

positive	comparative	
bald	eher	*sooner*
groß	größer	*bigger*
gut	besser	*better*

hoch	höher	*higher*
nah	näher	*nearer*
viel	mehr	*more*

Remember that **hoch** is a predicate adjective. When endings are added to **hoch**, it becomes **hoh-**. For example:

Er sieht den hohen Turm.	*He sees the tall tower.*

German comparatives can be translated in two ways. If the English translation is a short word of Anglo-Saxon origin, its comparative form is a single German word that ends in **-er** (e.g., **schneller** = *faster*). If the English translation is a long word, usually from a foreign source, it cannot be translated by adding the suffix *-er* to the adjective or adverb. Instead, the adverb *more* precedes the adjective or adverb (e.g., **interessanter** = *more interesting*). Take a look at these examples.

Er ist jünger.	*He's younger.*
Der schnellere Zug ist neuer.	*The faster train is newer.*

Dieses Buch ist interessanter.	*This book is* more *interesting.*
Tanja ist intelligenter als Maria.	*Tanja is* more *intelligent than Maria.*

To make a comparison between two people or objects, use **als** (*than*).

Sie war netter **als** ihre Schwester.	*She was nicer than her sister.*
Ist dein Zimmer kälter **als** meins?	*Is your room colder than mine?*

But **als** can also show a contrast between what is anticipated and the real situation. For example:

Der Chef war netter, **als** ich dachte.	*The boss was nicer than I thought.*
Seine Rede ist langweiliger, **als** wir erwarteten.	*His speech is more boring than we expected.*

Another useful expression is **je . . . desto**. It says that *the more* one thing occurs, *the more* another thing occurs. For example: *The more I complain, the more she ignores me. The faster he drives, the scarier the situation becomes.* Let's look at some examples in German.

Je größer die Hitze wird, desto stärker wird mein Durst.	*The greater the heat becomes, the stronger my thirst gets.*
Je kälter die Tage werden, desto mehr will ich nach dem Süden verreisen.	*The colder the days get, the more I want to travel south.*

You will notice that a clause introduced by **je** places the verb at the end of the clause just as with subordinating clauses. In the second clause, normal word order occurs with the second element being the verb. Sometimes **umso** replaces **desto** in sentences like these. For example:

Je größer die Hitze wird, **umso** stärker wird mein Durst.

It is common in English to use the words *more and more* or two comparatives stated side by side to emphasize a comparison. In German, the adverb **immer** precedes a comparative to achieve this meaning.

Es wurde **immer kälter**.	*It was getting* colder and colder.
Dieser Roman wird **immer interessanter**.	*This novel is getting* more and more *interesting*.

Superlatives

English superlatives are formed by adding the suffix **-est** to an adjective or adverb. However, if the adjective or adverb is a longer word, usually from a foreign source, the suffix is not used and the adverb *most* precedes the adjective or adverb. For example:

tallest	funniest
most fascinating	most flexible

German has only one superlative form. The suffix **-st-** plus any necessary adjective ending is added to the word. For example:

positive	superlative	
klein	kleinste	*smallest*
reich	reichste	*richest*
schnell	schnellste	*fastest*

If the superlative is used as a predicate adjective, it appears in a prepositional phrase with **an**.

Mein Vetter ist **am kleinsten**.	*My cousin is the smallest.*
Ist dieses Haus **am ältesten**?	*Is this house the oldest one?*

If the superlative is used as an adjective, it must have adjective endings. If it is used as an adverb, it is formed like a predicate adjective with the preposition **an**.

Frau Meier hat den schönsten Garten.   *Mrs. Meier has the prettiest garden.*
Diese Kinder lernen am schnellsten.   *These children learn the fastest.*

As with the comparative, some adjectives and adverbs add an umlaut to the vowel in the adjective or adverb when the superlative is formed. Here is a list of some of the commonly used adjectives and adverbs that require an umlaut in the superlative form.

positive	superlative	
alt	am ältesten	*oldest*
arm	am ärmsten	*poorest*
dumm	am dümmsten	*most stupid*
grob	am gröbsten	*coarsest*
hart	am härtesten	*hardest*
jung	am jüngsten	*youngest*
kalt	am kältesten	*coldest*
klug	am klügsten	*smartest*
krank	am kränksten	*sickest*
kurz	am kürzesten	*shortest*
lang	am längsten	*longest*
schwach	am schwächsten	*weakest*
stark	am stärksten	*strongest*
warm	am wärmsten	*warmest*

If adjectives or adverbs end in **-d, -t, -s, -ß,** or **-z,** an **-e-** is added to the superlative suffix. In the previous examples, you will find such words. Here are a few more examples.

positive	superlative	
breit	am breitesten	*broadest*
heiß	am heißesten	*hottest*
mild	am mildesten	*mildest*

A few superlatives have an irregular form.

positive	superlative	
bald	am ehesten	*soonest*
groß	am größten	*biggest*
gut	am besten	*best*
hoch	am höchsten	*highest*
nah	am nächsten	*nearest*
viel	am meisten	*most*

Exercise 140

Form the comparative and superlative of each adjective. For example:

klein *kleiner* *am kleinsten*

1. schön _____ _____
2. viel _____ _____
3. laut _____ _____
4. langweilig _____ _____
5. gut _____ _____
6. hässlich _____ _____
7. rot _____ _____
8. arm _____ _____
9. wenig _____ _____
10. angenehm _____ _____
11. langsam _____ _____
12. stolz _____ _____
13. teuer _____ _____
14. tief _____ _____
15. hoch _____ _____
16. scharf _____ _____
17. kühl _____ _____
18. weich _____ _____
19. hell _____ _____
20. berühmt _____ _____

Exercise 141

Using the adjective or adverb in parentheses, rewrite each sentence in the positive, comparative, and superlative. For example:

> (alt) Herr Bauer ist _____ .
> _Herr Bauer ist alt._
> _Herr Bauer ist älter._
> _Herr Bauer ist am ältesten._

1. (steil) Ist dieser Weg _____?

   _____

   _____

   _____

2. (gut) Frau Kessler ist die _____ Lehrerin.

   _____

   _____

   _____

3. (langsam) Warum gehst du_____?

   _____

   _____

   _____

4. (teuer) Diese großen Wagen sind _____ .

   _____

   _____

   _____

5. (hoch) Wir wohnen im _____ Wohnhaus.

   _____

   _____

   _____

6. (stark) Das _____ Zugtier ist ein Elefant.

   _____

   _____

   _____

7. (jung) Die _____ Schüler waren nicht so fleißig.

_____

_____

_____

8. (scharf) Er schneidet das Fleisch mit dem _____ Messer.

_____

_____

_____

9. (viel) Die Lehrlinge arbeiten _____ .

_____

_____

_____

10. (stolz) Der Mantel gefällt dem _____ Mann nicht.

_____

_____

_____

Exercise 142

Using the information in parentheses, compose three sentences: one with the given adjective or adverb in the positive, one in the comparative, and one in the superlative. For example:

> (klein, der Junge ist, das Mädchen, sein Sohn)
> *Der Junge ist klein.*
> *Das Mädchen ist kleiner als der Junge.*
> *Sein Sohn ist am kleinsten.*

1. (viel, mein Bruder raucht, mein Vater, Onkel Peter)

_____

_____

_____

2. (laut, Erik spricht, Thomas, mein Vater)

_____

_____

_____

3. (schöne Stadt, Berlin ist, Wien, Garmisch)

_____

_____

_____

4. (alt, meine Mutter ist, meine Großmutter, meine Urgroßmutter)

_____

_____

_____

5. (wenig Zeit, Frau Bauer hat, Herr Schmidt, Professor Keller)

_____

_____

_____

Exercise 143

Circle the letter of the word or phrase that best completes each sentence.

1. Ist ein VW besser _____ ein Audi?

a. wie

b. als

c. desto

d. beste

2. Mozart war ein _____ Musiker.

a. berühmter

b. wichtigere

c. am besten

d. jünger

3. Karins Bruder singt viel _____ .

a. allein

b. am schönsten

c. besser

d. laut

4. Sein Onkel ist _____ stolzesten.

a. als

b. am

c. je

d. desto

5. Die Straßen von Dortmund sind _____ als die Straßen von Hannover.

a. kleine

b. breiteste

c. am kürzesten

d. schmutziger

6. Ist Platin von allen Metallen _____ teuersten?

a. am meisten

b. als

c. am wenigsten

d. am

7. Die _____ Arbeiter fahren um sieben Uhr zur Arbeit.

a. wenige

b. ärmste

c. am reichsten

d. meisten

8. Die Mannschaft traf auf _____ härtesten Gegner.

a. den

b. am besten

c. schlechteste

d. als

9. Hier kann man _____ Informationen über Reisen erhalten.

a. weitere

b. die beste

c. guten

d. am wenigsten

10. _____ mehr der Mann fluchte, desto mehr weinte die Frau.

a. Als

b. Je

c. Am

d. Am meisten

11. Er hat _____ Probleme mit dem Computer.

a. am meisten

b. länger

c. viele

d. höher

12. Je länger sie darüber sprachen, _____ weniger überzeugte sie ihn.

a. besser

b. desto

c. am langweiligsten

d. langweiliger

13. Ich möchte einen _____ Mantel anprobieren.

a. längeren

b. am teuersten

c. billigere

d. schwerer

14. Wir brauchen eine _____ Wohnung.

a. kleinere

b. schönen

c. am größten

d. besser

15. Dieses Gebäude ist am _____ .

a. älter

b. älteren

c. hohen

d. höchsten

25

Passive Voice

The passive voice is so named because the subject of the active sentence moves to a *passive position*. The English passive voice consists of a form of the verb *to be* and a *past participle*: *is broken, was allowed, has been destroyed*, and so on. Let's look at a pair of sentences to contrast the active and passive voices.

active	The mayor attacked an alderman's reputation.
passive	An alderman's reputation was attacked by the mayor.

It is possible to omit the active subject from a passive sentence, thus relieving anyone of the responsibility of the action of the verb. For example:

active	The mayor attacked an alderman's reputation.
passive	An alderman's reputation was attacked.

The German passive voice functions in a similar manner. The basic components of the structure are the conjugation of the verb **werden** plus a *past participle* of a transitive verb. Intransitive verbs do not form a passive structure. The subject of the German active sentence becomes the object of the preposition **von** (*by*) in the passive sentence. Let's compare an active sentence that is changed into a passive sentence.

active	Die Schneiderin näht einen Anzug.	*The seamstress is sewing a suit.*
passive	Ein Anzug wird von der Schneiderin genäht.	*A suit is being sewn by the seamstress.*

Note carefully that the direct object **einen Anzug** in the active sentence changes to the nominative case (**Ein Anzug**) in the passive sentence, because it is the subject of that sentence.

Where in English the preposition *by* occurs in the passive sentence (*It was sewn* by *a seamstress.*), in German the dative preposition **von** is used to indicate the *person* or *force of nature* that carried out the action of the verb.

Das Dorf wurde von den Soldaten zerstört.	*The village was destroyed by the soldiers.*
Das Dorf wurde vom Erdbeben zerstört.	*The village was destroyed by the earthquake.*

But use **durch** in place of **von** to indicate *by what means* the action of the verb was carried out.

Sie ist durch einen Schuss getötet worden.	*She was killed by a shot.*
Sie ist durch einen Unfall getötet worden.	*She was killed in an accident.*

When an active sentence is made passive, the tense remains the same. The conjugation of **werden** in the various tenses determines the passive tenses. The main verb becomes a past participle, which remains constant throughout the tenses. For example:

present	Sie **wird** von ihm geküsst.	*She is being kissed by him.*
past	Sie **wurde** von ihm geküsst.	*She was kissed by him.*
present perfect	Sie **ist** von ihm geküsst **worden**.	*She has been kissed by him.*
past perfect	Sie **war** von ihm geküsst **worden**.	*She had been kissed by him.*
future	Sie **wird** von ihm geküsst **werden**.	*She will be kissed by him.*
future perfect	Sie **wird** von ihm geküsst **worden** sein.	*She will have been kissed by him.*

Be careful! The past participle of **werden** in the passive voice is **worden**. Use **geworden** only when **werden** means *to become* or *get*.

Compare the following pairs of active and passive sentences and the tenses used in them.

Er kaufte den VW. (past tense)	*He bought the VW.*
Der VW wurde von ihm gekauft. (past tense)	*The VW was bought by him.*

Karl hat das Gedicht gelernt. (present perfect)	*Karl has learned the poem.*
Das Gedicht ist von Karl gelernt worden. (present perfect)	*The poem has been learned by Karl.*

The passive voice occurs with transitive verbs—that is, verbs that have a direct object, which is in the accusative case. But dative verbs that require a dative object can also be made passive. Compare the following pairs of sentences.

active	Sie glaubten dem Mann nicht.	*They didn't believe the man.*
passive	Dem Mann wurde nicht geglaubt.	*The man wasn't believed.*

active	Man hilft ihr nicht.	*No one helps her.*
passive	Ihr wird nicht geholfen.	*She isn't being helped.*

Notice that the dative objects of the active sentences (**dem Mann** and **ihr**) remain in the dative case in the passive sentences. The new subject in the passive sentences is the elliptical word **es**, the reason for the third-person singular conjugation of **werden**.

Modal auxiliaries

The modal auxiliaries are frequently combined with an infinitive that is located at the end of a sentence. For example:

Sie kann dich gar nicht **verstehen**.	*She can't understand you at all.*
Warum musstet ihr **warten**?	*Why did you have to wait?*

In the same way, modal auxiliaries can combine with a *passive infinitive*. Passive infinitives consist of a **past participle** followed by **werden: geschlagen werden, gesagt werden, gefunden werden** (*to be hit, to be said, to be found*). When modals are followed by passive infinitives, it is only the modal auxiliary that is conjugated. For example:

Warum soll der Hund geschlagen werden?	*Why should the dog be beaten?*
Es durfte nicht gesagt werden.	*It wasn't permitted to be said.*
Die Kinder müssen sofort gefunden werden.	*The children must be found immediately.*

Exercise 144

Rewrite each passive infinitive phrase in the four tenses provided. Use the subject provided in parentheses. For example:

(das Haus) werden von den Bomben zerstört
present: *Das Haus wird von den Bomben zerstört.*
past: *Das Haus wurde von den Bomben zerstört.*
present perfect: *Das Haus ist von den Bomben zerstört worden.*
future: *Das Haus wird von den Bomben zerstört werden.*

1. (ich) werden von meinen Verwandten besucht

present: _____

past: _____

present perfect: _____

future: _____

2. (sie s.) werden von ihrem Bruder gebracht

present: _____

past: _____

present perfect: _____

future: _____

3. (sie pl.) werden niemals geglaubt

present: _____

past: _____

present perfect: _____

future: _____

4. (die Kinder) werden vom Reiseführer geführt

present: _____

past: _____

present perfect: _____

future: _____

5. (du) werden darum gebeten

present: _____

past: _____

present perfect: _____

future: _____

Exercise 145

Change the following active sentences to the passive voice. Keep the same tense as in the active sentence.

1. Der Bäcker bäckt das Brot.

_____

2. Die Eltern haben die Kinder sehr geliebt.

_____

3. Der alte Schuhmacher benutzte einen Hammer.

_____

4. Die Firma wird viele Angestellte entlassen.

_____

5. Unsere Lehrerin hat eine neue Klasse unterrichtet.

_____

6. Ein Bauer zog Kühe und Schweine auf.

_____

7. Sie fotografieren den berühmten Fußballspieler.

_____

8. Ein neuer Virus verursachte die Krankheit ihres Sohnes.

_____

9. Die Kellnerin wird zwei Gläser Wein bringen.

_____

10. Die Arbeiter beendeten um fünf Uhr die Arbeit.

_____

11. Frau Kamps hat zwei Einzelzimmer vermietet.

_____

12. Herr Schäfer muss die Heizung anstellen.

_____

13. Er wird das Licht anmachen.

_____

14. Ihr könnt die Schuhe beim Schuhmacher abholen.

_____

15. Man bot die meisten Waren zum halben Preis an.

_____

16. Der Dichter hatte viele schöne Gedichte geschrieben.

_____

17. Sie haben dem jungen Komponisten damit geholfen.

_____

18. Die Mutter muss noch das Baby füttern.

_____

19. Der Arzt wird ein Mittel gegen Husten verschreiben.

_____

20. Sie haben alle Gäste schnell bedient.

_____

Exercise 146

Circle the letter of the word or phrase that best completes each sentence.

1. Ein Glas Bier wurde _____ dem Kellner gebracht.

a. ist

b. war

c. von

d. kann

2. Das Museum _____ von den Touristen besucht.

a. waren

b. wird

c. worden

d. musste

3. Die neuen Sätze sind von dem Schüler gelernt _____ .

a. worden

b. werden

c. geworden

d. wurde

4. Eine heiße Suppe wurde _____ .

a. werden

b. worden

c. gekommen

d. bestellt

5. Wir _____ immer höflich gegrüsst worden.

a. können

b. sollten

c. sind

d. werden

6. _____ wurde für ihre Hilfe gedankt.

a. Ihn

b. Mich

c. Er

d. Ihr

7. Unsere Chancen _____ realistisch beurteilt werden.

a. sollten

b. kann

c. sind

d. wurden

8. _____ wurde von der Ärztin geheilt.

a. Ihm

b. Er

c. Mir

d. Euch

9. Sie ist von _____ zärtlich geküsst worden.

a. durch

b. sie

c. dich

d. ihm

10. _____ wird oft damit geholfen werden.

a. Ihrer Mutter

b. Er

c. Seinen Vater

d. Dich

11. Warum wurde mein Geburtstag wieder _____ ?

a. vergessen

b. schickte

c. gelacht

d. gehören

12. Viele Ostereier _____ von dem Kind bemalt worden.

a. war

b. wollen

c. werden

d. sind

13. Der Tisch wird _____ gedeckt.

a. von den Jungen

b. durch sie

c. gestern

d. werden

14. _____ das leicht geändert werden?

a. Kann

b. Müsst

c. Ist

d. War

15. Die Bevölkerung _____ davor gewarnt worden.

a. musste

b. war

c. soll

d. wird

Exercise 147

Using the passive infinitive phrases provided in parentheses, write original sentences in the passive voice.

1. (müssen abgeholt werden)

_____

2. (zerstört werden)

_____

3. (enttäuscht werden)

_____

4. (verhaftet werden)

_____

5. (können angestellt werden)

_____

6. (imponiert werden)

_____

7. (müssen abgerissen werden)

_____

8. (geglaubt werden)

_____

9. (verbessert werden)

_____

10. (verstanden werden)

_____

26

Subjunctive Mood

German has two subjunctive conjugational patterns, which simply are called *subjunctive I* and *subjunctive II*.

Subjunctive I

This conjugational pattern is also called the *present subjunctive*, because verbs conjugated in this pattern resemble the present-tense conjugation. But the conjugational endings in subjunctive I are somewhat different from the present-tense conjugation. The subjunctive I conjugational endings are -e, -est, -e, -en, -et, and -en. Let's look at some example verbs conjugated in subjunctive I.

	fragen (ask)	*fahren* (drive)	*bekommen* (receive)	*anstellen* (employ)
ich	frage	fahre	bekomme	stelle an
du	fragest	fahrest	bekommest	stellest an
er	frage	fahre	bekomme	stelle an
wir	fragen	fahren	bekommen	stellen an
ihr	fraget	fahret	bekommet	stellet an
sie	fragen	fahren	bekommen	stellen an

You will notice no difference in the conjugations of regular or irregular verbs or in the conjugations of verbs with prefixes. This is true with an overwhelming number of verbs.

Let's take a special look at modal auxiliaries. Their subjunctive I conjugation is derived from the infinitive.

	dürfen (may)	*können* (can)	*mögen* (like)	*wollen* (want)
ich	dürfe	könne	möge	wolle
du	dürfest	könnest	mögest	wollest
er	dürfe	könne	möge	wolle
wir	dürfen	können	mögen	wollen
ihr	dürfet	könnet	möget	wollet
sie	dürfen	können	mögen	wollen

Notice that the first-person plural (**wir**) and the third-person plural (**sie**) have a conjugation that is identical to the indicative present tense. This will be an important fact later on.

Three verbs must always be examined specially, because they play such significant roles in the German language: **haben**, **sein**, and **werden**. Let's look at their conjugations in subjunctive I.

	haben (have)	*sein* (be)	*werden* (become)
ich	habe	sei	werde
du	habest	seiest	werdest
er	habe	sei	werde
wir	haben	seien	werden
ihr	habet	seiet	werdet
sie	haben	seien	werden

German uses subjunctive I conjugations in *indirect discourse*. Let's look at some examples that compare direct discourse with indirect discourse.

direct	„Er glaubt ihr nicht."	*He doesn't believe her.*
indirect	Sie sagte, dass er ihr nicht glaube.	*She said that he doesn't believe her.*
direct	„Er glaubte ihr nicht."	*He didn't believe her.*
indirect	Sie sagte, dass er ihr nicht geglaubt habe.	*She said that he didn't believe her.*

Notice in the preceding example that the simple past tense is expressed in a *present perfect* structure in indirect discourse. This is done to avoid confusion with the present tense in indirect discourse.

Indirect questions follow the conjunction **ob** (*whether*) or other interrogatives used as a subordinating conjunction.

direct	„Ist Klaudia zu Hause?"
indirect	Er fragte, ob Klaudia zu Hause sei.
direct	„Wie viel Geld braucht der Mann?"
indirect	Er fragte, wie viel Geld der Mann brauche.

Subjunctive II

Subjunctive II conjugations are also called *past subjunctive* conjugations, because they are derived from the past tense of a verb. If a verb is regular, the subjunctive endings are **-te**, **-test**, **-te**, **-ten**, **-tet**, and **-ten** and resemble the past tense of the verb. For example:

	fragen (ask)	*stellen* (put)	*verkaufen* (sell)	*zumachen* (close)
ich	fragte	stellte	verkaufte	machte zu
du	fragtest	stelltest	verkauftest	machtest zu
er	fragte	stellte	verkaufte	machte zu
wir	fragten	stellten	verkauften	machten zu
ihr	fragtet	stelltet	verkauftet	machtet zu
sie	fragten	stellten	verkauften	machten zu

Modal auxiliaries use the same endings but add an umlaut to the verb stem's vowel if the infinitive has an umlaut. **Mögen**, however, is irregular.

	dürfen (may)	**können** (can)	**mögen** (like)	**wollen** (want)
ich	dürfte	könnte	möchte	wollte
du	dürftest	könntest	möchtest	wolltest
er	dürfte	könnte	möchte	wollte
wir	dürften	könnten	möchten	wollten
ihr	dürftet	könntet	möchtet	wolltet
sie	dürften	könnten	möchten	wollten

Irregular verbs use the past tense but add the endings -e, -est, -e, -en, -et, and -en. If the verb stem has an umlaut vowel (**a, o, u**), an umlaut is added.

	fahren (drive)	**gehen** (go)	**treffen** (meet)	**halten** (hold)
ich	führe	ginge	träfe	hielte
du	führest	gingest	träfest	hieltest
er	führe	ginge	träfe	hielte
wir	führen	gingen	träfen	hielten
ihr	führet	ginget	träfet	hieltet
sie	führen	gingen	träfen	hielten

	haben (have)	**sein** (be)	**werden** (become)
ich	hätte	wäre	würde
du	hättest	wärest	würdest
er	hätte	wäre	würde
wir	hätten	wären	würden
ihr	hättet	wäret	würdet
sie	hätten	wären	würden

Verbs that have a vowel change in the past tense and add the suffix **-te** have a special form in subjunctive II.

	senden (send)	*brennen* (burn)	*nennen* (name)	*wissen* (know)
ich	sendete	brennte	nennte	wüsste
du	sendetest	brenntest	nenntest	wüsstest
er	sendete	brennte	nennte	wüsste
wir	sendeten	brennten	nennten	wüssten
ihr	sendetet	brenntet	nenntet	wüsstet
sie	sendeten	brennten	nennten	wüssten

Subjunctive II conjugations are used in clauses that begin with **als ob** or **als wenn** (*as if*).

Sie tat so, als ob sie nicht hören könnte.	*She acted as if she couldn't hear.*
Das Kind lächelte, als wenn es sehr glücklich wäre.	*The child smiled as if he were very happy.*

The *conditional* consists of the subjunctive II conjugation of **werden** plus an infinitive. All verbs follow the same pattern. Look at these examples in the *present conditional*.

	haben (have)	*kaufen* (buy)	*finden* (find)
ich	würde haben	würde kaufen	würde finden
du	würdest haben	würdest kaufen	würdest finden
er	würde haben	würde kaufen	würde finden
wir	würden haben	würden kaufen	würden finden
ihr	würdet haben	würdet kaufen	würdet finden
sie	würden haben	würden kaufen	würden finden

Compare the previous examples with the following in the *past conditional*, which consist of the subjunctive II conjugation of **werden** plus a past participle followed by either **haben** or **sein**.

	haben (have)	*kaufen* (buy)	*gehen* (go)
ich	würde gehabt haben	würde gekauft haben	würde gegangen sein
du	würdest gehabt haben	würdest gekauft haben	würdest gegangen sein
er	würde gehabt haben	würde gekauft haben	würde gegangen sein
wir	würden gehabt haben	würden gekauft haben	würden gegangen sein
ihr	würdet gehabt haben	würdet gekauft haben	würdet gegangen sein
sie	würden gehabt haben	würden gekauft haben	würden gegangen sein

Compare the following pair of example sentences in the present conditional and the past conditional.

present conditional	Wenn er hier wäre, **würde** er mir helfen.	*If he were here, he would help me.*
past conditional	Wenn es nicht so weit gewesen wäre, **würde** sie dorthin gefahren sein.	*If it hadn't been so far, she would have driven there.*

Use subjunctive II to express unreal conditions. The conjunction **wenn** (*if*) is used to combine two subjunctive II clauses. The conditional **würde** plus **an infinitive** are commonly used in the main clause, especially when they are the only verbs in the clause.

Wenn es nicht so weit wäre, führe ich dorthin.	*If it weren't so far, I'd drive there.*

or

Wenn es nicht so weit wäre, würde ich dorthin fahren.

But when the tense is more complex, **würde** can be omitted.

Wenn sie genug Geld gehabt hätte, hätte sie ein neues Kleid gekauft.	*If she had had enough money, she would have bought a new dress.*

and

Wenn sie genug Geld verdienen könnte, könnte sie ein neues Kleid kaufen.	*If she earned enough money, she would be able to buy a new dress.*

If it introduces the sentence, the conjunction **wenn** can be omitted without changing the meaning of the sentence. In such a case, **dann** or **so** often introduce the main clause.

Hätte sie genug Geld, **dann** würde sie ein neues Kleid kaufen.	*If she had enough money, she would buy a new dress.*

When subjunctive I and the indicative are identical

When the subjunctive I conjugation in indirect discourse is the same as the present-tense indicative conjugation, subjunctive II is substituted. For example:

Er sagte, dass seine Eltern in diesem Haus **wohnen**.	*He said that his parents live in this house.*

changes to:

> Er sagte, dass seine Eltern in diesem Haus **wohnten.**

> Sie sagte, dass die Jungen die Vase gebrochen **haben.**   *She said that the boys broke the*
> *vase.*

changes to:

> Sie sagte, dass die Jungen die Vase gebrochen **hätten.**

Exercise 148

Write the present and past conditional forms of the following verbs with the subjects provided in parentheses.

	present conditional	past conditional
1. (er) finden		
2. (ich) glauben		
3. (du) fahren		
4. (wir) kommen		
5. (ihr) schlagen		
6. (das Kind) weinen		
7. (sie s.) helfen		
8. (sie pl.) singen		
9. (mein Vater) laufen		
10. (er) rennen		
11. (du) vertragen		
12. (Karin) werfen		
13. (Erik) spielen		
14. (ich) annehmen		
15. (wir) verstehen		

Exercise 149

Rewrite each sentence, replacing the past subjunctive with the present conditional in the main clause of each sentence. For example:

> Wenn es regnete, gingen sie ins Haus.
> *Wenn es regnete, würden sie ins Haus gehen.*

1. Er gäbe es mir, wenn er es hätte.

   _____

2. Wenn sie älter wäre, ginge sie zur Schule.

   _____

3. Wenn sie Zeit hätte, käme sie gern mit.

   _____

4. Hätten wir mehr Geld, dann kauften wir ein neues Haus.

   _____

5. Hätte sie mehr Zeit, so käme sie mit zur Party.

   _____

Exercise 150

Write each verb in the subjunctive I, subjunctive II, present conditional, and past conditional. Use the third-person singular **er** as the subject. For example:

infinitive	subjunctive I	subjunctive II	present conditional	past conditional
kaufen	*kaufe*	*kaufte*	*würde kaufen*	*würde gekauft haben*

1. schlagen _____ _____ _____ _____
2. trinken _____ _____ _____ _____
3. verbessern _____ _____ _____ _____
4. rauchen _____ _____ _____ _____
5. entlassen _____ _____ _____ _____
6. versprechen _____ _____ _____ _____
7. tun _____ _____ _____ _____
8. arbeiten _____ _____ _____ _____
9. bekommen _____ _____ _____ _____

10. ausgeben _____ _____ _____ _____

11. lernen _____ _____ _____ _____

12. verlieren _____ _____ _____ _____

13. probieren _____ _____ _____ _____

14. enthalten _____ _____ _____ _____

15. zählen _____ _____ _____ _____

16. bleiben _____ _____ _____ _____

17. essen _____ _____ _____ _____

18. bauen _____ _____ _____ _____

19. leihen _____ _____ _____ _____

20. anmachen _____ _____ _____ _____

21. kochen _____ _____ _____ _____

22. nennen _____ _____ _____ _____

23. brechen _____ _____ _____ _____

24. wissen _____ _____ _____ _____

25. gebrauchen _____ _____ _____ _____

Exercise 151

Revise each sentence from direct discourse to indirect discourse. Begin each statement with **Er sagte, dass.** Begin each question with **Sie fragte, ob** or **Sie fragte** with an interrogative word used as a subordinating conjunction. For example:

> „Martin spricht gut Deutsch.“
> *Er sagte, dass Martin gut Deutsch spreche.*

> „Kann Maria Geige spielen?“
> *Sie fragte, ob Maria Geige spielen könne.*

> „Wie sind sie wieder krank geworden?“
> *Sie fragte, wie sie wieder krank geworden seien.*

1. „Ihr Vetter wohnte damals in Heidelberg.“

_____

2. „Erik hat keinen Parkplatz gefunden.“

_____

3. „Herr Schneider kann die Führerscheinprüfung nicht bestehen."

_____

4. „Der Kranke wird aus dem Krankenhaus entlassen."

_____

5. „Die Handwerker haben für ihre Arbeit höhere Löhne gefordert."

_____

6. „Der Kanzler muss in der Hauptstadt bleiben."

_____

7. „Ihre Großmutter wohnt im Altersheim."

_____

8. „Man soll ihn täglich benachrichtigen."

_____

9. „Darf man im Kino rauchen?"

_____

10. „Wohin reisen diese Touristen?"

_____

11. „Was soll er Ihnen noch erklären?"

_____

12. „Wie viel wird das neue Haus kosten?"

_____

13. „Muss man hier umsteigen?"

_____

14. „Kommt Gudrun mit zur Party?"

_____

15. „Hat ihre Schwester das Buch langweilig gefunden?"

_____

Exercise 152

Complete each sentence with any appropriate phrase.

1. Er sprach so gut Deutsch, als ob _____

2. Das Mädchen tat so, als ob _____

3. Er führte ein Leben, als wenn _____

4. Der Kranke zitterte, als wenn _____

5. Der Mann lächelte, als ob _____

6. Ihre Augen sahen aus, als ob _____

7. Die Kinder schrien, als ob _____

8. Der Junge tat so, als wenn _____

9. Ihr Sohn benahm sich, als wenn _____

10. Die Frau machte ein Gesicht, als ob _____

Exercise 153

Combine the following pairs of sentences with **wenn**. For example:

> Sie kommt spät nach Hause. Vater ist böse.
> *Wenn sie spät nach Hause käme, würde Vater böse sein.*

1. Er hat mehr Zeit. Er hilft seinen Freunden.

_____

2. Die Verwandten können sie besuchen. Sie begrüßen es.

_____

3. Sie war gesund. Sie brauchte die Ärztin nicht.

_____

4. Seine Kusine kann ihm helfen. Er ist glücklich.

_____

5. Ich bin dorthin geflogen. Ich bin früher nach Hause gekommen.

_____

6. Es ist kalt geworden. Sie sind ins Haus gegangen.

_____

7. Wir haben nicht so viel Bier getrunken. Wir sind nicht krank geworden.

_____

8. Sie lernen mehr Deutsch. Sie können auch besser sprechen.

_____

9. Tante Gerda hat sie besucht. Sie sind sehr froh gewesen.

_____

10. Es ist heiß. Wir gehen schwimmen.

_____

11. Sie weiß das. Sie fragt nicht.

_____

12. Sie haben das neue Museum besucht. Sie sind in Berlin gewesen.

_____

13. Es regnet. Alles ist nass.

_____

14. Das Wetter ist schlecht gewesen. Ich bin nicht aufs Land gefahren.

_____

15. Der Student ist aufmerksam. Er macht keine Fehler.

_____

27

Infinitive Clauses

In infinitive clauses, the infinitive goes to the end of the clause and is preceded by **zu**. This resembles English infinitives such as *to speak*, *to help*, and so on, and occurs with verbs without a prefix or with an inseparable prefix.

zu sprechen	zu helfen
zu besprechen	zu verhelfen

If the verb has a separable prefix, **zu** is written together with the infinitive and stands between the prefix and the stem of the verb.

auszusprechen	mitzuhelfen

If the infinitive is a modal or other auxiliary, the modal or auxiliary follows the infinitive or participle in the verb phrase and is preceded by **zu**.

auxiliary as infinitive	**infinitive clause**
können arbeiten	arbeiten zu können
haben geschlafen	geschlafen zu haben
sein gefahren	gefahren zu sein
werden gebrochen	gebrochen zu werden

When two clauses have the same subject, it is often possible to change the second clause to an infinitive clause. For example:

Er hofft, dass er Sie bald wiedersieht.	*He hopes that he will see you soon.*
Er hofft Sie bald **wiederzusehen**.	*He hopes to see you soon.*

Or the object of a verb can often be changed to an infinitive clause.

Sie vergessen das Erzählen von Ihrem Aufenthalt in Paris.	*You're forgetting telling about your stay in Paris.*
Sie vergessen von Ihrem Aufenthalt in Paris **zu erzählen**.	*You're forgetting to tell about your stay in Paris.*

Certain words or phrases are signals that an infinitive clause will follow. An infinitive clause can be used after **etwas** or **nichts**.

Ich habe etwas zu sagen.   *I have something to say.*
Es gibt nichts zu essen.   *There's nothing to eat.*

The infinitive phrase occurs even when **etwas** or **nichts** is followed by an adjective.

Ich habe etwas Wichtiges zu sagen.   *I have something important to say.*
Es gibt nichts Gutes zu essen.   *There's nothing good to eat.*

You can also use an infinitive phrase after **vorhaben, versprechen, empört sein, glauben, behaupten,** and **sich freuen**, among numerous other verbs or phrases.

Sie hat vor eine Reise nach Berlin zu machen.   *She's planning on a trip to Berlin.*
Der Junge verspricht das Schlafzimmer   *The boy promises to straighten up the*
  aufzuräumen.   *bedroom.*
Sie war empört so lange auf Martin warten   *She was upset to have to wait so long*
  zu müssen.   *for Martin.*
Sie behauptete ein neues Heilmittel erfunden   *She claimed to have discovered a new*
  zu haben.   *remedy.*
Er freut sich den Rockstar kennen zu lernen.   *He's happy to get to know the rock star.*

When a prepositional adverb (**damit, darauf**) introduces or anticipates an infinitive, the infinitive clause must include **zu**.

Wir freuen uns darauf ins neue Museum   *We're looking forward to going to the*
  zu gehen.   *new museum.*
Ich bin daran interessiert eine Reise nach   *I'm interested in taking a trip to*
  Moskau zu machen.   *Moscow.*

Some important infinitive clauses are formed with the prepositions **um, ohne,** and **anstatt**. The preposition introduces the clause, and the infinitive goes to the end of the clause preceded by **zu**.

um . . . zu   *in order to (do something)*
ohne . . . zu   *without (doing something)*
anstatt . . . zu   *instead of (doing something)*

Unlike other infinitive clauses, those that begin with **um, ohne,** or **anstatt** are preceded by a comma.

Er tauchte ins Wasser, um seinen Bruder zu retten. *He dove into the water in order to save his brother.*

Erik sass am Tisch, ohne seiner Mutter zu helfen. *Erik sat at the table without helping his mother.*

Sie blieben im Lokal, anstatt nach Hause zu gehen. *They stayed in the tavern instead of going home.*

Exercise 154

Change each **dass**-clause to an infinitive clause. For example:

Wir wünschen, dass wir euch nächste Woche besuchen können.
Wir wünschen nächste Woche euch besuchen zu können.

1. Onkel Peter erlaubt seinem Sohn, dass er das Kino besucht.

_____

2. Sie empfahl ihren Studenten, dass sie einen Computer kaufen.

_____

3. Doktor Bauer ermahnt den kranken Mann, dass er das Rauchen sofort unterlässt.

_____

4. Tina bittet ihre Mutter, dass sie ein Märchen erzählt.

_____

5. Die Eltern warnen ihre Kinder, dass sie ihr Geld nicht verschwenden.

_____

6. Ich habe die Hoffnung, dass ich euch bald wiedersehe.

_____

7. Der kalte Winter zwingt die Leute, dass sie schwere Mäntel tragen.

_____

8. Ein Unglück zwang sie, dass sie ihren Besitz verkauften.

_____

9. Er verbietet dem verletzten Soldaten, dass er aufsteht.

_____

10. Der Chef befiehlt ihnen, dass sie die Arbeit schnell beenden.

_____

11. Wir freuen uns, dass wir dich besuchen können.

_____

12. Ein tapferer Mensch fürchtet nicht, dass er stirbt.

_____

13. Die Studenten fangen damit an, dass sie den Text ins Deutsche übersetzen.

_____

14. Sie hoffen, dass sie nach Freiburg mitreisen dürfen.

_____

15. Ich beabsichtige, dass ich nach dem Abendessen spazieren gehe.

_____

Exercise 155

Form infinitive clauses from the objects in the sentences. For example:

> Martin begann mit der Arbeit für das Staatsexamen.
> _Martin begann für das Staatsexamen zu arbeiten._

1. Wir haben Karl mit der Arbeit in der Küche geholfen.

_____

2. Sie hört spät in der Nacht mit dem Schreiben eines Aufsatzes auf.

_____

3. Herr Schmidt forderte von ihm die baldige Bezahlung der Miete.

_____

4. Das kleine Flugzeug machte auf dem Feld den Versuch einer Landung.

_____

5. Erik hat das Schreiben eines Dankbriefes an seine Gastgeber vergessen.

_____

Exercise 156

Complete each line with any appropriate infinitive clause.

1. Die Kinder brauchen etwas _____

2. Haben Sie nichts _____

3. Es freut mich _____

4. Es ist schade _____

5. Der Wissenschaftler behauptet _____

6. Es ist wichtig _____

7. Der Lehrer hat etwas Interessantes _____

8. Seine Frau war wieder empört _____

9. Der Mann glaubte _____

10. Es ist gar nicht wichtig _____

Exercise 157

Complete each sentence with any appropriate infinitive clause.

1. Ich freute mich darüber _____

2. Interessierst du dich dafür _____

3. Sie haben davon gesprochen _____

4. Meine Eltern sind darüber glücklich _____

5. Er ist nicht daran gewöhnt _____

6. Karl hat sich darauf gefreut _____

7. Hat sie davon gesprochen _____

?8. Haben Sie etwas dagegen _____

9. Ich denke nicht daran _____

10. Die Touristen sprechen darüber _____

Exercise 158

Complete each sentence with any appropriate infinitive clause. Note that these infinitive clauses will be formed from **um . . . zu, ohne . . . zu,** or **anstatt . . . zu.**

1. Der Vater ging zum Bett, ohne _____

2. Die Jungen sind zum Sportplatz gegangen, anstatt _____

3. Sie arbeitet bis spät abends, um _____

Review 3

Exercise 159

Rewrite each sentence, changing the subject to the new ones provided in parentheses. Make all the other necessary changes.

1. Der Dieb erfand die ganze Geschichte.

(ich) _____

(wir) _____

(ihr) _____

2. Meine Tante ruft den Arzt an.

(ich) _____

(du) _____

(wir) _____

3. Überzeugtest du den Mann?

(er) _____

(ihr) _____

(sie pl.) _____

Exercise 160

Fill in the blank with the inseparable prefix that best completes each verb: **be-, emp-, ent-, er-, ge-, miss-, ver-,** or **zer-.**

1. Während des Krieges haben sie das Dorf _____stört.

2. Er _____spricht die Wahrheit zu erzählen.

3. Wann habt ihr diese Briefe _____kommen?

4. Der Junge hat seine Handschuhe _____gessen.

5. Wie sieht er aus? Können Sie ihn _____schreiben?

Exercise 161

Circle the separable prefix in bold print that best completes the verbs in the following sentences.

1. Hoffentlich kannst du _____ kommen.	**auf**	**bei**	**mit**	**vor**	
2. Der Ritter hat den Drachen _____ gebracht.	**an**	**ein**	**um**	**zurück**	
3. Am Bahnhof müssen wir _____ steigen.	**um**	**mit**	**vor**	**voran**	
4. Hast du keinen Durst? Trink deine Milch _____ !	**an**	**auf**	**aus**	**zu**	
5. Sie konnte nur eine Lösung _____ schlagen.	**ab**	**aus**	**hin**	**vor**	

Exercise 162

Write each number as an Arabic numeral.

1. vierunddreißig _____

2. achtzig _____

3. einundfünfzig _____

4. sechshundertelf _____

5. fünfhundertdreiundzwanzig _____

Exercise 163

Write the given times in words. For example:

    1:00   *ein Uhr*

1. 10:10 _____

2. 12:30 _____

3. 2:40 _____

4. 6:45 _____

5. 8:55 _____

Exercise 164

Circle the letter of the word or phrase that best completes each sentence.

1. Der alte Mann kam um _____ Uhr um.

a. zehn

b. zehnten

c. vierte

d. Viertel

2. Kolumbus hat im _____ 1492 die neue Welt entdeckt.

a. Feiertag

b. Jahre

c. Amerika

d. Mittag

3. Ist sein Geburtstag am _____ ?

a. achtzehnten

b. Milliarde

c. August

d. vierundzwanzig

4. Vierzehn weniger vierzehn ist _____ .

a. eins

b. null

c. minus

d. durch

5. Darf ich eine _____ der Torte haben?

a. Hälfte

b. drei viertel

c. Viertel

d. halb

6. Meine Großmutter ist im _____ sehr krank geworden.

a. Montag

b. Januar

c. 2001

d. dritten

7. Mein Vater muss _____ Montag nach Bonn fliegen.

a. in

b. an

c. im

d. am

8. Meine _____ Frau wohnt in Bonn.

a. eins

b. zweiten

c. am zweiten

d. erste

9. Am einundzwanzigsten _____ bekam sie den ersten Brief.

a. Dienstag

b. 2005

c. Oktober

d. Jahre

10. Du musst bis _____ zehn wieder zu Hause sein!

a. halbes

b. elf

c. Hälfte

d. Viertel vor

Exercise 165

Rewrite each of the following sentences in the present and past tenses with the new subjects provided in parentheses. For example:

Ich will nichts.
(du)   *Du willst nichts.*   *Du wolltest nichts.*
(sie pl.)   *Sie wollen nichts.*   *Sie wollten nichts.*

1. Sie kann Deutsch und Englisch.

(wir) _____

_____

(du) _____

_____

2. Sie müssen ihm helfen.

(ihr) _____

_____

(du) _____

_____

3. Sie lässt den Wagen reparieren.

(wir) _____

_____

(ich) _____

_____

Exercise 166

Rewrite each sentence in the present tense with the verb provided in parentheses. For example:

Er spricht Deutsch.   (wollen) *Er will Deutsch sprechen.*

1. Wir erwarten einen Freund an der Ecke.

(sollen) _____

2. Wie lange arbeitet ihr jeden Tag?

(müssen) _____

3. Der Mann schneidet sich die Haare.

(lassen) _____

4. Was zeigt der Fremdenführer den Touristen?

(wollen) _____

5. Benutzt du die Volksbücherei?

(dürfen) _____

Exercise 167

Rewrite each sentence in the present perfect tense and the future tense.

1. Ich kann die Wörter nicht verstehen.

_____

_____

2. Warum muss er lügen?

_____

_____

3. Ihr seht sie im Garten arbeiten.

_____

_____

4. Der alte Hund hört Schritte kommen.

_____

_____

Exercise 168

Circle the letter of the word that best completes each sentence.

1. Der alte Herr _____ gesund werden.

a. gekonnt

b. muss

c. wollten

d. sollt

2. Der Student _____ die Arbeit nicht in der kurzen Zeit schaffen.

a. kann

b. musstet

c. dürft

d. gedurft

3. _____ ich weiß, ist der Mann ehrlich.

a. Damit

b. Wie

c. Falls

d. Soviel

4. _____ er mich liebt, will er mich nicht heiraten.

a. Wenn

b. Und

c. Obwohl

d. Indem

5. _____ sie die Kinder auf dem Bahnsteig sah, fing sie an zu weinen.

a. Falls

b. Wenn

c. Bis

d. Als

6. Sie _____ die Mädchen zum Tanz begleiten.

a. sollen

b. haben

c. werdet

d. hat

Exercise 169

Fill in the blank with the coordinating conjunction that makes the most sense: **aber, oder, denn, und,** or **sondern.**

1. Er bleibt lieber zu Hause, _____ es ist heute sehr kalt.

2. Sie kann nicht nur Russisch, _____ sie beherrscht auch Französisch.

3. Onkel Erhardt kommt morgen an _____ kann bis Freitag bei uns bleiben.

4. Ich lese den Satz, _____ ich verstehe ihn nicht.

Exercise 170

Rewrite each sentence by beginning with the subordinating clause. For example:

Er besucht uns, wenn er nach Deutschland kommt.
Wenn er nach Deutschland kommt, besucht er uns.

1. Karl konnte nicht fahren, da er betrunken war.

_____

2. Sie müssen sich beeilen, damit sie pünktlich ankommen.

_____

3. Wir kommen morgen vorbei, falls wir Zeit haben.

_____

4. Karin trägt eine Brille, damit sie besser sieht.

_____

5. Erik sah seine Verlobte an der Ecke stehen, als er vom Bahnhof ankam.

_____

Exercise 171

Rewrite each sentence in groups of four, changing the antecedents in bold print to the new antecedents in parentheses. Make all the other necessary changes. Follow the example provided with the antecedent (**der Junge**).

1. Er sieht **das Kind**, das in Amerika geboren ist.

Er sieht **das Kind**, das Gudrun fotografieren will.

Er sieht **das Kind**, mit dem Tanja spielt.

Er sieht **das Kind**, dessen Vater Zahnarzt ist.

(der Junge)

Er sieht den Jungen, der in Amerika geboren ist.

Er sieht den Jungen, den Gudrun fotografieren will.

Er sieht den Jungen, mit dem Tanja spielt.

Er sieht den Jungen, dessen Vater Zahnarzt ist.

(das Mädchen)

_____

_____

_____

_____

2. Sie findet **den Brief**, den Martin geschrieben hat.

Sie findet **den Brief**, nach dem ihre Schwester fragte.

Sie findet **den Brief**, dessen Inhalt ein Geheimnis ist.

Sie findet **den Brief**, der unter dem Tisch gelegen hat.

(die Ansichtskarte)

_____

_____

_____

_____

Exercise 172

Fill in the blanks with the appropriate form of the relative pronouns derived from definite articles.

1. Das Dorf, in _____ ich einmal wohnte, wurde vom Erdbeben zerstört.

2. Sie kaufte ein Fernrohr, mit _____ sie die Sterne beobachten kann.

3. Wir brauchen einen Tisch, auf _____ diese Lampe stehen kann.

4. Der Kranke, von _____ mein Onkel erzählte, war einmal Pianist.

5. Die Kleider, _____ Farbe rot ist, passen dir nicht.

Exercise 173

Circle the letter of the word that best completes each sentence.

1. Er kaufte _____ , was dir gefallen wird.

a. der

b. den

c. etwas

d. jemand

2. Der Rechtsanwalt, _____ sie alles glaubte, hat sie betrogen.

a. den

b. wem

c. dem

d. welchen

3. Ist das _____ , was er sagen kann?

a. wem

b. welcher

c. alles

d. nicht

4. Wir danken allen, _____ zum Faschingsball beigetragen haben.

a. was

b. die

c. denen

d. wer

5. Das sind die Sportler, _____ für die Olympischen Spiele trainieren.

a. welche

b. der

c. das

d. welcher

6. Das ist die Dame, _____ ich das Buch ausgeliehen habe.

a. deren

b. der

c. wessen

d. wem

7. Wo sind die Mieter, über _____ die Wirtin gesprochen hat?

a. die

b. was

c. wen

d. welches

8. Das ist alles, _____ sie sich erinnern können.

a. was

b. das

c. dass

d. woran

9. Das Mädchen, _____ Mutter gestorben ist, wird bei einer Tante wohnen.

a. deren

b. welches

c. dessen

d. denen

10. Der Dichter wohnt in einem Dorf, _____ er berühmt gemacht hatte.

a. das

b. dem

c. den

d. denen

Exercise 174

Form the comparative and superlative of each adjective. For example:

| klein | *kleiner* | *am kleinsten* |

1. scharf _____ _____
2. viel _____ _____
3. kühl _____ _____
4. hoch _____ _____
5. gut _____ _____
6. weich _____ _____
7. rot _____ _____
8. arm _____ _____
9. wenig _____ _____
10. bald _____ _____
11. groß _____ _____
12. stolz _____ _____
13. teuer _____ _____
14. tief _____ _____
15. schlecht _____ _____

Exercise 175

Using the information in parentheses, compose three sentences: one with the given adjective or adverb in the positive, one in the comparative, and one in the superlative. For example:

(klein, der Junge ist, das Mädchen, sein Sohn)
Der Junge ist klein.
Das Mädchen ist kleiner als der Junge.
Sein Sohn ist am kleinsten.

1. (alt, mein Vater ist, mein Großvater, mein Urgroßvater)

_____

_____

_____

2. (ein langer Fluss, die Weser ist, die Elbe, der Rhein)

_____

_____

_____

Exercise 176

Rewrite each passive infinitive phrase in the four tenses provided. Use the subject provided in parentheses. For example:

> (das Haus) werden von den Bomben zerstört
> _Das Haus wird von den Bomben zerstört._
> _Das Haus wurde von den Bomben zerstört._
> _Das Haus ist von den Bomben zerstört worden._
> _Das Haus wird von den Bomben zerstört werden._

1. (wir) werden von unseren Verwandten besucht

present: _____

past: _____

present perfect: _____

future: _____

2. (sie pl.) werden nicht geholfen

present: _____

past: _____

present perfect: _____

future: _____

3. (die Kinder) werden von einem neuen Lehrer unterrichtet

present: _____

past: _____

present perfect: _____

future: _____

Exercise 177

Change the following active sentences to the passive voice. Keep the same tense as in the active sentence.

1. Der Chef wird viele Angestellte entlassen.

_____

2. Sie fotografierte den berühmten Fußballspieler.

_____

3. Der Kellner hat zwei Gläser Bier gebracht.

_____

4. Herr Bauer muss die Heizung anstellen.

_____

5. Er hatte viele schöne Erzählungen geschrieben.

_____

Exercise 178

Circle the letter of the word that best completes each sentence.

1. Ein Glas Bier wurde _____ der Kellnerin gebracht.

a. ist

b. war

c. von

d. kann

2. Das Museum _____ von den Touristen besucht.

a. wart

b. wurde

c. worden

d. musste

3. Die neuen Sätze waren von dem Schüler gelernt _____.

a. worden

b. werden

c. geworden

d. wurde

4. Eine Tasse Kaffee wird _____.

a. werden

b. worden

c. gekommen

d. bestellt

5. Ich _____ immer höflich gegrüsst worden.

a. kann

b. bin

c. sollte

d. wurde

Exercise 179

Write the present and past conditional forms of the following verbs with the subject provided in parentheses.

	present conditional	past conditional
1. (er) glauben	_____	_____
2. (ich) weinen	_____	_____
3. (du) vertragen	_____	_____
4. (wir) kommen	_____	_____
5. (ihr) annehmen	_____	_____

Exercise 180

Replace the past subjunctive with the present conditional in the main clause of each sentence. For example:

> Wenn es regnete, gingen sie ins Haus.
> *Wenn es regnete, würden sie ins Haus gehen.*

1. Martin gäbe es uns, wenn er es hätte.

_____

2. Wenn Erik älter wäre, ginge er zur Schule.

_____

3. Hätten sie mehr Geld, dann kauften sie ein neues Haus.

_____

Exercise 181

Revise each sentence from direct discourse to indirect discourse. Begin each statement with **Er sagte, dass**. Begin each question with **Sie fragte, ob** or **Sie fragte** with an interrogative word used as a subordinating conjunction. For example:

> „Martin spricht gut Deutsch."
> *Er sagte, dass Martin gut Deutsch spreche.*

> „Kann Maria Geige spielen?"
> *Sie fragte, ob Maria Geige spielen könne.*

> „Wie sind sie wieder krank geworden?"
> *Sie fragte, wie sie wieder krank geworden seien.*

1. „Seine Kusine wohnte damals in Dänemark."

   _____

2. „Onkel Peter kann keinen Parkplatz finden."

   _____

3. „Der Bäcker war sehr alt."

   _____

4. „Darf man in diesem Restaurant rauchen?"

   _____

5. „Wie viel wird ein neuer Regenmantel kosten?"

   _____

Exercise 182

Combine the following pairs of sentences with **wenn**. For example:

> Sie kommt spät nach Hause. Vater ist böse.
> *Wenn sie spät nach Hause käme, würde Vater böse sein.*

1. Sie haben mehr Zeit. Sie helfen ihren Freunden.

   _____

2. Ich bin dorthin geflogen. Ich bin früher nach Hause gekommen.

   _____

3. Es ist sehr heiß geworden. Wir sind ins Haus gegangen.

   _____

Exercise 183

Change each **dass**-clause to an infinitive clause. For example:

Wir wünschen, dass wir euch nächste Woche besuchen können.
Wir wünschen nächste Woche euch besuchen zu können.

1. Doktor Bauer ermahnt den kranken Mann, dass er das Rauchen sofort unterlässt.

_____

2. Die Kinder bitten ihren Vater, dass er ein Lied singt.

_____

3. Tante Luise warnt Erik, dass er sein Geld nicht verschwendet.

_____

4. Der kalte Winter zwingt die Menschen, dass sie warme Kleidung tragen.

_____

5. Er verbietet dem verwundeten Offizier, dass er aufsteht.

_____

Exercise 184

Rewrite each sentence as an infinitive phrase, once with **um . . . zu, ohne . . . zu,** and **anstatt . . . zu.** The translate each phrase. For example:

Sie singt ein neues Lied.
um ein neues Lied zu singen	*in order to sing a new song*
ohne ein neues Lied zu singen	*without singing a new song*
anstatt ein neues Lied zu singen	*instead of singing a new song*

1. Er bringt uns zwei Gläser Wein.

_____   _____

_____   _____

2. Wir sprechen über die Lösung des Problems.

_____   _____

_____   _____

Final Review

Exercise 185

Identify the gender of the following nouns by supplying the missing definite article (**der**, **die**, or **das**).

1. _____ Situation
2. _____ Lehrerin
3. _____ Vorstellung
4. _____ Gemälde
5. _____ Blume
6. _____ Singen
7. _____ Gesundheit
8. _____ Silber
9. _____ Laden
10. _____ Einkommen

Exercise 186

Rewrite the following plural nouns as singular nouns. Provide the appropriate definite article.

1. die Fenster _____
2. die Brüder _____
3. die Zeitschriften _____
4. die Dörfer _____
5. die Mäntel _____

Exercise 187

Rewrite the following nouns as plural nouns.

1. der Garten _____
2. das Buch _____
3. der Lehrling _____

4. die Ärztin _____

5. das Singen _____

6. der Spiegel _____

7. die Tante _____

Exercise 188

Write the pronoun that substitutes for each noun: **er, sie s., es,** or **sie pl.**

1. Onkel _____

2. Stuhl _____

3. Pferd _____

4. Küche _____

5. Männer _____

6. Hefte _____

7. Tür _____

8. Mädchen _____

Exercise 189

Rewrite each of the following sentences as a question, appropriately changing the word or phrase in bold print to either **wer, wen, wem, wessen,** or **was.** For example:

Er ist ein Freund von Benno.   *Wer ist ein Freund von Benno?*

1. **Der Bahnhof** ist sehr weit von hier.

_____

2. Der Junge trinkt **keine Milch.**

_____

3. Tante Luise hatte etwas für **uns.**

_____

4. Er möchte **ein Butterbrot** essen.

_____

5. Ich warte auf **sie.**

_____

6. Herr Schäfer spricht mit **den Kindern**.

_____

7. **Sein** Sohn studiert in Berlin.

_____

8. **Ihr Vater** hat dagegen gesprochen.

_____

Exercise 190

Rewrite each of the following words or phrases in the accusative case and in the dative case.

nominative	accusative	dative
1. die Mutter	_____	_____
2. keine Gäste	_____	_____
3. sein Buch	_____	_____
4. Ihr Vetter	_____	_____
5. die Dörfer	_____	_____
6. ich	_____	_____
7. du	_____	_____
8. er	_____	_____
9. Sie	_____	_____
10. ihr	_____	_____

Exercise 191

Rewrite each phrase in the genitive case.

1. jener Baum _____

2. die Tante _____

3. keine Probleme _____

Exercise 192

Rewrite each sentence, using the word or phrase in parentheses as a possessive formed by the genitive case. Place the possessive in the blank provided. For example:

(der Mann)　　　　Der Pullover *des Mannes* ist weiß.

1. (unsere Tante)　Der Rock _____ passt ihr nicht.
2. (meine Brüder)　Das Schlafzimmer _____ war zu klein.
3. (der Offizier)　Die Stimme _____ ist laut.

Exercise 193

Fill in each blank with any appropriate adjective. Pay attention to the gender, number, and case.

1. Die Lehrerin wird diese _____ Schüler fragen.
2. Sie erinnerte sich an ihren _____ Onkel.
3. Die Frau kann dieser _____ Studentin nicht glauben.
4. Trinken Sie _____ Kaffee?
5. Meine Schwester hat ein _____ Auto.

Exercise 194

Rewrite each sentence as a question that could be answered with **ja** or **nein**. For example:

Er spricht kein Deutsch. *Spricht er kein Deutsch?*

1. Seine Geschwister haben im Park gespielt.

_____

2. Niemand geht ins Wohnzimmer.

_____

3. Sie sind am Fluss entlang gelaufen.

_____

Exercise 195

Write the present-tense and past-tense conjugation of each of the following verbs with the pronoun **er**.

versuchen	*werden*	*gehen*	*schreiben*
1. _____	_____	_____	_____
2. _____	_____	_____	_____

bekommen	*fressen*	*wissen*	*verstehen*
3. _____	_____	_____	_____
4. _____	_____	_____	_____

sein	*glauben*	*nennen*	*haben*
5. _____	_____	_____	_____
6. _____	_____	_____	_____

Exercise 196

Circle the letter of the word that best completes each sentence.

1. _____ hat sein Geld gestohlen?

a. Mochte

b. Wer

c. Waren

d. Wessen

2. _____ wollte ihr helfen.

a. Was

b. Ihr

c. Du

d. Niemand

3. _____ siehst du hinter der Tür?

a. Wer

b. Wann

c. Wo

d. Was

4. Warst _____ mit dem Zug gekommen?

a. sie

b. Sie

c. du

d. ihr

5. Sie _____ sehr weit gefahren.

a. hat

b. hatte

c. wart

d. ist

Exercise 197

Write the present perfect and past perfect conjugation for each of the following verbs with the pronoun **er**.

kennen	*sagen*	*laufen*	*schreiben*
1. _____	_____	_____	_____
2. _____	_____	_____	_____

Exercise 198

Rewrite each present-tense sentence in the present perfect tense.

1. Die Männer sind in der Stadt.

_____

2. Sehen Sie jemand?

_____

3. Die Jungen fangen einen Igel.

_____

4. Sie gehen mit ihren Freunden ins Kino.

_____

Exercise 199

Change the following present-tense sentences to the future tense with **werden**. Then write a present-tense sentence that infers the future tense with the adverb **morgen**. For example:

> Sie spielen Fußball.
> *Sie werden Fußball spielen.*
> *Morgen spielen sie Fußball.*

1. Sie fahren in die Schweiz.

_____

_____

2. Es geht ihm besser.

_____

_____

Exercise 200

Write the three imperative forms for each of the following verbs.

	lernen	*sein*	*sprechen*	*behalten*
1. du	_____	_____	_____	_____
2. ihr	_____	_____	_____	_____
3. Sie	_____	_____	_____	_____

Exercise 201

Rewrite each sentence, changing the object in bold print to the appropriate reflexive pronoun.

1. Fragen Sie **Ihre Mutter,** warum es nicht regnet?

_____

2. Hast du **deinem Vater** einen Schlips gekauft?

_____

3. Warum muss er **uns** widersprechen?

_____

4. Legt **die Dokumente** hin!

_____

5. Ich habe **ihm** die Suppe bestellt.

_____

Exercise 202

Circle the separable prefix that best completes the verbs in the following sentences.

1. Hoffentlich kann Erik _____ kommen.

a. auf

b. bei

c. mit

d. vor

2. Sie hat die Blumen _____ genommen.

a. an

b. ein

c. um

d. ver

3. In der Hauptstraße muss man _____ steigen.

a. mit

b. ent

c. be

d. aus

4. Machen Sie die Fenster _____ !

a. an

b. mit

c. aus

d. zu

5. Ich habe viel Geld _____ gegeben.

a. ab

b. aus

c. hin

d. vor

Exercise 203

Write the given times in words. For example:

      1:00   *ein Uhr*

1. 1:10 _____

2. 12:45 _____

3. 2:30 _____

4. 6:40 _____

5. 4:45 P.M. _____

6. 11:30 P.M. _____

Exercise 204

Circle the word or phrase that best completes each sentence.

1. Ist die Party am _____ ?

a. Zehnten

b. heute

c. Dezember

d. vierundzwanzig

2. Acht weniger acht ist _____ .

a. eins

b. plus

c. durch

d. null

3. Viele Leute sind im _____ krank geworden.

a. Samstag

b. März

c. gestern

d. Jahr

4. Ich muss _____ Dienstag in Bremen bleiben.

a. in

b. an

c. bis

d. auf

5. Am dritten _____ bekam sie den ersten Brief.

a. Dienstag

b. 1999

c. Februar

d. Jahre

6. Das war ihr _____ Gedicht.

a. halb

b. erstes

c. Hälfte

d. dritte

Exercise 205

Rewrite each sentence in the present tense with the verb provided in parentheses. For example:

Er spricht Deutsch.   (wollen) *Er will Deutsch sprechen.*

1. Wir helfen unseren Nachbarn.

(sollen) _____

2. Wie lange schlaft ihr?

(müssen) _____

3. Herr Bauer repariert seinen Wagen.

(lassen) _____

4. Rauchen Sie hier?

(dürfen) _____

Exercise 206

Rewrite each sentence in the present perfect tense and the future tense.

1. Wer kann Arabisch verstehen?

_____

_____

2. Du musst eine Stunde warten.

_____

_____

3. Wir sehen sie im Park spielen.

_____

_____

Exercise 207

Circle the letter of the word that best completes each sentence.

1. Er liest den Brief, _____ er versteht ihn nicht.

a. weil

b. wie

c. als

d. aber

2. _____ ich weiß, wohnt sie noch in Amerika.

a. Falls

b. Damit

c. Wie

d. Soviel

3. _____ er wieder gesund ist, bleibt er zu Hause.

a. Wenn

b. Und

c. Obwohl

d. Indem

4. Das ist alles, _____ ich brauche.

a. was

b. woran

c. das

d. dass

5. Der Junge, _____ Vater gestorben ist, muss bei einem Onkel wohnen.

a. der

b. welches

c. dessen

d. denen

6. _____ er das verlorene Geld fand, fing er an zu lachen.

a. Falls

b. Als

c. Wenn

d. Bis

Exercise 208

Fill in the blank with the appropriate form of the relative pronouns derived from definite articles.

1. Er kaufte ein Fernrohr, mit _____ er die Schiffe beobachten kann.

2. Er brachte uns ein Radio, _____ kaputt war.

3. Die Dame, von _____ mein Onkel erzählte, war einmal Pianistin.

4. Die Schuhe, _____ Farbe rot ist, passen dir nicht.

5. Eine Witwe ist eine Frau, _____ Mann gestorben ist.

6. Kennst du den Künstler, über _____ der Reporter berichtet hat?

Exercise 209

Form the comparative and superlative of each adjective. For example:

klein   *kleiner*   *am kleinsten*

1. gut   _____   _____

2. bald   _____   _____

3. kühl   _____   _____

4. hoch   _____   _____

5. schnell   _____   _____

6. groß   _____   _____

7. schlecht   _____   _____

8. arm   _____   _____

9. warm   _____   _____

10. kalt   _____   _____

Exercise 210

Rewrite the passive infinitive phrase in the four tenses shown. Use the subject provided in parentheses. For example:

(das Haus) werden von den Bomben zerstört
present: *Das Haus wird von den Bomben zerstört.*
past: *Das Haus wurde von den Bomben zerstört.*
present perfect: *Das Haus ist von den Bomben zerstört worden.*
future: *Das Haus wird von den Bomben zerstört werden.*

(er) werden von seiner Freundin besucht

1. present: _____

2. past: _____

3. present perfect: _____

4. future: _____

Exercise 211

Circle the letter of the word that best completes each sentence.

1. Ein Teller Suppe wurde _____ dem Kellner gebracht.

a. ist

b. war

c. kann

d. von

2. Das neue Museum _____ von den Kindern besucht.

a. waren

b. wird

c. worden

d. könnte

3. Das lange Gedicht ist von ihm gelernt _____ .

a. würden

b. geworden

c. wurde

d. worden

4. Wird eine Torte _____ werden?

a. würden

b. worden

c. gegangen

d. bestellt

5. Die Lehrerin_____ immer höflich gegrüsst worden.

a. könnte

b. soll

c. war

d. werde

Exercise 212

Conjugate the following verbs in subjunctive I and II with the pronoun **er**.

	haben	*kaufen*	*ausstellen*	*werden*
1. subjunctive I	_____	_____	_____	_____
2. subjunctive II	_____	_____	_____	_____

	brechen	*anfangen*	*sein*	*fahren*
3. subjunctive I	_____	_____	_____	_____
4. subjunctive II	_____	_____	_____	_____

	kennen	*dürfen*	*gehen*	*wissen*
5. subjunctive I	_____	_____	_____	_____
6. subjunctive II	_____	_____	_____	_____

Exercise 213

Replace the past subjunctive with the present conditional in the main clause of each sentence. For example:

> Wenn es regnete, gingen sie ins Haus.
> *Wenn es regnete, würden sie ins Haus gehen.*

1. Er führe nach Hause, wenn er genug Geld hätte.

_____

2. Wenn sie einen Wagen hätte, reiste sie ins Ausland.

_____

Exercise 214

Revise each sentence from direct discourse to indirect discourse. Begin each statement with **Er sagte, dass**. For example:

> „Martin spricht gut Deutsch.“
> *Er sagte, dass Martin gut Deutsch spreche.*

1. „Die Touristen kommen aus England.“

_____

2. „Sie kann ihn kaum verstehen.“

_____

3. „Frau Kamps war einmal Schauspielerin.“

_____

Exercise 215

Rewrite each sentence as an infinitive phrase, once with **um . . . zu, ohne . . . zu,** and **anstatt . . . zu,** for example

> Sie singt ein neues Lied.
> *um ein neues Lied zu singen*
> *ohne ein neues Lied zu singen*
> *anstatt ein neues Lied zu singen*

1. Er ist schnell nach Hause gelaufen.

_____

_____

_____

2. Wir können darüber sprechen.

_____

_____

_____

Answer Key

N/A is used throughout to indicate no change is needed.

Exercise 1

1. der 2. der 3. die 4. das 5. die 6. das 7. die 8. das 9. die 10. das 11. das 12. die 13. die 14. der 15. die 16. die 17. das 18. die 19. der 20. das 21. die 22. das 23. der 24. der 25. der

Exercise 2

These are sample answers. 1. Verständnis 2. Gesundheit 3. Gesicht 4. Bitte 5. Museum 6. Kellner 7. Mantel 8. Einsamkeit 9. Frühling 10. der König 11. Eigentum 12. Schauspielerin 13. Laden 14. Büchlein 15. Situation

Exercise 3

1. die Tanne 2. der Fluss 3. das Buch 4. die Übung 5. die Zeit 6. der Baum 7. der Arm 8. das Kind 9. die Freundin 10. der König 11. die Zeitung 12. das Land 13. der Ball 14. der Finger 15. das Mädchen

Exercise 4

1. die Mäntel 2. die Frauen 3. die Häuser 4. die Fräulein 5. die Küsten 6. N/A 7. die Wagen 8. die Lehrer 9. die Richterinnen 10. die Bleistifte 11. die Plätze 12. die Sitten 13. N/A 14. die Nasen 15. die Lautsprecher

Exercise 5

These are sample answers.

1. der Gärtner	der Tisch
der Soldat	der Wagen
der Arzt	der Wald
der Vater	der Computer
der Tourist	der Führerschein
2. die Tante	die Lampe
die Tochter	die Kreide
die Lehrerin	die Zeitung
die Tänzerin	die Schule
die Physikerin	die Bücherei
3. das Kind	das Geheimnis
das Mädchen	das Bild
das Fräulein	das Gesicht
das Pferd	das Fundament
das Schwein	das Gebäude

Exercise 6

1. die Vögel 2. die Spiegel 3. die Gärtner 4. die Briefe 5. die Lehrlinge 6. die Physiker 7. die Läden 8. die Käfige 9. die Hämmer 10. die Schuhe

Exercise 7

1. die Mäuse 2. die Schülerinnen 3. die Kassen 4. die Landkarten 5. die Hausarbeiten 6. die Mächte 7. die Würste 8. die Schwestern 9. die Tafeln 10. die Tannen

Exercise 8

1. die Hefte 2. die Wörter 3. die Hotels 4. die Kinder 5. die Räder 6. die Gesichte 7. die Beine 8. die Blätter 9. die Büchlein 10. die Zimmer

Exercise 9

1. die Schule 2. der Lehrer 3. das Kino 4. die Hütte 5. der Band 6. das Würstchen 7. die Eule 8. der Name 9. der Wurm 10. die Straße 11. die Sache 12. der Laden 13. der Wolf 14. das Schwein 15. der Franzose

Exercise 10

1. P 2. P 3. S 4. S 5. S 6. B 7. P 8. P 9. S 10. P 11.B 12. B 13. S 14. S 15. B 16. P 17. B 18. P 19. S 20. P 21. B 22. S 23. P 24. P 25. P

Exercise 11

1. sie s. 2. er 3. es 4. sie pl. 5. sie s. 6. es 7. sie s. 8. sie pl. 9. er 10. er

Exercise 12

1. Sie 2. sie 3. Sie 4. Wir 5. es 6. Sie 7. Sie 8. Er 9. er 10. Es 11. Sie 12. sie 13. Er 14. Er 15. Wir

Exercise 13

These are sample answers. 1. **Der Wagen** ist alt aber fährt gut. 2. Ist **der Rechtsanwalt** ein guter Freund von euch? 3. **Die Männer** spielen gern Schach. 4. Wo wird **Ihre Tante** wohnen? 5. **Das Kind** ist nur sechs Jahre alt und kann schon lesen und schreiben. 6. **Meine Kusine** kann Englisch und Arabisch. 7. Liegt **das Buch** auf dem Tisch? 8. **Unser Bruder** hat sein Fahrrad verkaufen müssen. 9. **Das Mädchen** glaubt mir nicht. 10. Ist **die Maschine** kaputt? 11. Wo ist **dein Heft**? 12. **Die Krankenschwester** will uns nicht stören. 13. **Mein Mann und ich** wohnen in der Goethestraße. 14. Ist **die neue Lampe** grün? 15. **Der alte Hund** schläft in einer Ecke der Küche.

Exercise 14

1. Man kann nicht jedem gefallen. 2. In unserem Klassenzimmer spricht man nur Deutsch. 3. Was man verspricht, das muss man halten. 4. Hat man an die Tür geklopft? 5. Warum muss man so lange warten? 6. Bei grün darf man über die Straße gehen. 7. Damals war man großzügiger. 8. Man hat sie davor gewarnt. 9. Man soll nicht fluchen. 10. Man wird es schnell vergessen. 11. Man muss im Wartesaal warten. 12. Man soll nicht vergessen. 13. Man steht an der Tür und weint. 14. Während der Krise war man hoffnungslos. 15. Man darf nicht lachen.

Exercise 15

1. Jemand hat das Geld gefunden. Niemand hat das Geld gefunden. 2. Ist jemand da? Ist niemand da? 3. Jemand hat etwas zu sagen. Niemand hat etwas zu sagen. 4. Jemand hat den roten Sportwagen gekauft. Niemand hat den roten Sportwagen gekauft. 5. Jemand wird dir helfen. Niemand wird dir helfen. 6. Jemand hat das Geld verloren. Niemand hat das Geld verloren. 7. Heute kommt jemand zu Besuch. Heute kommt niemand zu Besuch. 8. Jemand wartet an der Ecke. Niemand wartet an der Ecke.

Exercise 16

1. N 2. S 3. S 4. P 5. P 6. S 7. P 8. S 9. N 10. S

Exercise 17

1. Haben deine (meine) Eltern sehr lange darauf gewartet? 2. War Onkel Franz in Dänemark? 3. Hast du mit deinem (Habe ich mit meinem) Professor gesprochen? 4. Ist die junge Krankenschwester eine Bekannte von

ihm? 5. Liegt Hamburg an der Elbe? 6. Helfen die Brüder einander? 7. Ist das neue Gebäude in der Hauptstraße ein Museum? 8. Ist die Brücke ziemlich weit von hier? 9. Versteht er das nicht? 10. Waren sie gestern noch in Paris?

Exercise 18

1. Er 2. Sie 3. Er 4. Sie 5. er 6. sie 7. Niemand (Er) 8. Sie 9. es 10. Er 11. Wir 12. sie 13. Er 14. sie 15. Es

Exercise 19

1. es 2. sie pl. 3. sie 4. sie 5. sie pl. 6. er 7. es 8. er 9. es 10. sie 11. er 12. sie pl. 13. sie 14. es/sie pl. 15. es/sie pl. 16. es/sie pl. 17. er 18. er 19. sie 20. sie pl.

Exercise 20

1. die Kinder, Kinder, keine Kinder 2. das Buch, ein Buch, kein Buch 3. der Mensch, ein Mensch, kein Mensch 4. die Tische, Tische, keine Tische 5. die Dame, eine Dame, keine Dame 6. die Schule, eine Schule, keine Schule 7. der Wecker, ein Wecker, kein Wecker/die Wecker, Wecker, keine Wecker 8. der Fluss, ein Fluss, kein Fluss 9. die Männer, Männer, keine Männer 10. das Theater, ein Theater, kein Theater/die Theater, Theater, keine Theater 11. die Übungen, Übungen, keine Übungen 12. die Straße, eine Straße, keine Straße 13. der Arm, ein Arm, kein Arm 14. der Stuhl, ein Stuhl, kein Stuhl 15. das Stück, ein Stück, kein Stück

Exercise 21

1. S 2. S 3. DO 4. DO 5. DO 6. DO 7. S 8. DO 9. DO 10. DO

Exercise 22

1. **Wer** durchzieht die Stadt? 2. **Was** schreibt das Kind? 3. **Wen** legte die junge Mutter aufs Bett? 4. **Was** baut man in der Schillerstraße? 5. **Was** trinke ich gern? (**Was** trinkst du gern?) 6. **Wer** bringt uns Würstchen und Kartoffeln? 7. **Wer** hat ein paar neue Gedichte geschrieben? 8. **Was** möchten die Gäste essen? 9. Für **wen** habe ich drei alte Briefmarken? (Für **wen** hast du drei alte Briefmarken?) 10. **Was** bäckt Herr Schäfer? 11. **Wer** hat ein Stein ins Fenster geworfen? 12. **Was** fängt seine Tochter mit einer Hand? 13. **Was** stand früher an dieser Ecke? 14. **Was** wollen die Studenten trinken? 15. Gegen **wen** hat ihr Vater gesprochen?

Exercise 23

These are sample answers. 1. Haben Sie **Ihre Handschuhe** verloren? 2. Meine Tante stellte **den Blumenstrauß** auf den Tisch. 3. Ich muss **diese Briefe** unterschreiben. 4. Die Läufer erreichen **das Ziel**. 5. Sie hat **das Buch** in der Bibliothek gelesen. 6. Kennst du **meine Schwester** nicht? 7. Onkel Peter wird **die Kinder und mich** besuchen. 8. Das Hochwasser hat **die Brücke** zerstört. 9. Ich verstehe **den Professor** überhaupt nicht. 10. Die Kinder wollen **zwei Gläser Milch** trinken. 11. Herr Bauer wird **das Fleisch** braten. 12. Haben Sie **Ihre Eltern** angerufen? 13. Ich möchte **meinen Cousin** vorstellen. 14. Mein Bruder hat **den neuen VW** noch nicht gekauft. 15. Die jungen Eltern lieben **ihr Kind** sehr.

Exercise 24

1. für sie 2. gegen ihn 3. dagegen 4. darum 5. dadurch 6. ohne sie 7. um es 8. dafür 9. ohne ihn 10. dadurch

Exercise 25

These are sample answers. 1. Wir fahren gerade durch einen Tunnel. 2. Wie viel Uhr ist es? Um elf Uhr muss ich nach Hause gehen. 3. Können Sie bis nächsten Donnerstag bleiben? 4. Ich habe wirklich nichts gegen den Mann. 5. Erik spielt Klavier für die Gäste. 6. Warum ist dein Freund ohne seine Frau gekommen? 7. Ein Vogel flog durch das Fenster. 8. Der arme Mann sorgt und arbeitet für seine Familie. 9. Wir gehen den Bach entlang. 10. Alle kämpfen gegen den Feind.

Exercise 26

1. Bleibst du eine Woche lang in Paris? 2. Sie kam letzten Montag vorbei. 3. Er ist jede Woche zwei Tage in der Hauptstadt. 4. Wir bleiben dieses Jahr in Bremen. 5. Ich begegnete ihr einen Augenblick zuvor. 6. Wir fahren nächsten Samstag nach Ulm. 7. Er arbeitete einen Monat lang in einer Fabrik. 8. Waren Sie ein paar Monate in Italien? 9. Benno hat den ganzen Abend auf dem Sofa geschlafen. 10. Wir haben ihn letzte Woche gesehen.

Exercise 27

1. den Lehrer	dem Lehrer
2. keinen Mann	keinem Mann
3. die Leute	den Leuten
4. seine Mutter	seiner Mutter
5. deinen Wagen	deinem Wagen
6. das Heft	dem Heft
7. ein Zimmer	einem Zimmer
8. Tische	Tischen
9. keine Tasse	keiner Tasse
10. keine Tassen	keinen Tassen
11. meinen Bruder	meinem Bruder
12. einen Schrank	einem Schrank
13. ein Schiff	einem Schiff
14. ihre Geschwister	ihren Geschwistern
15. die Gäste	den Gästen

Exercise 28

1. Was hast du **deinem Bruder** geschickt? Was hast du **deiner Tante** geschickt? Was hast du **meinen Eltern** geschickt? Was hast du **dem Mädchen** geschickt? Was hast du **deiner Freundin** geschickt? 2. Ich möchte mit **meiner Lehrerin** sprechen. Ich möchte mit **den Schülern** sprechen. Ich möchte mit **euch** sprechen. Ich möchte mit **ihnen** sprechen. Ich möchte mit **dir** sprechen. 3. Niemand kann **mir** helfen. Niemand kann **ihm** helfen. Niemand kann **der Frau** helfen. Niemand kann **den Touristen** helfen. Niemand kann **dem Verbrecher** helfen.

Exercise 29

1. b 2. c 3. a 4. d 5. a 6. a 7. b 8. d 9. b 10. a

Exercise 30

1. c 2. d 3. a 4. a 5. d 6. a 7. a 8. b 9. d 10. b

Exercise 31

These are sample answers. 1. Es gehört nicht deinem Vater. 2. Sein Bruder hat mit meiner Mutter getanzt. 3. Was hat sie dem alten Mann gegeben? 4. In der Straßenbahn sitzt er einem berühmten Schauspieler gegenüber. 5. Herr Schneider kommt vom Bahnhof. 6. Morgen fahren wir zu unseren Verwandten. 7. Ihre Ohrringe waren aus Silber. 8. Nach dem Abendessen gingen wir sofort ins Kino. 9. Haben Sie lange bei Herrn Bauer gewohnt? 10. Der Anzug passt dem Jungen gar nicht. 11. Ich habe meiner Freundin dafür gedankt. 12. Wer hat der Dame die Blumen geschenkt? 13. Alle sprechen von den Touristen. 14. Die Würstchen schmecken dem Kind nicht. 15. Tante Gerda hat ihrer Kusine eine Ansichtskarte geschickt.

Exercise 32

These are sample answers. 1. Wem wirst du diesen Pullover geben? 2. Ich wohne lieber bei einem Freund. 3. Der Rundfunk teilt uns die Nachrichten mit. 4. Erik hat seinem Onkel für das schöne Hemd gedankt. 5. Brauchst du es nicht? 6. Ich werde nie gegen meinen eigenen Vater sprechen. 7. Benno arbeitet seit drei Monaten in Amerika. 8. Die Reiseleiterin hat es den amerikanischen Touristen gezeigt. 9. Kannst du mir damit helfen? 10. Die Jungen wollen mit dem schönen Mädchen tanzen. 11. Wir haben ein Paket von unseren Verwandten bekommen. 12. Der Diener bringt der Königin eine Tasse Tee. 13. Warum soll ich euch glauben? 14. Die Frau gibt dem weinenden Kind eine Münze. 15. Was machst du am Wochenende?

Exercise 33

1. den Professor	dem Professor	des Professors
2. die Lehrerin	der Lehrerin	der Lehrerin
3. das Gebäude	dem Gebäude	des Gebäudes

4. Bücher	Büchern	Bücher
5. meine Kinder	meinen Kindern	meiner Kinder
6. kein Brot	keinem Brot	keines Brotes
7. eine Tür	einer Tür	einer Tür
8. die Leute	den Leuten	der Leute
9. keinen Krieg	keinem Krieg	keines Krieges
10. den Verbrecher	dem Verbrecher	des Verbrechers

Exercise 34

1. mein 2. dein 3. sein 4. ihr 5. sein 6. unser 7. euer 8. ihr 9. Ihr 10. wessen

Exercise 35

1. Die Lautsprecher des Radios sind kaputt. 2. Das Kleid meiner Kusine passt ihr nicht. 3. Das Spielzeug der Kinder ist überall auf dem Boden. 4. Das Schlafzimmer meiner Brüder war zu klein. 5. Die Stimme des Mädchens ist süß. 6. Der Sohn der Ärztin wurde Rechtsanwalt. 7. Die Handschuhe meines Gastes sind unter dem Bett. 8. Das ist die Unterschrift einer Freundin von mir. 9. Hast du die Briefe des Dichters gelesen? 10. Der Eingang des Museums ist frisch gestrichen.

Exercise 36

1. b 2. d 3. c 4. b 5. a or d 6. d 7. a 8. c 9. c or d 10. d

Exercise 37

1. Seine Beschreibung **seiner Afrikareise** war ausführlich. Seine Beschreibung **der Idee** war ausführlich. Seine Beschreibung **des Verbrechens** war ausführlich. Seine Beschreibung **des Urlaubs** war ausführlich. Seine Beschreibung **der Krisen** war ausführlich. Seine Beschreibung **des Unfalls** war ausführlich.
2. Die neue Wohnung **meiner Eltern** ist in einem Vorort. Die neue Wohnung **einer Freundin** ist in einem Vorort. Die neue Wohnung **des Arztes** ist in einem Vorort. Die neue Wohnung **meiner Verwandten** ist in einem Vorort. Die neue Wohnung **eines Freundes** ist in einem Vorort. Die neue Wohnung **der Pflegerin** ist in einem Vorort.
3. Hast du die Reden **der Schauspielerin** gehört? Hast du die Reden **der Politiker** gehört? Hast du die Reden **des Bürgermeisters** gehört? Hast du die Reden **meines Chefs** gehört? Hast du die Reden **der Manager** gehört? Hast du die Reden **meiner Tochter** gehört?

Exercise 38

1. Ein altes Porträt hing über **dem Schrank**. Ein altes Porträt hing über **einer Lampe**. Ein altes Porträt hing über **dem Sofa**. Ein altes Porträt hing über **den Stühlen**.
2. Ihre Katze schläft gern auf **dem Tisch**. Ihre Katze schläft gern auf **einem Kissen**. Ihre Katze schläft gern auf **der Couch**. Ihre Katze schläft gern auf **dem Fensterbrett**.
3. Der neue Wagen steht hinter **der Garage**. Der neue Wagen steht hinter **den Bäumen**. Der neue Wagen steht hinter **einem Gebäude**. Der neue Wagen steht hinter **dem Supermarkt**.
4. Ist die Milch in **dem (im) Kühlschrank**? Ist die Milch in **der Küche**? Ist die Milch in **einer Flasche**? Ist die Milch in **dem (im) Esszimmer**?
5. Hier sind wir unter unseren **Schulkameraden**. Hier sind wir unter unseren **Verwandten**. Hier sind wir unter unseren **Geschwistern**. Hier sind wir unter unseren **Nachbarn**.

Exercise 39

1. Wir fahren vor **das Kino**. Wir fahren vor **die Schule**. Wir fahren vor **einen Laden**. Wir fahren vor **das Museum**.
2. Denkst du niemals an **deine Kinder**? Denkst du niemals an **deine Freundin**? Denkst du niemals an **deine Eltern**? Denkst du niemals an **deinen Sohn**?
3. Eine kleine Maus kroch unter **den Tisch**. Eine kleine Maus kroch unter **das Kissen**. Eine kleine Maus kroch unter **den Ofen**. Eine kleine Maus kroch unter **die Decke**.
4. Er hat sich neben **seinen Freund** gesetzt. Er hat sich neben **meine Schwester** gesetzt. Er hat sich neben **unseren Rechtsanwalt** gesetzt. Er hat sich neben **seine Kinder** gesetzt.

5. Ich stelle mein Fahrrad hinter **einen Baum**. Ich stelle mein Fahrrad hinter **die Garage**. Ich stelle mein Fahrrad hinter **die Türen**. Ich stelle mein Fahrrad hinter **das Tor**.

Exercise 40

1. daran, woran 2. auf ihn, auf wen 3. in sie, in wen 4. daran, woran 5. davor, wovor 6. neben ihr, neben wem 7. auf ihn/auf ihm, auf wen/auf wem 8. hinter sie, hinter wen 9. darauf, worauf 10. darin, worin 11. zwischen uns, zwischen wen 12. unter sie, unter wen 13. darüber, worüber 14. darüber, worüber 15. darunter, worunter

Exercise 41

1. b 2. a 3. b 4. d 5. a 6. c 7. d 8. d 9. a 10. c 11. b 12. c 13. c 14. d 15. a

Exercise 42

These are sample answers. 1. Die Wanderer wollen auf den Berg steigen. 2. Die Zeitungen waren unter dem großen Wörterbuch. 3. Neben wem sitzt Professor Bingen? 4. Warum stehst du so lange vor diesem Spiegel? 5. Wir mussten wieder auf unsere Kusine warten. 6. Der Kranke leidet an einer Lungenentzündung. 7. Sie wird die Blumen auf den Esstisch stellen. 8. Ich habe das alte Buch hinter dem Sessel gefunden. 9. Vor zwei Jahren wohnten wir noch in Hamburg. 10. Die Jungen reden über das Fußballspiel. 11. Ich freue mich schon auf die Ferien. 12. Das weinende Mädchen ist in den Garten gelaufen. 13. Karl wird eine Postkarte an seinen Bruder schreiben. 14. Was machst du in dem (im) Keller? 15. Ein großer Wagen steht vor dem Hotel. 16. Der Hund sitzt an der Tür und wartet auf seinen Herrn. 17. Wir essen nur selten in einem Restaurant. 18. Das schlafende Baby liegt auf dem Bett. 19. Sie hat oft an ihren Mann gedacht. 20. Der Junge stellte sich zwischen seine beiden Freunde und lächelte.

Exercise 43

These are sample answers. 1. accusative: Wir warten noch auf den Zug.
dative: Eine Spinne steht auf dem Fensterbrett.
2. accusative: Eine Maus ist unter den Tisch gelaufen.
dative: Die Schwestern leben jahrelang unter einem Dach.
3. accusative: Wir fuhren vor das Kino.
dative: Warum steht ein Krankenwagen vor unserem Haus?
4. accusative: Ich stelle eine Laterne hinter die Gardinen.
dative: Sie hat sich hinter dem Zaun verborgen.
5. accusative: Setzen Sie sich zwischen uns!
dative: Mein Platz ist zwischen meinen Eltern.

Exercise 44

1. keine Blume	keine Blume	keiner Blume	keiner Blume
2. meine Kinder	meine Kinder	meinen Kindern	meiner Kinder
3. jene Freunde	jene Freunde	jenen Freunden	jener Freunde
4. welcher Zug	welchen Zug	welchem Zug	welches Zuges
5. unser Arzt	unseren Arzt	unserem Arzt	unseres Arztes
6. einige Tassen	einige Tassen	einigen Tassen	einiger Tassen
7. viele Leute	viele Leute	vielen Leuten	vieler Leute
8. jedes Stück	jedes Stück	jedem Stück	jedes Stücks
9. deine Kusine	deine Kusine	deiner Kusine	deiner Kusine
10. beide Länder	beide Länder	beiden Ländern	beider Länder

Exercise 45

1. Sie wohnen nicht in **dieser** Straße, sondern in **jener**. 2. Sie stand nicht an **dieser** Tür, sondern an **jener**. 3. Ich kaufte nicht **dieses** Bild, sondern **jenes**. 4. Die Kinder gehen nicht zu **dieser** Schule, sondern zu **jener**. 5. Wir verkaufen nicht **diesen** VW, sondern **jenen**. 6. Sie fahren nicht mit **diesem** Bus, sondern mit **jenem**. 7. Martin wird nicht an **dieser** Ecke stehen, sondern an **jener**. 8. Ich warte nicht auf **diesen** Zug, sondern auf **jenen**.

9. Er spricht nicht über **diese** Probleme, sondern über **jene**. 10. Sie haben nicht **diesen** Mann verhaftet, sondern **jenen**.

Exercise 46

1. Ich habe **diesen** Professor noch nicht kennen gelernt. Ich habe **seinen** Professor noch nicht kennen gelernt. Ich habe **Ihren** Professor noch nicht kennen gelernt. Ich habe **jenen** Professor noch nicht kennen gelernt. Ich habe **eu(e)rn** Professor noch nicht kennen gelernt.
2. Meine Schwester will **diese** Romane lesen. Meine Schwester will **viele** Romane lesen. Meine Schwester will **keine** Romane lesen. Meine Schwester will **meine** Romane lesen. Meine Schwester will **beide** Romane lesen.
3. Sie liebt **solche** Menschen nicht. Sie liebt **diese** Menschen nicht. Sie liebt **viele** Menschen nicht. Sie liebt **beide** Menschen nicht. Sie liebt **mehrere** Menschen nicht.
4. Ich sorge mich um **alle** Kinder. Ich sorge mich um **beide** Kinder. Ich sorge mich um **eure** Kinder. Ich sorge mich um **meine** Kinder. Ich sorge mich um **keine** Kinder.
5. Warum hast du **dieses** Haus gekauft? Warum hast du **ihr** Haus gekauft? Warum hast du **jenes** Haus gekauft? Warum hast du **kein** Haus gekauft? Warum hast du **solch ein** Haus gekauft?

Exercise 47

1. **Jede Schülerin** muss vorsichtig sein. **Jeder Tourist** muss vorsichtig sein. **Jeder Soldat** muss vorsichtig sein. **Jeder Gast** muss vorsichtig sein. **Jedes Mädchen** muss vorsichtig sein. **Jede Krankenschwester** muss vorsichtig sein. **Jedes Kind** muss vorsichtig sein. **Jeder Mensch** muss vorsichtig sein.
2. Vor solch **einem Rechtsanwalt** muss man sich hüten. Vor solch **einer Frau** muss man sich hüten. Vor solch **einem Menschen** muss man sich hüten. Vor solch **einem Dieb** muss man sich hüten. Vor solch **einer Lehrerin** muss man sich hüten. Vor solch **einem Kind** muss man sich hüten. Vor solch **einer Gefahr** muss man sich hüten. Vor solch **einem Unglück** muss man sich hüten.

Exercise 48

These are sample answers. 1. Diese Familie wohnt in Stuttgart. 2. Ich möchte jenen Mantel kaufen. 3. Jedes Kind muss geimpft werden. 4. Welchen Anzug werden Sie tragen? 5. Alle Touristen müssen ein Visum haben. 6. Beide Freunde spielen gern Schach. 7. Ich kenne mehrere Ausländer. 8. Ich brauche viele Briefmarken. 9. Ist dein neuer Wagen ein Sportwagen? 10. Solch einem Mann kann man nicht trauen. 11. Ich habe keine Zeit dazu. 12. Wo ist meine neue Bluse? 13. Ihre Geschwister wohnen jetzt in der Hauptstadt. 14. Sie kann unsere Verwandten in Bonn besuchen. 15. Eu(e)re Eltern sind sehr nett.

Exercise 49

1. der 2. der 3. die 4. das 5. die 6. das 7. die 8. das 9. die 10. das 11. das 12. die 13. die 14. der 15. die

Exercise 50

1. die Schule 2. der Fluss 3. das Haus 4. die Übung 5. das Kind 6. der Baum 7. der Wagen 8. die Lehrerin 9. die Zeitschrift 10. der König

Exercise 51

1. die Vögel 2. die Hefte 3. die Söhne 4. die Schülerinnen 5. die Wörter 6. die Gärtner 7. die Landkarten 8. die Kinder 9. die Hausarbeiten 10. die Läden 11. die Käfige 12. N/A 13. die Richterinnen 14. die Gespräche 15. die Einheiten

Exercise 52

1. **Er** wohnt jetzt in Frankreich. 2. Wo sind **sie**? 3. **Er** will eine Afrikareise machen. 4. Ist **es** eine Bekannte von dir? 5. **Er** ist sehr interessant.

Exercise 53

These are sample answers. 1. Der BMW 2. diese Frau 3. Die Kinder 4. der Brief 5. das Messer

Exercise 54

1. Man kann nicht jedem gefallen. 2. Warum muss man so lange warten? 3. Bei Grün darf man über die Straße gehen. 4. Man hat sie davor gewarnt. 5. Man soll nicht fluchen.

Exercise 55

1. Jemand hat etwas zu sagen. Niemand hat etwas zu sagen. 2. Jemand wird euch helfen. Niemand wird euch helfen.

Exercise 56

1. N 2. S 3. S 4. N 5. N 6. P

Exercise 57

1. Wer durchzieht die Stadt? 2. Was trinken die Männer gern? 3. Wer wird ein neues Gedicht schreiben? 4. Was möchten die Jungen essen? 5. Für wen habe ich (hast du) ein Geschenk? 6. Was bäckt Herr Schäfer? 7. Wer hat ein Stein ins Fenster geworfen? 8. Gegen wen hat ihr Vater gesprochen? 9. Was kommt in fünf Minuten? 10. Was hänge ich (hängst du) über das Bett?

Exercise 58

1. für sie 2. gegen ihn 3. dagegen 4. darum 5. wider ihn 6. ohne sie 7. um es 8. dafür 9. ohne sie 10. dadurch

Exercise 59

1. die Lehrerin	der Lehrerin
2. keine Männer	keinen Männern
3. die Zeitung	der Zeitung
4. seine Tante	seiner Tante
5. deinen Wagen	deinem Wagen
6. das Auto	dem Auto
7. ein Zimmer	einem Zimmer
8. Bücher	Büchern
9. keine Frage	keiner Frage
10. mich	mir
11. dich	dir
12. ihn	ihm
13. sie	ihr
14. es	ihm
15. uns	uns

Exercise 60

1. Was hast du seinem Bruder gezeigt? 2. Was hast du deiner Schwester gezeigt? 3. Was hast du meinen Verwandten gezeigt? 4. Was hast du dem Kind gezeigt? 5. Was hast du deiner Freundin gezeigt?

Exercise 61

1. den Ausländer	dem Ausländer	des Ausländers
2. die Ärztin	der Ärztin	der Ärztin
3. das Gebäude	dem Gebäude	des Gebäudes
4. keine Gesetze	keinen Gesetzen	keiner Gesetze
5. wen	wem	wessen

Exercise 62

1. Der Rock meiner Kusine passt ihr nicht. 2. Das Schlafzimmer meines Bruders war zu klein. 3. Die Stimme des Mädchens ist laut. 4. Der Sohn der Kellnerin wurde Rechtsanwalt. 5. Der Wagen unseres Gasts ist rot.

Exercise 63

1. b 2. a 3. c 4. c 5. b 6. d

Exercise 64

1. Ein altes Porträt hing über **dem Schrank**. Ein altes Porträt hing über **einer Lampe**. Ein altes Porträt hing über **dem Sofa**. Ein altes Porträt hing über **den Tischen**. 2. Erik hat einen Brief an **seine Freundin** geschrieben. Erik hat einen Brief an **seinen Vater** geschrieben. Erik hat einen Brief an **seinen Bruder** geschrieben. Erik hat einen Brief an **seine Geschwister** geschrieben. 3. Ich habe **diesen** Professor noch nicht kennen gelernt. Ich habe **Ihren** Professor noch nicht kennen gelernt. Ich habe **jenen** Professor noch nicht kennen gelernt. Ich habe **euren** Professor noch nicht kennen gelernt.

Exercise 65

1. ein netter Herr	diese kleine Katze____	unsere neue Freundin
2. meine gute Tasse	jener schnelle Wagen	welche alten Männer
3. heißer Kaffee____	die schöne Blume	alle deutschen Autos
4. das kleine Dorf	meine neuen Hefte	einige gute Weine
5. jeder kluge Student	ihr erstes Gedicht	kalte Suppe
6. den letzten Zug	diesen kurzen Bleistift	einen langen Weg
7. seinen besten Freund	unsere reichen Freunde____	meine Kinder
8. warmen Tee____	einen stolzen Mann	eure armen Nachbarn
9. jenes schwarze Hemd	jede nette Dame	deine neue Lehrerin
10. ein____ großes Haus	warme Milch____	ihre braunen Hunde
11. diesem kleinen Jungen	unserem alten Fahrrad	seinen neuen Schuhen
12. weißem Wein____	vielen alten Zeitungen	beiden guten Kindern
13. einem schlechten Tag	deiner jungen Schwester	kranken Leuten
14. diesem scharfen Messer	jeder neuen Studentin	kaltem Bier
15. einer engen Straße____	jenem kleinen Zimmer	meiner dummen Bekannten
16. eines großen Problems	dieser jungen Frau____	
17. vieler alter Menschen____	jedes armen Kindes	
18. kalten Bieres	weniger neuer Schüler____	
19. unseres besten Läufers	keiner deutschen Zeitung____	
20. welches stolzen Professors	deines neuen Autos	

Exercise 66

1. **Jener Mann** war einmal Richter. **Mein Mann** war einmal Richter. **Ihr Mann** war einmal Richter. **Welcher Mann** war einmal Richter?
2. **Mein guter Freund** wohnt jetzt in Japan. **Mein alter Freund** wohnt jetzt in Japan. **Mein neuer Freund** wohnt jetzt in Japan. **Mein amerikanischer Freund** wohnt jetzt in Japan.
3. Ist **seine neue Freundin** Krankenschwester geworden? Ist **diese neue Freundin** Krankenschwester geworden? Ist **eure neue Freundin** Krankenschwester geworden? Ist **jene neue Freundin** Krankenschwester geworden?
4. **Diese jungen Leute** spielen gern Tennis. **Alle jungen Leute** spielen gern Tennis. **Keine jungen Leute** spielen gern Tennis. **Einige junge Leute** spielen gern Tennis.
5. Trinkt ihr **heißen Kaffee**? Trinkt ihr **warmen Kaffee**? Trinkt ihr **türkischen Kaffee**? Trinkt ihr **starken Kaffee**?
6. Hast du **ihr neues Auto** gesehen? Hast du **jenes neue Auto** gesehen? Hast due **ein neues Auto** gesehen? Hast due **dieses neue Auto** gesehen?

Exercise 67

1. Wie oft besuchen Sie **einen deutschen Freund**? Wie oft besuchen Sie **einen deutschen Verwandten**? Wie oft besuchen Sie **eine deutsche Freundin**? Wie oft besuchen Sie **eine deutsche Kunstausstellung**?
2. Ich habe **keine neuen Teller** (**keinen neuen Teller**). Ich habe **keine neue Jacke**. Ich habe **kein neues Auto**. Ich habe **keinen neuen Mantel**.

3. Sie wollen mit **dieser armen Frau** sprechen. Sie wollen mit **diesem armen Kind** sprechen. Sie wollen mit **diesen armen Leuten** sprechen. Sie wollen mit **diesen armen Männern** sprechen.

4. Ich denke oft an **meine ausgewanderte Schwester**. Ich denke oft an **meine ausgewanderten Geschwister**. Ich denke oft an **meinen ausgewanderten Onkel**. Ich denke oft an **meinen ausgewanderten Bruder**.

5. Er trinkt nicht gern **kalten Tee**. Er trinkt nicht gern **kalte Milch**. Er trinkt nicht gern **kaltes Bier**. Er trinkt nicht gern **kaltes Wasser**.

6. Das ist das neue Haus **einer alten Freundin** von mir. Das ist das neue Haus **eines alten Freundes** von mir. Das ist das neue Haus **eines alten Rechtsanwalts** von mir. Das ist das neue Haus **eines alten Lehrers** von mir.

Exercise 68

These are sample answers. 1. Solch einen Mann will ich nicht einladen. 2. Karl möchte jenes hübsche Mädchen kennen lernen. 3. Viele alte Menschen leben im Altersheim. 4. Diese gesunden Kinder dürfen wieder zur Schule gehen. 5. Morgen reisen alle Touristen in die Schweiz. 6. Ich habe keine einzige Münze bei mir. 7. Diese eleganten Damen sind Schauspielerinnen. 8. Einige ausländische Gäste kommen aus Schweden. 9. Wegen eines langen Tages ging Martin sofort ins Bett. 10. Die Eltern der fleißigen Schülerin sind erfreut. 11. Dieser eifrige Kaufmann muss viel reisen. 12. Frau Huber kaufte jenen schicken Mantel. 13. Wenige neue Studenten gehen ins Lokal. 14. Leibniz hat diese berühmte Akademie begründet. 15. Ein Fußgänger hat seine verlorene Tasche gefunden.

Exercise 69

These are sample answers. 1. Mein Sohn hat ein langes Gedicht auswendig gelernt. 2. Der Lehrer wird diesen neuen Schüler fragen. 3. Welchem Bruder gleicht jener ältere Mann? 4. Sie erinnert sich gern an einige alte Freunde. 5. Die Frau kann diesem fleißigen Handwerker vertrauen. 6. Trinkst du deutsches Bier? 7. In diesem Zimmer sind zu viele helle Lampen. 8. Sind eure englischen Übungen schwer? 9. Die Touristen reisen durch mehrere interessante Städte. 10. Dieses Dorf hat wenige breite Straßen. 11. Meine Großmutter hat einen kleinen Garten. 12. Diese zwei großen Bäume tragen viele süße Birnen. 13. Der Park ist auch ein Opfer des letzten Krieges gewesen. 14. Das neugierige Kind stellt tausend schwere Fragen. 15. Über der Tür des kleinen Ladens hängt ein Schild.

Exercise 70

1. am Fenster 2. ums Haus 3. zum Klavier 4. beim Schwimmen 5. ans Tor 6. zur Ausstellung 7. im Keller 8. vom Professor 9. aufs Buch 10. fürs Kind 11. ins Haus

Exercise 71

1. für den Kranken 2. ans Fenster 3. ums Gefängnis 4. in der Tasche 5. beim Packen 6. von den Eltern 7. zur Universität 8. am Tisch 9. zum Arzt 10. an der Tür 11. aufs Sofa 12. ins Schloss 13. fürs Geschenk 14. um die Sonne 15. bei der Tür 16. vom Sportplatz 17. zu den Bürgern 18. an der Wand 19. auf den Bus 20. im Walde 21. für den alten Mann 22. bei der Tür 23. vom Wetter 24. zur Kirche

Exercise 72

1. Hat er den Ofen noch nicht geheizt? 2. Kämpfen sie gegen ihre Feinde? 3. Trinkt der Student ein Glas Bier? 4. Ist Deutschland arm an Silber und Gold? 5. War der Professor nicht zufrieden? 6. Wird der Zustand des Kranken von Tag zu Tag besser? 7. Kennt niemand den geretteten Mann? 8. Ist sein Bruder ebenso alt wie meine Schwester? 9. Gibt es viele große Geschäfte mit sehenswerten Schaufenstern? 10. Liegen die Oberhemden auf dem Boden?

Exercise 73

These are sample answers. 1. Ja, ich bleibe noch ein paar Tage in Bonn. 2. Nein, die schwarze Tinte ist besser dafür. 3. Ja, sie kann Geige spielen. 4. Nein, der Hund ist nicht über den Zaun gesprungen. 5. Ja, die Wanderer singen Volkslieder. 6. Nein, die Hunde waren einem kleinen Jungen treu. 7. Ja, der Schriftsteller hat ein neues Buch geschrieben. 8. Nein, wir werden eine Wohnung in Ulm suchen. 9. Ja, die lange Trockenheit war dem Wachstum der Bäume schädlich. 10. Nein, die schlechten Waren sind den Kunden nicht angenehm gewesen.

Exercise 74

1. Was ist ihm äußert peinlich? 2. Wer hat uns oft angerufen? 3. Wer hat in Mathematik eine gute Note bekommen? 4. Wer gibt abends Englischunterricht? 5. Wer studiert an der Universität Hamburg? 6. Was muss sofort landen? 7. Was zählt zu den Naturwissenschaften? 8. Wer muss jetzt mehr Geld ausgeben? 9. Was ist zu schwer? 10. Wer hat seine Ferien in Italien verbracht?

Exercise 75

1. Wessen Tante ist Physikerin? 2. Wer ist ein Freund des neuen Bürgermeisters? 3. Wem können wir nicht glauben? 4. Mit wem möchte der Hauptmann sprechen? 5. Wessen Geschwister sind in der Schule? 6. Wen versucht Martin zu küssen? 7. Auf wen haben wir wieder gewartet? 8. Wer hat seine Mappe verloren? 9. Wem gibt der Bäcker zwei Plätzchen? 10. Wer bittet um ihre Fahrkarten?

Exercise 76

1. Für wen ist der Eintritt kostenlos? 2. Was können wir sehen? 3. An wen möchte ich eine Ansichtskarte schicken? 4. Wer hat eine gute Stimme? 5. Wessen alten Wagen hast du gekauft? 6. Wann gehen wir italienisch essen? 7. Warum bleiben wir zu Hause? 8. Wo haben sie ein Häuschen? 9. Wohin fährt mein Bruder mit der Straßenbahn? 10. Was hat die Polizei unter Kontrolle gehabt? 11. Wie viel Einwohner hat Hamburg? 12. Wie oft fahren die Kaufleute nach Bremen? 13. Was hat dieser treulose Mensch gebrochen? 14. Wohin fallen die Blätter und vertrocknen? 15. Was ist in der Wärme verdorben? 16. Wem helfen seine Nachbarn? 17. Wo steht der Lehrer? or Woran steht der Lehrer? 18. Warum sagt er nichts? 19. Wen will der Hund warnen? 20. Was sehen die Reisenden in den Bahnhof kommen? 21. Über wen redet Frau Schneider? 22. Wessen Verwandte wohnen seit zwanzig Jahren in Heidelberg? 23. Was ist ein teures Metall? 24. Wodurch erhält man ein warmes Haus? 25. Wie alt ist seine Schwester jetzt?

Exercise 77

1. **Du gibst** meinem Freund ein paar Euro. **Martin gibt** meinem Freund ein paar Euro. **Meine Eltern geben** meinem Freund ein paar Euro. **Sie gibt** meinem Freund ein paar Euro. **Ihr gebt** meinem Freund ein paar Euro. 2. **Er wartet** auf Gudrun und Angela. **Sie warten** auf Gudrun und Angela. **Der Kellner wartet** auf Gudrun und Angela. **Unsere Freunde warten** auf Gudrun und Angela. 3. **Wir müssen** vorsichtig sein. **Frau Bauer muss** vorsichtig sein. **Die Kinder müssen** vorsichtig sein. **Du musst** vorsichtig sein. 4. **Seid ihr** noch in Köln? **Sind sie** noch in Köln? **Ist Herr Schmidt** noch in Köln? **Bist du** noch in Köln? 5. **Sie hat** heute keine Zeit. **Andrea hat** heute keine Zeit. **Du hast** heute keine Zeit. **Ihr habt** heute keine Zeit. 6. **Wir wollen** eine alte Freundin besuchen. **Sie will** eine alte Freundin besuchen. **Karl und Benno wollen** eine alte Freundin besuchen. **Wer will** eine alte Freundin besuchen? 7. **Mein Vater weiß** nicht, wo er wohnt. **Seine Eltern wissen** nicht, wo er wohnt. **Du weißt** nicht, wo er wohnt. **Sie wissen** nicht, wo er wohnt.

Exercise 78

1. b 2. a 3. d 4. a 5. a 6. a 7. a 8. b 9. b 10. c 11. d 12. a 13. b 14. d 15. a

Exercise 79

1. wir, sie, or Sie 2. Ich 3. du 4. es 5. Er, Sie, or Ihr 6. wir, sie, or Sie 7. Ihr 8. Sie 9. Er or Sie 10. er or sie 11. ihr 12. Sie 13. ihr 14. Wer 15. Er 16. Was 17. Er or Sie 18. Sie 19. Sie 20. du 21. Sie 22. Ich, Er, or Sie 23. du 24. Es 25. ihr

Exercise 80

1. **Ich ging** langsam nach Hause. **Ihr gingt** langsam nach Hause. **Der Arzt ging** langsam nach Hause. **Du gingst** langsam nach Hause. 2. **Er war** vier Wochen in den USA. **Sie waren** vier Wochen in den USA. **Wer war** vier Wochen in den USA? **Ihre Verwandten waren** vier Wochen in den USA. 3. **Warum kam** sie nicht mit? **Warum kamt** ihr nicht mit? **Warum kam** Ihr Bruder nicht mit? **Warum kamen** Sie nicht mit? 4. Am Freitag **starb sie.** Am Freitag **starben die Soldaten.** Am Freitag **starben sie.** Am Freitag **starb Frau Bauer.**

5. **Ich lief** ins Wohnzimmer. **Du liefst** ins Wohnzimmer. **Wer lief** ins Wohnzimmer? **Die Hunde** liefen ins Wohnzimmer.

6. **Du musstest** einer Freundin damit helfen. **Felix und Gudrun mussten** einer Freundin damit helfen. **Andrea musste** einer Freundin damit helfen. **Ihr musstet** einer Freundin damit helfen.

7. **Wer kannte** den Gast nicht? **Sie kannten** den Gast nicht. **Doktor Braun kannte** den Gast nicht. **Meine Eltern kannten** den Gast nicht.

Exercise 81

1. b 2. b 3. c 4. d 5. b 6. a 7. c 8. b 9. d 10. c 11. b 12. a 13. d 14. a 15. d

Exercise 82

1. Viele Krankheiten quälten die Menschen. 2. Aßen Sie nur Obst und Gemüse? 3. Sie gab dem Kellner das Trinkgeld. 4. Man hatte das Recht zu schweigen. 5. Es wurde wieder regnerisch. 6. Wir fanden ein paar Euro auf der Straße. 7. Sie klagten vor Gericht gegen ihren Mieter. 8. Konntest du diesen Fluss nennen? 9. Felix brachte seiner Freundin einen Blumenstrauß. 10. Wir saßen am Strand und beobachteten die großen Wellen. 11. Die anderen Kinder lachten über ihn. 12. Die Sterne leuchteten. 13. Es blitzte und donnerte. 14. Er lächelte und machte mir ein Kompliment. 15. Herr Bauer bat sie um diesen Tanz. 16. Wer befahl der Armee anzugreifen? 17. Wir sammelten Briefmarken und Ansichtskarten. 18. Mein Schlafzimmer war sehr klein und dunkel. 19. Der Student hatte eine kleine Zweizimmerwohnung unter dem Dach. 20. Fuhrt ihr nach Hannover? 21. Mein Onkel kam aus Basel. 22. Die Eltern liebten ihre Kinder über alles. 23. Diese Jungen trieben viel Sport. 24. Ich dachte oft an meine alten Freunde in Deutschland.

Exercise 83

1. Ich habe mit dem Hund gespielt. Ich hatte mit dem Hund gespielt.
Ihr habt mit dem Hund gespielt. Ihr hattet mit dem Hund gespielt.
Du hast mit dem Hund gespielt. Du hattest mit dem Hund gespielt.
Die Jungen haben mit dem Hund gespielt. Die Jungen hatten mit dem Hund gespielt.
2. Hast du genug Zeit gehabt? Hattest du genug Zeit gehabt?
Haben sie genug Zeit gehabt? Hatten sie genug Zeit gehabt?
Hat Karl genug Zeit gehabt? Hatte Karl genug Zeit gehabt?
Haben Felix und Benno genug Zeit gehabt? Hatten Felix und Benno genug Zeit gehabt?
3. Ich bin wieder gesund geworden. Ich war wieder gesund geworden.
Wir sind wieder gesund geworden. Wir waren wieder gesund geworden.
Ihr seid wieder gesund geworden. Ihr wart wieder gesund geworden.
Du bist wieder gesund geworden. Du warst wieder gesund geworden.
4. Wie hat er das gewusst? Wie hatte er das gewusst?
Wie haben sie das gewusst? Wie hatten sie das gewusst?
Wie hat sie das gewusst? Wie hatte sie das gewusst?
Wie haben die Wissenschaftler das gewusst? Wie hatten die Wissenschaftler das gewusst?
5. Ich habe es nie gekonnt. Ich hatte es nie gekonnt.
Du hast es nie gekonnt. Du hattest es nie gekonnt.
Wir haben es nie gekonnt. Wir hatten es nie gekonnt.
Ihr habt es nie gekonnt. Ihr hattet es nie gekonnt.

Exercise 84

1. Wir waren schon fertig. Wir sind schon fertig gewesen. 2. Glaubten Sie, dass diese Idee gut ist (war)? Haben Sie geglaubt, dass diese Idee gut ist? 3. Peter fing den Ball nicht. Peter hat den Ball nicht gefangen. 4. Ich kannte den neuen Studenten nicht. Ich habe den neuen Studenten nicht gekannt. 5. Tante Gerda stellte die Vase aufs Klavier. Tante Gerda hat die Vase aufs Klavier gestellt. 6. Er ging mit seiner Freundin auf eine Party. Er ist mit seiner Freundin auf eine Party gegangen. 7. Wir redeten mit Herrn Müller. Wir haben mit Herrn Müller geredet. 8. Sie warf ein Stein ins Fenster. Sie hat ein Stein ins Fenster geworfen. 9. Alle kritisierten diese Politiker. Alle haben diese Politiker kritisiert. 10. Wer schwamm besser? Maria oder Tanja? Wer ist besser geschwommen? Maria oder Tanja?

Exercise 85

1. c 2. b 3. d 4. a 5. c 6. a 7. a 8. b 9. d 10. a 11. a 12. d 13. d 14. d 15. b

Exercise 86

1. Ich kann ihnen gar nicht helfen. 2. Sie sitzen am Fenster und trinken Kaffee. 3. Warum stellt er den Sessel ins Wohnzimmer? 4. Das Mädchen ist sehr müde. 5. Kommen Ihre Gäste mit der Straßenbahn? 6. Peter spielt Klavier für sie. 7. Ich lächele aber sage nichts. 8. An wen schreibt sie diesen Brief? 9. Wir denken selten an jene schlechten Tage. 10. Wer arrangiert diesen Ausflug?

Exercise 87

werde lachen	werde kennen	werde gehen	werde schreiben
wirst lachen	wirst kennen	wirst gehen	wirst schreiben
wird lachen	wird kennen	wird gehen	wird schreiben
werden lachen	werden kennen	werden gehen	werden schreiben
werdet lachen	werdet kennen	werdet gehen	werdet schreiben
werden lachen	werden kennen	werden gehen	werden schreiben

Exercise 88

1. Die Mädchen werden auf eine Party gehen. Morgen gehen die Mädchen auf eine Party. 2. Doktor Schneider wird in einem großen Krankenhaus arbeiten. Morgen arbeitet Doktor Schneider in einem großen Krankenhaus. 3. Ein Auslandsbrief wird 1 Euro kosten. Morgen kostet ein Auslandsbrief 1 Euro. 4. Der kleine Felix wird seinen Großeltern dafür danken. Morgen dankt der kleine Felix seinen Großeltern dafür. 5. Martin wird mit seiner Verlobten nach Hause kommen. Morgen kommt Martin mit seiner Verlobten nach Hause.

Exercise 89

1. Er wird über die Lage in Afghanistan berichten. 2. Wir werden sie über die Gefahren dieser Industrie informieren. 3. Werden Sie eine Nachrricht von Ihrem Sohn erhalten? 4. Ich werde sie im Garten treffen. 5. Wo wirst du den Schatz finden? 6. Ich werde kein Wort sagen. 7. Die Jungen werden dorthin wandern. 8. Der Dieb wird mir den Mantel stehlen. 9. Wird er den Nagel in die Wand schlagen? 10. Sie wird ihr Leben riskieren. 11. Wer wird für die alte Frau sorgen? 12. Katrina wird ihr Spielzeug mit den anderen Kindern teilen. 13. Der reiche Mann wird in einem riesigen Haus wohnen. 14. Wirst du die Röcke selbst machen? 15. Die Studenten werden nach Paris fahren.

Exercise 90

1. present: Ihr Haus wird für sie zu klein.
past: Ihr Haus wurde für sie zu klein.
present perfect: Ihr Haus ist für sie zu klein geworden.
future: Ihr Haus wird für sie zu klein werden.
2. present: Die Haustür ist oft offen.
past: Die Haustür war oft offen.
present perfect: Die Haustür ist oft offen gewesen.
future: Die Haustür wird oft offen sein.
3. present: Diese Treppe führt in den Keller.
past: Diese Treppe führte in den Keller.
present perfect: Diese Treppe hat in den Keller geführt.
future: Diese Treppe wird in den Keller führen.
4. present: Sie renovieren die ganze Wohnung.
past: Sie renovierten die ganze Wohnung.
present perfect: Sie haben die ganze Wohnung renoviert.
future: Sie werden die ganze Wohnung renovieren.
5. present: Sie erbt die Ringe von ihrer Mutter.
past: Sie erbte die Ringe von ihrer Mutter.

present perfect: Sie hat die Ringe von ihrer Mutter geerbt.
future: Sie wird die Ringe von ihrer Mutter erben.

Exercise 91

1. Er wird es gesagt haben. 2. Sie wird mich gefragt haben. 3. Ich werde nichts gekauft haben. 4. Wirst du mitgekommen sein? 5. Werden Sie darüber gelacht haben? 6. Die Frauen werden Karten gespielt haben. 7. Werdet ihr dorthin gefahren sein? 8. Tina wird geweint haben. 9. Sie wird zum Ziel gelaufen sein. 10. Ich werde das Geld geborgt haben.

Exercise 92

1. Arbeite!	Singe!	Fahre!	Verkaufe!
2. Arbeitet!	Singt!	Fahrt!	Verkauft!
3. Arbeiten Sie!	Singen Sie!	Fahren Sie!	Verkaufen Sie!
4. Sei!	Nimm an!	Gib zu!	Störe!
5. Seid!	Nehmt an!	Gebt zu!	Stört!
6. Seien Sie!	Nehmen Sie an!	Geben Sie zu!	Stören Sie!

Exercise 93

1. Singt in einem Chor! 2. Sprich über den Wildwestfilm! 3. Erzählen Sie von einer Reise nach China! 4. Brate die Würstchen in Öl! 5. Schneiden Sie das Brot für Butterbrote! 6. Iss Hähnchen mit Pommes frites! 7. Nehmt eine Suppe vor dem Hauptgericht! 8. Ziehe einen braunen Gürtel an! 9. Bügele die Hemden und Hosen! 10. Grabt ein tiefes Loch! 11. Sei artig! 12. Ziehen Sie den schmutzigen Pullover aus! 13. Decke das Kind mit der Bettdecke gut zu! 14. Werfen Sie den harten Käse weg! 15. Sieh den komischen Mann an!

Exercise 94

1. Zurückbleiben! 2. Hier umsteigen! 3. Das Gepäck aufmachen! 4. Bitte schweigen! 5. Nicht sprechen!

Exercise 95

1. Sie fragte **sich**, warum es so kalt ist. 2. Ich erinnere **mich** an die Schularbeit. 3. Wir waschen **uns** im Keller. 4. Warum willst du **dich** so ärgern? 5. Setze **dich** auf einen Stuhl! 6. Legt **euch** hin! 7. Mutter will **sich** vor einer Erkältung schützen. 8. Wir brauchen das Geld für **uns**. 9. Siehst du **dich** im Spiegel? 10. Felix und Karl denken nur an **sich**.

Exercise 96

1. Wir suchen **uns** gute Plätze in der ersten Reihe. 2. Wer hat **sich** ein Glas Wein bestellt? 3. Wirst du **dir** diese Arbeit zutrauen? 4. Ich konnte **mir** diese Dummheit nicht verzeihen. 5. Der alte Mann verbirgt die Blumen hinter **sich**. 6. Wie könnt ihr **euch** helfen? 7. Haben Sie **sich** einen Pelzmantel gekauft? 8. Ich helfe **mir**, so gut ich kann. 9. Warum musst du **dir** widersprechen? 10. Wer kaufte **sich** die Rosen?

Exercise 97

These are sample answers. 1. Wirst du deinem Sohn ein Fahrrad kaufen? Wirst du dir ein Fahrrad kaufen? 2. Wo kann ich die Kinder waschen? Wo kann ich mich waschen? 3. Onkel Martin hat seiner Schwester ein Telegramm geschickt. Onkel Martin hat sich ein Telegramm geschickt. 4. Der Vater muss die Jungen daran erinnern. Der Vater muss sich daran erinnern. 5. Trauen Sie dem Lehrling diese Arbeit zu? Trauen Sie sich diese Arbeit zu? 6. Die Kinder ärgerten ihren Vater nicht. Die Kinder ärgerten sich nicht. 7. Ich will meine Patienten vor der Grippe schützen. Ich will mich vor der Grippe schützen. 8. Widersprich dem Professor nicht! Widersprich dir nicht! 9. Sie half den armen Menschen, so gut sie konnte. Sie half sich, so gut sie konnte. 10. Herr Schneider hat ein Geschenk für seine Frau. Herr Schneider hat ein Geschenk für sich.

Exercise 98

1. ein netter Mann	diese kleine Katze____	unsere neue Schule
2. eine gute Tasse	jener schnelle Wagen	welche alten Leute

3. den letzten Platz   diesen kurzen Bleistift   einen langen Stock
4. seine besten Freunde   unseren reichen Freund   meine Kinder
5. einem schlechten Tag   deiner jungen Schwester   kranken Leuten
6. diesem scharfen Messer   jeder neuen Studentin   kaltem Bier
7. eines großen Problems   dieser jungen Dame____
8. vieler alter Frauen____   jenes armen Kindes

Exercise 99

1. **Jene** Frau war einmal Richterin. **Meine** Frau war einmal Richterin. **Welche** Frau war einmal Richterin? 2. Ist **ihr neuer** Freund Reporter geworden? Ist **dieser neue** Freund Reporter geworden? Ist **jener neue** Freund Reporter geworden? 3. Er trinket night gern **kalten** Tee. Er trinket night gern **kalte** Milch. Er trinket night gern **kaltes** Bier.

Exercise 100

These are sample answers. 1. Die Lehrerin wird diesen neuen Schüler fragen. 2. Sie erinnerte sich gern an einige deutsche Verwandte. 3. Die Frau kann diesem arroganten Politiker vertrauen. 4. Trinkst du kaltes Wasser? 5. Meine Mutter hat einen schönen Garten.

Exercise 101

1. ums Haus 2. zum Klavier 3. beim Schwimmen 4. ans Tor 5. zur Ausstellung 6. vom Professor 7. aufs Buch

Exercise 102

1. Ist dieses Land arm an Silber und Gold? 2. War Frau Schneider nicht zufrieden? 3. Hat niemand den geretteten Mann gekannt? 4. Ist seine Schwester ebenso alt wie mein Bruder? 5. Möchten die Touristen das Schloss fotografieren?

Exercise 103

1. Wer ist Physikerin? 2. Wer ist ein Freund des neuen Bürgermeisters? 3. Was hat sie für mich gekauft? 4. Was sieht jetzt sehr schön aus? 5. Wem gibt der Bäcker eine Torte? 6. Wer bittet um ihre Fahrkarten? 7. Wen sah er an der Ecke?

Exercise 104

1.	suchst	wirst	fährst	liest
2.	suchtest	wurdest	fuhrst	lasest
3.	sucht	wird	fährt	liest
4.	suchte	wurde	fuhr	las
5.	suchen	werden	fahren	lesen
6.	suchten	wurden	fuhren	lasen

Exercise 105

1. **Ich muss** vorsichtig sein. **Die Kinder müssen** vorsichtig sein. **Du musst** vorsichtig sein. 2. **Seid ihr** noch in Ulm? **Sind sie** noch in Ulm? **Bist du** noch in Ulm? 3. **Sie hat** keine Zeit. **Du hast** keine Zeit. **Ihr habt** keine Zeit.

Exercise 106

1. **Ich ging** langsam nach Hause. **Der Lehrer ging** langsam nach Hause. **Du gingst** langsam nach Hause. 2. **Sie waren** vier Wochen in Madrid. **Wer war** vier Wochen in Madrid? **Ihre Verwandten waren** vier Wochen in Madrid. 3. Warum **kam** sie nicht mit? Warum **kamt** ihr nicht mit? Warum **kamen** Sie nicht mit? 4. Am Montag Abend **starben die Soldaten.** Am Montag Abend **starben sie.** Am Montag Abend **starb Frau Bauer.**

Exercise 107

1. b 2. c 3. a 4. d 5. c 6. d 7. a 8. b

Exercise 108

1. habe gekannt	habe gesagt	bin gelaufen	habe geschrieben
2. hatte gekannt	hatte gesagt	war gelaufen	hatte geschrieben
3. hat gekannt	hat gesagt	ist gelaufen	hat geschrieben
4. hatte gekannt	hatte gesagt	war gelaufen	hatte geschrieben
5. habt gekannt	habt gesagt	seid gelaufen	habt geschrieben
6. hattet gekannt	hattet gesagt	wart gelaufen	hattet geschrieben

Exercise 109

1. Die Jungen waren fertig. Die Jungen sind fertig gewesen. 2. Glaubtest du, dass diese Idee gut ist (war)? Hast du geglaubt, dass diese Idee gut ist (gewesen ist)? 3. Sein Bruder fing den Ball nicht. Sein Bruder hat den Ball nicht gefangen. 4. Sie ging mit ihren Freundinnen zur Party. Sie ist mit ihren Freundinnen zur Party gegangen. 5. Alle kritisierten seine Politik. Alle haben seine Politik kritisiert.

Exercise 110

1. Er kann ihr nicht helfen. 2. Wir sitzen in der Küche und trinken Kaffee. 3. Warum stellen Sie diesen Tisch ins Wohnzimmer? 4. Die Kinder sind sehr müde. 5. An wen schreibt er die Ansichtskarte?

Exercise 111

1. Auslandsbriefe werden 1 Euro kosten. Morgen kosten Auslandsbriefe 1 Euro. 2. Er wird spät nach Hause kommen. Morgen kommt er spät nach Hause. 3. Du wirst gesund sein. Morgen bist du gesund.

Exercise 112

1. present: Diese Treppe führt in den Keller.
past: Diese Treppe führte in den Keller.
present perfect: Diese Treppe hat in den Keller geführt.
future: Diese Treppe wird in den Keller führen.
2. present: Sie spielen Fußball.
past: Sie spielten Fußball.
present perfect: Sie haben Fußball gespielt.
future: Sie werden Fußball spielen.
3. present: Sie kommt mit dem Zug.
past: Sie kam mit dem Zug.
present perfect: Sie ist mit dem Zug gekommen.
future: Sie wird mit dem Zug kommen.
4. present: Ihre Tante nennt sie Geli.
past: Ihre Tante nannte sie Geli.
present perfect: Ihre Tante hat sie Geli genannt.
future: Ihre Tante wird sie Geli nennen.

Exercise 113

1. Sei!	Nimm an!	Gib aus!	Werde!
2. Seid!	Nehmt an!	Gebt aus!	Werdet!
3. Seien Sie!	Nehmen Sie an!	Geben Sie aus!	Werden Sie!

Exercise 114

1. Sie fragte **sich**, warum es so kalt ist. 2. Ich erinnere **mich** an die Schularbeit. 3. Er wäscht **sich** im Keller. 4. Setze **dich** auf diesen Stuhl! 5. Hat sie **sich** einen Pelzmantel gekauft? 6. Warum musst du **dir** widersprechen? 7. Legt **euch** hin! 8. Wer hat **sich** ein Glas Wein bestellt? 9. Wie kannst du **dir** helfen? 10. Ich kaufte **mir** eine neue Brille.

Exercise 115

1. Was befehlen Sie? Was befiehlt er? Was befiehlt sie? Was befehlen sie? Was befiehlst du?
2. Ich erfand die ganze Geschichte. Wir erfanden die ganze Geschichte. Ihr erfandet die ganze Geschichte. Sie erfanden die ganze Geschichte. Du erfandest die ganze Geschichte.
3. Die Gäste rufen die Polizei an. Ich rufe die Polizei an. Du rufst die Polizei an. Er ruft die Polizei an. Wir rufen die Polizei an.
4. Sie schlief gleich ein. Du schliefst gleich ein. Die Kinder schliefen gleich ein. Alle schliefen gleich ein. Niemand schlief gleich ein.

Exercise 116

1. entflohen 2. verblutete 3. erwarte 4. errötete 5. zerstört 6. verspreche 7. bekommen 8. vergessen 9. empfangen 10. beschreiben

Exercise 117

1. c 2. c 3. d 4. b 5. a 6. a 7. c 8. d 9. d 10. c

Exercise 118

These are sample answers. 1. Ich habe nur einen Satz übersetzt. 2. Der Wirt verlangt mehr Geld. 3. Wann kommst du von der Party zurück? 4. Felix benimmt sich sehr schlecht. 5. Wir gehorchen unseren Eltern. 6. Mach die Fenster zu! 7. Herr Bauer unterrichtet Geschichte. 8. Das Kind sieht sehr krank aus. 9. Wie kannst du dein Benehmen erklären? 10. Ich muss einen Aufsatz vorbereiten.

Exercise 119

1. Sechs plus vier ist zehn. *or* Sechs und vier ist zehn. 2. Wie viel ist achtzehn minus zehn? 3. Vier mal drei ist zwölf. 4. Wie viel ist fünfzehn geteilt durch fünf? 5. Dreiundzwanzig weniger dreizehn ist zehn. 6. Wie viel ist sechzehn plus vier? *or* Wie viel ist sechzehn und vier? 7. Einundzwanzig geteilt durch sieben ist drei. 8. Wie viel ist einunddreißig mal vier? 9. Neun und acht ist siebzehn. *or* Neun plus acht ist siebzehn. 10. Wie viel ist hundert geteilt durch zehn?

Exercise 120

1. fünfzehnte 2. zweite 3. hundertste 4. fünfundsiebzigste 5. zwanzigste 6. elfte 7. erste 8. dritte 9. dreißigste 10. tausendste

Exercise 121

1. Ist heute **der erste** Dezember? Ist heute **der zweite** Dezember? Ist heute **der dritte** Dezember? Ist heute **der einunddreißigste** Dezember?
2. Meine Schwester ist **am fünften** Juli geboren. Meine Schwester ist **am zwanzigsten** Juli geboren. Meine Schwester ist **am dreiundzwanzigsten** Juli geboren. Meine Schwester ist **am neunundzwanzigsten** Juli geboren.

Exercise 122

1. fünf Uhr 2. sieben Uhr 3. zehn Uhr zehn/zehn Minuten nach zehn 4. halb eins 5. halb zwei 6. zwanzig vor vier 7. Viertel vor sieben (drei viertel sieben) 8. fünf Minuten vor neun 9. fünf Minuten nach vier 10. achtzehn Minuten nach fünf 11. drei Minuten vor halb neun 12. drei Minuten nach halb zehn 13. achtzehn Minuten vor zwölf 14. null Uhr eins 15. vierundzwanzig Uhr (Mitternacht)

Exercise 123

1. Um wie viel Uhr beginnt die nächste Vorlesung? 2. Um wie viel Uhr fährst du nach Hause? 3. Um wie viel Uhr seid ihr auf eine Party gegangen? 4. Um wie viel Uhr starb der alte Herr? 5. Um wie viel Uhr ist Frau Schneider eingeschlafen?

Exercise 124

1. um 2. am 3. In 4. N/A 5. N/A 6. N/A *or* im Jahre 7. im 8. am 9. im 10. N/A

Exercise 125

1. c 2. a 3. d 4. a 5. b 6. a 7. b 8. a 9. d 10. b

Exercise 126

1. Wir können Deutsch und Spanisch. Wir konnten Deutsch und Spanisch. Sie können Deutsch und Spanisch. Sie konnten Deutsch und Spanisch.
2. Ihr müsst schneller lernen. Ihr musstet schneller lernen. Du musst schneller lernen. Du musstest schneller lernen.
3. Was hört er? Was hörte er? Was hören Sie? Was hörten Sie?
4. Wir lassen den neuen Wagen waschen. Wir ließen den neuen Wagen waschen. Ich lasse den neuen Wagen waschen. Ich ließ den neuen Wagen waschen.
5. Ihr wollt die Kinder warnen. Ihr wolltet die Kinder warnen. Sie will die Kinder warnen. Sie wollte die Kinder warnen.
6. Das darfst du nicht tun. Das durftest du nicht tun. Das dürfen Sie nicht tun. Das durften Sie nicht tun.

Exercise 127

1. Der Ausländer kann den Brief nicht lesen. 2. Darf man hier rauchen? 3. Was mögen Sie zu Ihrem Essen trinken? 4. Sie sollen ihren Freund an der Ecke erwarten. 5. Wie lange müsst ihr jeden Tag arbeiten? 6. Der Mann lässt sich die Haare schneiden. 7. Was will der Fremdenführer den Touristen zeigen? 8. Dürft ihr die Volksbücherei benutzen? 9. Was können wir am Abend tun? 10. Sie sollen jetzt Ihre Pflicht tun.

Exercise 128

1. Ich habe die Prüfung nicht bestehen können. Ich werde die Prüfung nicht bestehen können. 2. Warum hat er sterben müssen? Warum wird er sterben müssen? 3. Wir haben ihn im Garten arbeiten sehen. Wir werden ihn im Garten arbeiten sehen. 4. In diesem Abteil hat man nicht rauchen dürfen. In diesem Abteil wird man nicht rauchen dürfen. 5. Er hat das norddeutsche Klima nicht vertragen können. Er wird das norddeutsche Klima nicht vertragen können. 6. Der alte Hund hat Schritte kommen hören. Der alte Hund wird Schritte kommen hören. 7. Die Lehrerin hat die Fehler nicht finden können. Die Lehrerin wird die Fehler nicht finden können. 8. Wir haben ihnen die Bücher tragen helfen. Wir werden ihnen die Bücher tragen helfen. 9. Sie hat die Schüler einen Aufsatz schreiben lassen. Sie wird die Schüler einen Aufsatz schreiben lassen. 10. Hat die kranke Frau die Reise nicht machen dürfen? Wird die kranke Frau die Reise nicht machen dürfen?

Exercise 129

1. present: Ich kann gut Mundharmonika spielen.
past: Ich konnte gut Mundharmonika spielen.
present perfect: Ich habe gut Mundharmonika spielen können.
future: Ich werde gut Mundharmonika spielen können.
2. present: Wir wollen in die Berge fahren.
past: Wir wollten in die Berge fahren.
present perfect: Wir haben in die Berge fahren wollen.
future: Wir werden in die Berge fahren wollen.
3. present: Die Kinder dürfen nicht streiten.
past: Die Kinder durften nicht streiten.
present perfect: Die Kinder haben nicht streiten dürfen.
future: Die Kinder werden nicht streiten dürfen.
4. present: Sie hört ihre Eltern in der Küche sprechen.
past: Sie hörte ihre Eltern in der Küche sprechen.
present perfect: Sie hat ihre Eltern in der Küche sprechen hören.
future: Sie wird ihre Eltern in der Küche sprechen hören.
5. present: Du sollst dich besser benehmen.
past: Du solltest dich besser benehmen.

present perfect: Du hast dich besser benehmen sollen.

future: Du wirst dich besser benehmen sollen.

6. present: Er muss seine Verwandten in Berlin besuchen.

past: Er musste seine Verwandten in Berlin besuchen.

present perfect: Er hat seine Verwandten in Berlin besuchen müssen.

future: Er wird seine Verwandten in Berlin besuchen müssen.

7. present: Seht ihr die Flugzeuge über der Stadt fliegen?

past: Saht ihr die Flugzeuge über der Stadt fliegen?

present perfect: Habt ihr die Flugzeuge über der Stadt fliegen sehen?

future: Werdet ihr die Flugzeuge über der Stadt fliegen sehen?

8. present: Er lässt sich einen neuen Anzug machen.

past: Er ließ sich einen neuen Anzug machen.

present perfect: Er hat sich einen neuen Anzug machen lassen.

future: Er wird sich einen neuen Anzug machen lassen.

9. present: Sie helfen mir den alten Wagen reparieren.

past: Sie halfen mir den alten Wagen reparieren.

present perfect: Sie haben mir den alten Wagen reparieren helfen.

future: Sie werden mir den alten Wagen reparieren helfen.

10. present: Wir können seine Theorie nicht verstehen.

past: Wir konnten seine Theorie nicht verstehen.

present perfect: Wir haben seine Theorie nicht verstehen können.

future: Wir werden seine Theorie nicht verstehen können.

Exercise 130

1. b 2. b 3. a 4. d 5. d 6. b 7. a 8. a 9. d 10. d 11. a 12. d 13. d 14. a 15. d

Exercise 131

1. aber 2. denn 3. sondern 4. und 5. oder

Exercise 132

1. Da er betrunken war, konnte Karl nicht fahren. 2. Damit sie pünktlich ankommen, müssen sie sich beeilen. 3. Falls wir Zeit haben, kommen wir morgen vorbei. 4. Damit sie besser sieht, trägt Karin eine Brille. 5. Als er vom Bahnhof ankam, sah Erik seine Verlobte an der Ecke stehen. 6. Wenn es nicht regnet, spielen die Jungen gern Fußball. 7. Nachdem er gegessen hatte, wollte er sich eine Weile hinlegen. 8. Da das Klima dort besser ist, verreisen viele Leute nach dem Süden.

Exercise 133

1. d 2. a 3. d 4. b 5. a 6. b 7. d 8. a 9. a 10. c 11. b 12. b 13. c 14. c 15. d

Exercise 134

These are sample answers. 1. Ich wusste nicht, dass du in England geboren bist. 2. Können Sie mir sagen, ob das Museum noch offen ist? 3. Sie sind nicht zum Park gegangen, sondern sie sind zu Hause geblieben. 4. Ich bedauere es sehr, dass dein Vater so krank ist. 5. Sobald ich seine Wunde sah, rief ich den Artz an. 6. Wir bleiben in Kiel, bis das Wetter besser ist. 7. Sie können kommen, sooft Sie wollen. 8. Während er in Amerika war, fing der Krieg an. 9. Mein Vater ist wieder gesund, aber er kann noch nicht arbeiten. 10. Ich kann dich nicht hören, denn der Lärm ist zu groß. 11. Wissen Sie, ob Professor Schmidt in der Nähe wohnt? 12. Sie hat die Klingel abgestellt, damit sie nicht gestört wird. 13. Beabsichtigt ihr ein Haus zu mieten oder ein Haus zu kaufen? 14. Sie können in der Küche essen, weil die Küche sehr groß ist. 15. Wir heizen im Schlafzimmer, wenn es sehr kalt wird.

Exercise 135

1. Er sieht das Mädchen, das in Amerika geboren ist.

Er sieht das Mädchen, das Gudrun fotografieren will.

Er sieht das Mädchen, mit dem Tanja spielt.

Er sieht das Mädchen, dessen Vater Zahnarzt ist.

Er sieht die Kinder, die in Amerika geboren sind.

Er sieht die Kinder, die Gudrun fotografieren will.

Er sieht die Kinder, mit denen Tanja spielt.

Er sieht die Kinder, deren Vater Zahnarzt ist.

Er sieht die Schülerin, die in Amerika geboren ist.

Er sieht die Schülerin, die Gudrun fotografieren will.

Er sieht die Schülerin, mit der Tanja spielt.

Er sieht die Schülerin, deren Vater Zahnarzt ist.

2. Sie findet die Briefe, die Martin geschrieben hat.

Sie findet die Briefe, nach denen ihre Schwester fragte.

Sie findet die Briefe, deren Inhalt ein Geheimnis ist.

Sie findet die Briefe, die unter dem Tisch gelegen haben.

Sie findet das Telegramm, das Martin geschrieben hat.

Sie findet das Telegramm, nach dem ihre Schwester fragte.

Sie findet das Telegramm, dessen Inhalt ein Geheimnis ist.

Sie findet das Telegramm, das unter dem Tisch gelegen hat.

Sie findet die Postkarte, die Martin geschrieben hat.

Sie findet die Postkarte, nach der ihre Schwester fragte.

Sie findet die Postkarte, deren Inhalt ein Geheimnis ist.

Sie findet die Postkarte, die unter dem Tisch gelegen hat.

3. Liebst du das Mädchen, das schon verlobt ist?

Liebst du das Mädchen, von dem deine Tante gesprochen hat?

Liebst du das Mädchen, gegen das Lilo etwas hat?

Liebst du das Mädchen, dessen Bruder ein Dieb ist?

Liebst du den Mann, der schon verlobt ist?

Liebst du den Mann, von dem deine Tante gesprochen hat?

Liebst du den Mann, gegen den Lilo etwas hat?

Liebst du den Mann, dessen Bruder ein Dieb ist?

Liebst du den Studenten, der schon verlobt ist?

Liebst du den Studenten, von dem deine Tante gesprochen hat?

Liebst du den Studenten, gegen den Lilo etwas hat?

Liebst du den Studenten, dessen Bruder ein Dieb ist?

Exercise 136

1. Er sieht das Kind, welches in Amerika geboren ist.

Er sieht das Kind, welches Gudrun fotografieren will.

Er sieht das Kind, mit welchem Tanja spielt.

Er sieht das Kind, dessen Vater Zahnarzt ist.

2. Sie findet den Brief, welchen Martin geschrieben hat.

Sie findet den Brief, nach welchem ihre Schwester fragte.

Sie findet den Brief, dessen Inhalt ein Geheimnis ist.

Sie findet den Brief, welcher unter dem Tisch gelegen hat.

3. Sie haben einige Bücher, welche sehr alt und teuer sind.

Sie haben einige Bücher, welche sie verkaufen wollen.

Sie haben einige Bücher, in welchen sie alte Ansichtskarten gefunden haben.

Sie haben einige Bücher, deren Verlag sich in Bonn befindet.

Exercise 137

1. das 2. den 3. dem 4. dem 5. dem 6. dem 7. deren 8. dem 9. deren 10. die 11. deren 12. die 13. dem 14. die 15. dem

Exercise 138

1. was 2. Wen 3. was 4. Wem 5. was 6. was 7. was 8. was 9. was 10. Wer 11. was 12. was 13. Was 14. was 15. was

Exercise 139

1. c 2. c 3. c 4. d 5. a 6. b 7. a 8. b 9. c 10. b

Exercise 140

1. schöner, am schönsten 2. mehr, am meisten 3. lauter, am lautesten 4. langweiliger, am langweiligsten 5. besser, am besten 6. hässlicher, am hässlichsten 7. röter, am rötesten 8. ärmer, am ärmsten 9. weniger, am wenigsten 10. angenehmer, am angenehmsten 11. langsamer, am langsamsten 12. stolzer, am stolzesten 13. teurer, am teuersten 14. tiefer, am tiefsten 15. höher, am höchsten 16. schärfer, am schärfsten 17. kühler, am kühlsten 18. weicher, am weichsten 19. heller, am hellsten 20. berühmter, am berühmtesten

Exercise 141

1. Ist dieser Weg **steil**? Ist dieser Weg **steiler**? Ist dieser Weg **am steilsten**?
2. Frau Kessler ist die **gute** Lehrerin. Frau Kessler ist die **bessere** Lehrerin. Frau Kessler ist die **beste** Lehrerin.
3. Warum gehst du **langsam**? Warum gehst du **langsamer**? Warum gehst du **am langsamsten**?
4. Diese großen Wagen sind **teuer**. Diese großen Wagen sind **teurer**. Diese großen Wagen sind **am teuersten**.
5. Wir wohnen im **hohen** Wohnhaus. Wir wohnen im **höheren** Wohnhaus. Wir wohnen im **höchsten** Wohnhaus.
6. Das **starke** Zugtier ist ein Elefant. Das **stärkere** Zugtier ist ein Elefant. Das **stärkste** Zugtier ist ein Elefant.
7. Die **jungen** Schüler waren nicht so fleißig. Die **jüngeren** Schüler waren nicht so fleißig. Die **jüngsten** Schüler waren nicht so fleißig.
8. Er schneidet das Fleisch mit dem **scharfen** Messer. Er schneidet das Fleisch mit dem **schärferen** Messer. Er schneidet das Fleisch mit dem **schärfsten** Messer.
9. Die Lehrlinge arbeiten **viel**. Die Lehrlinge arbeiten **mehr**. Die Lehrlinge arbeiten **am meisten**.
10. Der Mantel gefällt dem **stolzen** Mann nicht. Der Mantel gefällt dem **stolzeren** Mann nicht. Der Mantel gefällt dem **stolzesten** Mann nicht.

Exercise 142

1. Mein Bruder raucht viel. Mein Vater raucht mehr als mein Bruder. Onkel Peter raucht am meisten.
2. Erik spricht laut. Thomas spricht lauter als Erik. Mein Vater spricht am lautesten.
3. Berlin ist eine schöne Stadt. Wien ist eine schönere Stadt als Berlin. Garmisch ist die schönste Stadt.
4. Meine Mutter ist alt. Meine Großmutter ist älter als meine Mutter. Meine Urgroßmutter ist am ältesten.
5. Frau Bauer hat wenig Zeit. Herr Schmidt hat weniger Zeit als Frau Bauer. Professor Keller hat am wenigsten Zeit.

Exercise 143

1. b 2. a 3. c 4. b 5. d 6. d 7. d 8. a 9. a 10. b 11. c 12. b 13. a 14. a 15. d

Exercise 144

1. present: Ich werde von meinen Verwandten besucht.
past: Ich wurde von meinen Verwandten besucht.
present perfect: Ich bin von meinen Verwandten besucht worden.
future: Ich werde von meinen Verwandten besucht werden.
2. present: Sie wird von ihrem Bruder gebracht.
past: Sie wurde von ihrem Bruder gebracht.
present perfect: Sie ist von ihrem Bruder gebracht worden.
future: Sie wird von ihrem Bruder gebracht werden.
3. present: Ihnen werden niemals geglaubt.
past: Ihnen wurden niemals geglaubt.
present perfect: Ihnen sind niemals geglaubt worden.
future: Ihnen werden niemals geglaubt werden.

4. present: Die Kinder werden vom Reiseführer geführt.

past: Die Kinder wurden vom Reiseführer geführt.

present perfect: Die Kinder sind vom Reiseführer geführt worden.

future: Die Kinder werden vom Reiseführer geführt werden.

 5. present: Du wirst darum gebeten.

past: Du wurdest darum gebeten.

present perfect: Du bist darum gebeten worden.

future: Du wirst darum gebeten werden.

Exercise 145

1. Das Brot wird von dem Bäcker gebacken. 2. Die Kinder sind von den Eltern sehr geliebt worden. 3. Ein Hammer wurde von dem alten Schuhmacher benutzt. 4. Viele Angestellte werden von der Firma entlassen werden. 5. Eine neue Klasse ist von unserer Lehrerin unterrichtet worden. 6. Kühe und Schweine wurden von einem Bauer aufgezogen. 7. Der berühmte Fußballspieler wird von ihnen fotografiert. 8. Die Krankheit ihres Sohnes wurde durch einen neuen Virus verursacht. 9. Zwei Gläser Wein werden von der Kellnerin gebracht werden. 10. Die Arbeit wurde um fünf Uhr von den Arbeitern beendet. 11. Zwei Einzelzimmer sind von Frau Kamps vermietet worden. 12. Die Heizung muss von Herrn Schäfer angestellt werden. 13. Das Licht wird von ihm angemacht werden. 14. Die Schuhe können von euch beim Schuhmacher abgeholt werden. 15. Die meisten Waren wurden zum halben Preis angeboten. 16. Viele schöne Gedichte waren von dem Dichter geschrieben worden. 17. Dem jungen Komponisten ist damit geholfen worden. 18. Das Baby muss noch von der Mutter gefüttert werden. 19. Ein Mittel gegen Husten wird von dem Arzt verschrieben werden. 20. Alle Gäste sind schnell bedient worden.

Exercise 146

1. c 2. b 3. a 4. d 5. c 6. d 7. a 8. b 9. d 10. a 11. a 12. d 13. a 14. a 15. b

Exercise 147

These are sample answers. 1. Die Touristen müssen vom Bahnhof abgeholt werden. 2. Ein großer Teil der Stadt wurde zerstört. 3. Mein Vater ist wieder enttäuscht worden. 4. Ein Taschendieb wurde gestern verhaftet. 5. Zwei neue Manager konnten angestellt werden. 6. Ihr wurde davon sehr imponiert. 7. Das alte Haus muss bald abgerissen werden. 8. Dem Mann wird nie geglaubt werden. 9. Die Prüfungen werden von dem Lehrer verbessert werden. 10. Seine Rede wurde nicht vom Publikum verstanden.

Exercise 148

1. würde finden	würde gefunden haben
2. würde glauben	würde geglaubt haben
3. würdest fahren	würdest gefahren sein
4. würden kommen	würden gekommen sein
5. würdet schlagen	würdet geschlagen haben
6. würde weinen	würde geweint haben
7. würde helfen	würde geholfen haben
8. würden singen	würden gesungen haben
9. würde laufen	würde gelaufen sein
10. würde rennen	würde gerannt sein
11. würdest vertragen	würdest vertragen haben
12. würde werfen	würde geworfen haben
13. würde spielen	würde gespielt haben
14. würde annehmen	würde angenommen haben
15. würden verstehen	würden verstanden haben

Exercise 149

1. Er würde es mir geben, wenn er es hätte. 2. Wenn sie älter wäre, würde sie zur Schule gehen. 3. Wenn sie Zeit hätte, würde sie gern mitkommen. 4. Hätten wir mehr Geld, dann würden wir ein neues Haus kaufen. 5. Hätte sie mehr Zeit, so würde sie mit zur Party kommen.

Exercise 150

1. schlage	schlüge	würde schlagen	würde geschlagen haben
2. trinke	tränke	würde trinken	würde getrunken haben
3. verbessere	verbesserte	würde verbessern	würde verbessert haben
4. rauche	rauchte	würde rauchen	würde geraucht haben
5. entlasse	entließe	würde entlassen	würde entlassen haben
6. verspreche	verspräche	würde versprechen	würde versprochen haben
7. tue	täte	würde tun	würde getan haben
8. arbeite	arbeitete	würde arbeiten	würde gearbeitet haben
9. bekomme	bekäme	würde bekommen	würde bekommen haben
10. gebe aus	gäbe aus	würde ausgeben	würde ausgegeben haben
11. lerne	lernte	würde lernen	würde gelernt haben
12. verliere	verlöre	würde verlieren	würde verloren haben
13. probiere	probierte	würde probieren	würde probiert haben
14. enthalte	enthielte	würde enthalten	würde enthalten haben
15. zähle	zählte	würde zählen	würde gezählt haben
16. bleibe	bliebe	würde bleiben	würde geblieben sein
17. esse	äße	würde essen	würde gegessen haben
18. baue	baute	würde bauen	würde gebaut haben
19. leihe	liehe	würde leihen	würde geliehen haben
20. mache an	machte an	würde anmachen	würde angemacht haben
21. koche	kochte	würde kochen	würde gekocht haben
22. nenne	nennte	würde nennen	würde genannt haben
23. breche	bräche	würde brechen	würde gebrochen haben
24. wisse	wüsste	würde wissen	würde gewusst haben
25. gebrauche	gebrauchte	würde gebrauchen	würde gebraucht haben

Exercise 151

1. Er sagte, dass ihr Vetter damals in Heidelberg gewohnt habe. 2. Er sagte, dass Erik keinen Parkplatz gefunden habe. 3. Er sagte, dass Herr Schneider die Führerscheinprüfung nicht bestehen könne. 4. Er sagte, dass der Kranke aus dem Krankenhaus entlassen werde. 5. Er sagte, dass die Handwerker für ihre Arbeit höhere Löhne gefordert hätten. 6. Er sagte, dass der Kanzler in der Hauptstadt bleiben müsse. 7. Er sagte, dass ihre Großmutter im Altersheim wohne. 8. Er sagte, dass man ihn täglich benachrichtigen solle. 9. Sie fragte, ob man im Kino rauchen dürfe. 10. Sie fragte, wohin diese Touristen reisten. 11. Sie fragte, was er Ihnen noch erklären solle. 12. Sie fragte, wie viel das neue Haus kosten werde. 13. Sie fragte, ob man hier umsteigen müsse. 14. Sie fragte, ob Gudrun mit zur Party komme. 15. Sie fragte, ob ihre Schwester das Buch langweilig gefunden habe.

Exercise 152

These are sample answers. 1. Er sprach so gut Deutsch, als ob er Deutscher wäre. 2. Das Mädchen tat so, als ob sie mich nicht sähe. 3. Er führte ein Leben, als wenn er ein reicher Mann wäre. 4. Der Kranke zitterte, als wenn es kalt im Zimmer wäre. 5. Der Mann lächelte, als ob er einen komischen Witz gehört hätte. 6. Ihre Augen sahen aus, als ob sie weinen wollte. 7. Die Kinder schrien, als ob man sie verprügelt hätte. 8. Der Junge tat so, als wenn es nicht regnete. 9. Ihr Sohn benahm sich, als wenn er taub wäre. 10. Die Frau machte ein Gesicht, als ob ihr die Suppe nicht schmeckte.

Exercise 153

1. Wenn er mehr Zeit hätte, würde er seinen Freunden helfen. 2. Wenn die Verwandten sie besuchen könnten, würden sie es begrüßen. 3. Wenn sie gesund gewesen wäre, hätte sie die Ärztin nicht gebraucht. 4. Wenn seine Kusine ihm helfen könnte, würde er glücklich sein. 5. Wenn ich dorthin geflogen wäre, wäre ich früher nach Hause gekommen. 6. Wenn es kalt geworden wäre, wären sie ins Haus gegangen. 7. Wenn wir nicht so viel Bier getrunken hätten, wären wir nicht krank geworden. 8. Wenn sie mehr Deutsch lernten, könnten sie auch besser sprechen. 9. Wenn Tante Gerda sie besucht hätte, wären sie sehr froh gewesen. 10. Wenn es heiß wäre, würden wir schwimmen gehen. 11. Wenn sie das wüsste, würde sie nicht fragen. 12. Sie hätten das neue Museum

besucht, wenn sie in Berlin gewesen wären. 13. Wenn es regnete, würde alles nass sein. 14. Wenn das Wetter schlecht gewesen wäre, wäre ich nicht aufs Land gefahren. 15. Wenn der Student aufmerksam wäre, würde er keine Fehler machen.

Exercise 154

1. Onkel Peter erlaubt seinem Sohn das Kino zu besuchen. 2. Sie empfahl ihren Studenten einen Computer zu kaufen. 3. Doktor Bauer ermahnt den kranken Mann das Rauchen sofort zu unterlassen. 4. Tina bittet ihre Mutter ein Märchen zu erzählen. 5. Die Eltern warnen ihre Kinder ihr Geld nicht zu verschwenden. 6. Ich habe die Hoffnung euch bald wiederzusehen. 7. Der kalte Winter zwingt die Leute schwere Mäntel zu tragen. 8. Ein Unglück zwang sie ihren Besitz zu verkaufen. 9. Er verbietet dem verletzten Soldaten aufzustehen. 10. Der Chef befiehlt ihnen die Arbeit schnell zu beenden. 11. Wir freuen uns dich besuchen zu können. 12. Ein tapferer Mensch fürchtet nicht zu sterben. 13. Die Studenten fangen damit an den Text ins Deutsche zu übersetzen. 14. Sie hoffen nach Freiburg mitreisen zu dürfen. 15. Ich beabsichtige nach dem Abendessen spazieren zu gehen.

Exercise 155

1. Wir haben Karl geholfen in der Küche zu arbeiten. 2. Sie hört spät in der Nacht auf einen Aufsatz zu schreiben. 3. Herr Schmidt forderte von ihm die Miete bald zu bezahlen. 4. Das kleine Flugzeug versuchte auf dem Feld eine Landung zu machen. 5. Erik hat vergessen einen Dankbrief an seine Gastgeber zu schreiben.

Exercise 156

These are sample answers. 1. Die Kinder brauchen etwas zu essen. 2. Haben Sie nichts im Garten zu tun? 3. Es freut mich von Ihnen eingeladen zu werden. 4. Es ist schade morgen abfahren zu müssen. 5. Der Wissenschaftler behauptet das Problem gelöst zu haben. 6. Es ist wichtig fit und gesund zu bleiben. 7. Der Lehrer hat etwas Interessantes zu erzählen. 8. Seine Frau war wieder empört so lange an der Ecke stehen zu müssen. 9. Der Mann glaubte ein Ufo gesehen zu haben. 10. Es ist gar nicht wichtig wieder darüber zu sprechen.

Exercise 157

These are sample answers. 1. Ich freute mich darüber wieder in London gewesen zu sein. 2. Interessierst du dich dafür Briefmarken zu sammeln? 3. Sie haben davon gesprochen ihren Urlaub in Spanien zu verbringen. 4. Meine Eltern sind darüber glücklich so viel Geld gewonnen zu haben. 5. Er ist nicht daran gewöhnt so beleidigt zu werden. 6. Karl hat sich darauf gefreut wieder mit Maria tanzen zu dürfen. 7. Hat sie davon gesprochen eine Reise nach Indien zu machen? 8. Haben Sie etwas dagegen heute Abend italienisch zu essen? 9. Ich denke nicht daran nach Kanada umziehen zu müssen. 10. Die Touristen sprechen darüber einen anderen Ausflug zu machen.

Exercise 158

These are sample answers. 1. Der Vater ging zum Bett, ohne sich die Hände zu waschen. 2. Die Jungen sind zum Sportplatz gegangen, anstatt zur Schule zu gehen. 3. Sie arbeitet bis spät abends, um den langen Aufsatz zu schreiben.

Exercise 159

1. **Ich erfand** die ganze Geschichte. **Wir erfanden** die ganze Geschichte. **Ihr erfandet** die ganze Geschichte. 2. **Ich rufe** den Arzt an. **Du rufst** den Arzt an. **Wir rufen** den Arzt an. 3. **Überzeugte er** den Mann? **Überzeugtet ihr** den Mann? **Überzeugten sie** den Mann?

Exercise 160

1. zerstört 2. verspricht 3. bekommen 4. vergessen 5. beschreiben

Exercise 161

1. **mit**kommen 2. **um**gebracht 3. **um**steigen 4. Trink . . . **aus** 5. **vor**schlagen

Exercise 162

1. 34 2. 80 3. 51 4. 611 5. 523

Exercise 163

1. zehn Uhr zehn/zehn Minuten nach zehn 2. halb eins 3. zwanzig vor drei 4. Viertel vor sechs/drei Viertel sechs 5. fünf vor neun

Exercise 164

1. a 2. b 3. a 4. b. 5. a 6. b 7. d 8. d 9. c 10. d

Exercise 165

1. Wir können Deutsch und Englisch. Wir konnten Deutsch und Englisch. Du kannst Deutsch und Englisch. Du konntest Deutsch und Englisch.
2. Ihr müsst ihm helfen. Ihr musstet ihm helfen. Du musst ihm helfen. Du musstest ihm helfen.
3. Wir lassen den Wagen reparieren. Wir ließen den Wagen reparieren. Ich lasse den Wagen reparieren. Ich ließ den Wagen reparieren.

Exercise 166

1. Wir sollen einen Freund an der Ecke erwarten. 2. Wie lange müsst ihr jeden Tag arbeiten? 3. Der Mann lässt sich die Haare schneiden. 4. Was will der Fremdenführer den Touristen zeigen? 5. Darfst du die Volksbücherei benutzen?

Exercise 167

1. Ich habe die Wörter nicht verstehen können. Ich werde die Wörter nicht verstehen können. 2. Warum hat er lügen müssen? Warum wird er lügen müssen? 3. Ihr habt sie im Garten arbeiten sehen. Ihr werdet sie im Garten arbeiten sehen. 4. Der alte Hund hat Schritte kommen hören. Der alte Hund wird Schritte kommen hören.

Exercise 168

1. b 2. a 3. d 4. c 5. d 6. a

Exercise 169

1. denn 2. sondern 3. und 4. aber

Exercise 170

1. Da er betrunken war, konnte Karl nicht fahren. 2. Damit sie pünktlich ankommen, müssen sie sich beeilen. 3. Falls wir Zeit haben, kommen wir morgen vorbei. 4. Damit sie besser sieht, trägt Karin eine Brille. 5. Als er vom Bahnhof ankam, sah Erik seine Verlobte an der Ecke stehen.

Exercise 171

1. Er sieht das Mädchen, das in Amerika geboren ist.
Er sieht das Mädchen, das Gudrun fotografieren will.
Er sieht das Mädchen, mit dem Tanja spielt.
Er sieht das Mädchen, dessen Vater Zahnarzt ist.
2. Sie findet die Ansichtskarte, die Martin geschrieben hat.
Sie findet die Ansichtskarte, nach der ihre Schwester fragte.
Sie findet die Ansichtskarte, deren Inhalt ein Geheimnis ist.
Sie findet die Ansichtskarte, die unter dem Tisch gelegen hat.

Exercise 172

1. dem 2. dem 3. dem 4. dem 5. deren

Exercise 173

1. c 2. c 3. c 4. b 5. a 6. b 7. a 8. d 9. c 10. a

Exercise 174

1. schärfer, am schärfsten 2. mehr, am meisten 3. kühler, am kühlsten 4. höher, am höchsten 5. besser, am besten 6. weicher, am weichsten 7. röter, am rötesten 8. ärmer, am ärmsten 9. weniger, am wenigsten 10. eher, am ehesten 11. größer, am größten 12. stolzer, am stolzesten 13. teurer, am teuersten 14. tiefer, am tiefsten 15. schlechter, am schlechtesten

Exercise 175

1. Mein Vater ist alt. Mein Großvater ist älter als mein Vater. Mein Urgroßvater ist am ältesten.
2. Die Weser ist ein langer Fluss. Die Elbe ist länger als die Weser. Der Rhein ist der längste Fluss.

Exercise 176

1. present: Wir werden von unseren Verwandten besucht.
past: Wir wurden von unseren Verwandten besucht.
present perfect: Wir sind von unseren Verwandten besucht worden.
future: Wir werden von unseren Verwandten besucht werden.
2. present: Ihnen wird nicht geholfen.
past: Ihnen wurde nicht geholfen.
present perfect: Ihnen ist nicht geholfen worden.
future: Ihnen wird nicht geholfen werden.
3. present: Die Kinder werden von einem neuen Lehrer unterrichtet.
past: Die Kinder wurden von einem neuen Lehrer unterrichtet.
present perfect: Die Kinder sind von einem neuen Lehrer unterrichtet worden.
future: Die Kinder werden von einem neuen Lehrer unterrichtet werden.

Exercise 177

1. Viele Angestellte werden von dem Chef entlassen werden. 2. Der berühmte Fußballspieler wurde von ihr fotografiert. 3. Zwei Gläser Bier sind von dem Kellner gebracht worden. 4. Die Heizung muss von Herrn Bauer angestellt werden. 5. Viele schöne Erzählungen waren von ihm geschrieben worden.

Exercise 178

1. c 2. b 3. a 4. d 5. b

Exercise 179

1. würde glauben   würde geglaubt haben
2. würde weinen   würde geweint haben
3. würdest vertragen   würdest vertragen haben
4. würden kommen   würden gekommen sein
5. würdet annehmen   würdet angenommen haben

Exercise 180

1. Martin würde es uns geben, wenn er es hätte. 2. Wenn Erik älter wäre, würde er zur Schule gehen. 3. Hätten sie mehr Geld, dann würden sie ein neues Haus kaufen.

Exercise 181

1. Er sagte, dass seine Kusine damals in Dänemark gewohnt habe. 2. Er sagte, dass Onkel Peter keinen Parkplatz finden könne. 3. Er sagte, dass der Bäcker sehr alt gewesen sei. 4. Sie fragte, ob man in diesem Restaurant rauchen dürfe. 5. Sie fragte, wie viel ein neuer Regenmantel kosten werde.

Exercise 182

1. Wenn sie mehr Zeit hätten, würden sie ihren Freunden helfen. 2. Wenn ich dorthin geflogen wäre, wäre ich früher nach Hause gekommen. 3. Wenn es sehr heiß geworden wäre, wären wir ins Haus gegangen.

Exercise 183

1. Doktor Bauer ermahnt den kranken Mann das Rauchen sofort zu unterlassen. 2. Die Kinder bitten ihren Vater ein Lied zu singen. 3. Tante Luise warnt Erik sein Geld nicht zu verschwenden. 4. Der kalte Winter zwingt die Menschen warme Kleidung zu tragen. 5. Er verbietet dem verwundeten Offizier aufzustehen.

Exercise 184

1. um uns zwei Gläser Wein zu bringen	in order to bring us two glasses of wine
ohne uns zwei Gläser Wein zu bringen	without bringing us two glasses of wine
anstatt uns zwei Gläser Wein zu bringen	instead of bringing us two glasses of wine
2. um über die Lösung des Problems zu sprechen	in order to speak about the solution of the problem
ohne über die Lösung des Problems zu sprechen	without speaking about the solution of the problem
anstatt über die Lösung des Problems zu sprechen	instead of speaking about the solution of the problem

Exercise 185

1. die 2. die 3. die 4. das 5. die 6. das 7. die 8. das 9. der 10. das

Exercise 186

1. das Fenster 2. der Bruder 3. die Zeitschrift 4. das Dorf 5. der Mantel

Exercise 187

1. die Gärten 2. die Bücher 3. die Lehrlinge 4. die Ärztinnen 5. N/A 6. die Spiegel 7. die Tanten

Exercise 188

1. er 2. er 3. es 4. sie s. 5. sie pl. 6. sie pl. 7. sie s. 8. es

Exercise 189

1. Was ist sehr weit von hier? 2. Was trinkt der Junge nicht? 3. Für wen hatte Tante Luise etwas? 4. Was möchte er essen? 5. Auf wen warte ich (wartest du)? 6. Mit wem spricht Herr Schäfer? 7. Wessen Sohn studiert in Berlin? 8. Wer hat dagegen gesprochen?

Exercise 190

1. die Mutter	der Mutter
2. keine Gäste	keinen Gästen
3. sein Buch	seinem Buch
4. Ihren Vetter	Ihrem Vetter
5. die Dörfer	den Dörfern
6. mich	mir
7. dich	dir
8. ihn	ihm
9. Sie	Ihnen
10. euch	euch

Exercise 191

1. jenes Baumes 2. der Tante 3. keiner Probleme

Exercise 192

1. Der Rock unserer Tante passt ihr nicht. 2. Das Schlafzimmer meiner Brüder war zu klein. 3. Die Stimme des Offiziers ist laut.

Exercise 193

These are sample answers. 1. Die Lehrerin wird diese neuen Schüler fragen. 2. Sie erinnerte sich an ihren alten Onkel. 3. Die Frau kann dieser faulen Studentin nicht glauben. 4. Trinken Sie heißen Kaffee? 5. Meine Schwester hat ein altes Auto.

Exercise 194

1. Haben seine Geschwister im Park gespielt? 2. Geht niemand ins Wohnzimmer? 3. Sind sie am Fluss entlang gelaufen?

Exercise 195

1. versucht	wird	geht	schreibt
2. versuchte	wurde	ging	schrieb
3. bekommt	frisst	weiß	versteht
4. bekam	fraß	wusste	verstand
5. ist	glaubt	nennt	hat
6. war	glaubte	nannte	hatte

Exercise 196

1. b 2. d 3. d 4. c 5. d

Exercise 197

1. hat gekannt	hat gesagt	ist gelaufen	hat geschrieben
2. hatte gekannt	hatte gesagt	war gelaufen	hatte geschrieben

Exercise 198

1. Die Männer sind in der Stadt gewesen. 2. Haben Sie jemand gesehen? 3. Die Jungen haben einen Igel gefangen. 4. Sie sind mit ihren Freunden ins Kino gegangen.

Exercise 199

1. Sie werden in die Schweiz fahren. Morgen fahren sie in die Schweiz. 2. Es wird ihm besser gehen. Morgen geht es ihm besser.

Exercise 200

1. Lerne!	Sei!	Sprich!	Behalte!
2. Lernt!	Seid!	Sprecht!	Behaltet!
3. Lernen Sie!	Seien Sie!	Sprechen Sie!	Behalten Sie!

Exercise 201

1. Fragen Sie **sich**, warum es nicht regnet? 2. Hast du **dir** einen Schlips gekauft? 3. Warum muss er **sich** widersprechen? 4. Legt **euch** hin! 5. Ich habe **mir** die Suppe bestellt.

Exercise 202

1. c 2. a 3. d 4. d 5. b

Exercise 203

1. ein Uhr zehn/zehn Minuten nach eins 2. Viertel vor eins/drei viertel eins 3. halb drei 4. zwanzig Minuten vor sieben 5. sechzehn Uhr fünfundvierzig 6. dreiundzwanzig Uhr dreißig

Exercise 204

1. a 2. d 3. b 4. c 5. c 6. b

Exercise 205

1. Wir sollen unseren Nachbarn helfen. 2. Wie lange müsst ihr schlafen? 3. Herr Bauer lässt seinen Wagen reparieren. 4. Dürfen Sie hier rauchen?

Exercise 206

1. Wer hat Arabisch verstehen können? Wer wird Arabisch verstehen können? 2. Du hast eine Stunde warten müssen. Du wirst eine Stunde warten müssen. 3. Wir haben sie im Park spielen sehen. Wir werden sie im Park spielen sehen.

Exercise 207

1. d 2. d 3. c 4. a 5. c 6. b

Exercise 208

1. dem 2. das 3. der 4. deren 5. deren 6. den

Exercise 209

1. besser, am besten 2. eher, am ehesten 3. kühler, am kühlsten 4. höher, am höchsten 5. schneller, am schnellsten 6. größer, am größten 7. schlechter, am schlechtesten 8. ärmer, am ärmsten 9. wärmer, am wärmsten 10. kälter, am kältesten

Exercise 210

1. Er wird von seiner Freundin besucht. 2. Er wurde von seiner Freundin besucht. 3. Er ist von seiner Freundin besucht worden. 4. Er wird von seiner Freundin besucht werden.

Exercise 211

1. d 2. b 3. d 4. d 5. c

Exercise 212

1. habe	kaufe	stelle aus	werde
2. hätte	kaufte	stellte aus	würde
3. breche	fange an	sei	fahre
4. bräche	finge an	wäre	führe
5. kenne	dürfe	gehe	wisse
6. kennte	dürfte	ginge	wüsste

Exercise 213

1. Er würde nach Hause fahren, wenn er genug Geld hätte. 2. Wenn sie einen Wagen hätte, würde sie ins Ausland reisen.

Exercise 214

1. Er sagte, dass die Touristen aus England kämen. 2. Er sagte, dass sie ihn kaum verstehen könne. 3. Er sagte, dass Frau Kamps einmal Schauspielerin gewesen sei.

Exercise 215

1. um schnell nach Hause gelaufen zu sein
ohne schnell nach Hause gelaufen zu sein
anstatt schnell nach Hause gelaufen zu sein
2. um darüber sprechen zu können
ohne darüber sprechen zu können
anstatt darüber sprechen zu können

Answer Key

Page 63

1. line; 2. ray; 3. line segment;
4. ray; 5. line segment; 6. line;
7. ray; 8. ray; 9. perpendicular;
10. parallel; 11. intersecting; 12.
parallel; 13. False; 14. False; 15. True;
16. False; 17. True

Page 64

1. 70°, acute; 2. 170°, obtuse; 3. 30°,
acute; 4. 10°, acute; 5. 120°, obtuse;
6. 90°, right; 7. 50°, acute; 8. 110°,
obtuse; 9. 130°, obtuse

Page 65

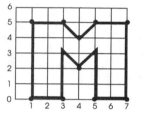

MATH IS ONE OF THE
INGREDIENTS FOR MAKING LIFE
FUN!

Page 66

1. rhombus; 2. octagon;
3. quadrilateral; 4. triangle; 5. square;
6. pentagon; 7. rectangle;
8. parallelogram; 9. hexagon;
10. triangle; 11. quadrilateral;
12. parallelogram; 13. rectangle;
14. pentagon; 15. quadrilateral;
16. square

Page 67

1. 32 in.; 2. 26 cm; 3. 24 m; 4. 28 ft.;
5. 22 cm; 6. 25 cm; 7. 31 ft.; 8. 31 cm;
9. 20 m; 10. 29 m; 11. 13 cm; 12. 15
cm; 13. 17 cm; 14. 27 cm; 15. 11 cm;
16. 25 cm

Page 68

1. 16 ft.^{2}; 2. 100 m^2; 3. 96 in.^{2}; 4. 44
m^2; 5. 9 ft.^{2}; 6. 40 m^2; 7. 105 in.^{2}; 8. 25
cm^2; 9. 91 ft.^{2}; 10. 24 cm^2; 11. 24 cm^2;
12. 40 m^2; 13. 70 m^2; 14. 84 in.^{2}; 15.
40 m^2; 16. 25 in.^{2}; 17. 49 m^2; 18. 30
cm^2; 19. 66 m^2; 20. 70 in.^{2}; 21. 54
cm^2; 22. 150 m^2

Page 69

1. 12 m^2; 2. 30 ft.^{2}; 3. 54 ft.^{2}; 4. 105
cm^2; 5. 130 m^2; 6. 28 in.^{2}; 7. 40 m^2;
8. 120 cm^2; 9. 10 in.^{2}; 10. 16 ft.^{2}; 11.
42 in.^{2}; 12. 54 in.^{2}; 13. 9 in.^{2}; 14. 25

m^2; 15. 35 ft.^{2}; 16. 12 mm^2; 17. 24 m^2;
18. 225 m^2; 19. 18 cm^2; 20. 49 m^2; 21.
30 mm^2; 22. 300 ft.^{2}

Page 70

1. radius; 2. chord; 3. diameter;
4. radius; 5. chord; 6. 6 cm; 7. 8 cm;
8. 16 cm; 9. 12 cm; 10. 10 cm; 11. 5
cm; 12. 4 cm; 13. 8 cm; 14. 5 cm;
15. 6 cm; 16. 6.28 cm; 17. 9.42 cm

Page 71

1. 72 cm^3; 2. 30 m^3; 3. 36 m^3; 4. 12.5
in.^{3}; 5. 42 m^3; 6. 280 cm^3; 7. 20 m^3;
8. 120 in.^{3}; 9. 18 mm^3; 10. 108 in.^{3};
11. 6 mm^3; 12. 120 m^3; 13. 24 cm^3;
14. 60 m^3; 15. 150 in.^{3}; 16. 7 ft.^{3};
17. 60 m^3; 18. 200 cm^3; 19. 42 yd.^{3};
20. 160 cm^3; 21. 34 m^3; 22. 80 yd.^{3}

Page 72

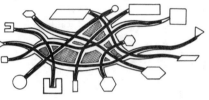

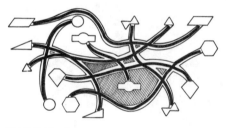

Unit 5 Test

1. B; 2. C; 3. A; 4. D; 5. B; 6. C; 7. D;
8. C; 9. A; 10. B; 11. D; 12. A; 13. C;
14. A; 15. C; 16. C; 17. B; 18. A; 19. C;
20. D; Constructed response: A
rectangle is a type of quadrilateral
because it has four sides.; A triangle
can never be a quadrilateral because
it only has three sides.

Page 77

1. 2; 2. 5; 3. 8; 4. 12; 5. 2/3; 6. 5/6;
7. 8/9; 8. 1/2; 9. 3/5; 10. 5/12; 11. 2/3;
12. 2/5; 13. 3/4; 14. 1/2; 15. 1/3;
16. 7/10; 17. 1/3; 18. 5/9; 19. 1/2

Page 78

1. 2 = 2, 4, 6, 8, 10, 12; 3 = 3, 6, 9,
12, 15, 18; LCM = 6; 2. 3 = 3, 6, 9,
12, 15, 18; 4 = 4, 8, 12, 16, 20, 24;
LCM = 12; 3. 4 = 4, 8, 12, 16, 20, 24;

5 = 5, 10, 15, 20, 25, 30; LCM = 20;
4. 4 = 4, 8, 12, 16, 20, 24; 6 = 6, 12,
18, 24, 30, 36; LCM = 12; 5. 5/10,
2/10, LCM = 10; 6. 4/12, 3/12, LCM =
12; 7. 7/14, 2/14, LCM = 14; 8. 8/24,
3/24, LCM = 24; 9. 6/30, 5/30, LCM =
30; 10. 9/18, 2/18, LCM = 18;
11. 7/21, 3/21, LCM = 21; 12. 7/28,
4/28, LCM = 28; 13. 11/33, 3/33, LCM
= 33

Page 79

1. 4/5; 2. 5/8; 3. 5/7; 4. 7/10; 5. 5/6;
6. 7/10; 7. 10/21; 8. 5/6; 9. 5/18;
10. 11/12; 11. 4/9; 12. 4/9; 13. 3/4;
14. 3/7; 15. 9/20

Page 80

1. 4 4/5; 2. 9 4/5; 3. 9 9/14; 4. 6 1/2;
5. 11 5/12; 6. 3 3/8; 7. 9 2/9; 8. 7 1/6;
9. 13 2/5; 10. 4 1/2; 11. 8 2/15; 12. 6
1/12

Page 81

1. 3/8; 2. 7/10; 3. 1/2; 4. 7/12;
5. 13/24; 6. 1/8; 7. 1/4; 8. 1/20; 9. 2/7;
10. 1/9; 11. 13/56; 12. 2/7; 13. 11/20;
14. 1/2; 15. 2/5

Page 82

1. 2 5/8; 2. 4 3/5; 3. 3/10; 4. 9; 5. 5
8/9; 6. 4 3/4; 7. 4 5/18; 8. 5; 9. 3 9/10;
10. 1 9/14; 11. 4; 12. 1 7/12; 13. 1
33/35; 14. 3 11/21; 15. 8 7/8; 16. 17
7/12

Page 83

1. 5 5/8; 2. 4 6/7; 3. 11 11/16; 4. 7 4/7;
5. 26 3/10; 6. 9 8/15; 7. 7 2/5; 8. 13
1/6; 9. 51 8/9; 10. 14 1/6; 11. 41 1/8;
12. 20 1/4; 13. 49 5/8; 14. 60 4/9;
15. 2 7/8; 16. 8 4/7

Page 84

1. 1 1/2; 2. 3/16; 3. 3/40; 4. 1 3/7;
5. 3/14; 6. 10/27; 7. 5/16; 8. 4; 9. 1
1/7; 10. 3; 11. 2/15; 12. 1/2; 13. 5/21;
14. 1/6; 15. 3/20; 16. 1/14; 17. 2/15;
18. 1/12; 19. 1 1/4; 20. 3

Page 85

1. 4 1/2; 2. 7/12; 3. 1; 4. 3 1/40; 5. 11
2/3; 6. 3 15/16; 7. 13 1/2; 8. 1 1/4;
9. 7 7/12; 10. 9 5/8; 11. 3 1/3; 12. 3
3/10; 13. 1 1/27; 14. 12; 15. 8 2/3

Answer Key

Page 86

1. 15; 2. 24; 3. 4; 4. 35; 5. 12; 6. 25;
7. 12; 8. 6; 9. 16; 10. 8; 11. 8; 12. 9

Unit 6 Test

1. D; 2. B; 3. A; 4. B; 5. D; 6. C; 7. A;
8. B; 9. C; 10. A; 11. A; 12. B; 13. D;
14. A; 15. B; 16. B; 17. A; 18. A; 19. C;
20. A; Constructed-response answers
will vary.

Page 91

1. 12 h 7 min; 2. 36 min 55 s; 3. 31
min 1 s; 4. 10 h 13 min; 5. 41 min 8 s;
6. 13 h 10 min; 7. 18 h 50 min; 8. 11
s; 9. 1 h 50 s; 10. 1 h 44 min; 11. 1
min 50 s; 12. 6 min 50 s

Page 92

1.–12. Check students' lengths.;
13. <; 14. =; 15. =; 16. >; 17. <; 18. >;
19. =; 20. >; 21. <; 22. >; 23. >; 24. =;
25. <; 26. >; 27. >

Page 93

1. <; 2. =; 3. >; 4. <; 5. >; 6. <; 7. =;
8. >; 9. <; 10. >; 11. >; 12. >; 13. =;
14. <; 15. >; 16. 1 g; 17. 1 kg; 18. 1 g;
19. 5 mg; 20. 40 mL; 21. 4 L; 22. 5
mL; 23. 355 mL

Page 94

1. 1; 2. 3; 3. 1/2.; 4. 1 1/2; 5. 5; 6. 3
1/2; 7. 4 1/2; 8. 36; 9. 4; 10. 12; 11. 5;
12. 3,520; 13. 18; 14. 5; 15. 2; 16. 2;
17. 3; 18. 12; 19. 4; 20. 6; 21. 16;
22. 1; 23. 2; 24. 32; 25. 6,000; 26. 80;
27. 48; 28. 5

Page 95

1. 50°; 2. 60°; 3. 202°; 4. 60°; 5. 32°;
6. 212°; 7. 100°; 8. -20°; 9. 55°;
10. 45°; 11. 66.6°; 12. 180°; 13. 100°

Page 96

1. 4.3; 2. 8 L; 3. 4 mm; 4. 10 ft.;
5. 76.1; 6. 335 lb.; 7. 13 m; 8. 9; 9. 5;
10. 87 m; 11. 14 mL: 12. 4.5; 13. 16
oz.; 14. 6 t.; 15. 4 in.; 16. 26; 17. 36;
18. 1; 19. 3, 3; 20. 8, 4.5; 21. 5, 5

Page 97

1. 15.8; 2. 7.5; 3. 38.6; 4. 95.8%;
5. 4.5; 6. 5; 7. 38.25; 8. 5; 9. 9.5;
10. 149; 11. 70; 12. 83; 13. 16.4;
14. 49.2; 15. 245; 16. 18; 17. 85.5;
18. 2.5; 19. 516; 20. 34; 21. 6; 22.
4.775; 23. 10.45; 24. 6.9; 25. 6.78;

26. 3.33

Page 98

Pictograph: 1. Strawberry Juice;
2. Grape Juice and Orange Juice;
3. Apple Juice; 4. Cherry Juice;
5. 12

Double Bar Graph: 1. Garrett, 14;
2. 6; 3. Garrett; 4. September

Page 99

Circle: 1. yellow; 2. blue; 3. red;
4. pink and blue; 5. 40%; 6. 10%;
7. 100%; 8. 90%

Line: 1. 4th; 2. 5th and 6th; 3. 1st and
2nd; 4. 115; 5. 6th; 6. 5th; 7. 2nd and
3rd; 8. 10; 9. 15; 10. down 5; 11. 25

Page 100

1. 1/2; 2. 1/4; 3. 2/6 = 1/3; 4. 4/8 = 1/2;
5. 2/3; 6. 1/3; 7. 2/8 = 1/4; 8. 5/8; 9.
3/10; 10. 3/5; 11. 1/11; 12. red, 3/7;
13. yellow, 2/4 = 1/2; 14. blue, 5/9

Unit 7 Test

1. A; 2. C; 3. A; 4. C; 5. D; 6. C; 7. A;
8. C; 9. D; 10. B; 11. B; 12. A; 13. B;
14. C; 15. B; 16. C; 17. C; 18. D;
19. B; 20. C; Constructed response:
Because the probability is 1/6; no.

Page 105

1. addition, 32 invitations; 2. division,
20 singers; 3. subtraction, 13/24 want
pets; 4. multiplication, $972.36;
5. addition, 5/8 own rabbits or dogs;
6. multiplication, 3,200 apples

Page 106

1. 6 choices; 2. 12 choices; 3. 8
choices; 4. 12 choices; 5. 8 decisions

Page 107

1. 3 = $1.35, 4 = $1.80, 5 = $2.25, 6
= $2.70, 7 = $3.15, 8 = $3.60, 9 =
$4.05, 10 = $4.50; 2. 4th = 2.1, 5th =
2.4, 6th = 2.7; 3. 3 = 3.3, 4 = 4.4, 5 =
5.5, 6 = 6.6, 7 = 7.7, 8 = 8.8, 9 = 9.9,
10 = 10.10

Page 108

1. 2 3/8 cups; 2. 5 5/8 cups; 3. turkey
pot pie; 4. 7/8 cup; 5. 10 cups; 6. 1
5/8 cups; 8. baked chicken and
vegetables combined with baked
zucchini sticks with onions

Page 109

1. $20, $4; 2. 2 hours 15 minutes;
3. second and third; 4. $2.45, $4.90;
5. 7/12, 1 5/12; 6. 10.71 oz.

Page 110

1. 100 in.³; 2. 17 people; 3. 7 11/15
lbs.; 4. 1.44 miles; 5. 8.1 hours;
6. 97.5 oz.

Page 111

1. D or E, 11 cm; 2. C or A, 7 cm;
3. 18 cm; 4. 15 cm; 5. A. 26 cm, B. 10
cm; 6. A. 18 cm, B. 12 cm; 7. D or B,
7 cm; 8. Answers will vary.

Page 112

1. 3/6 = n/12, n = 6 pints; 2. 5/10 =
n/30, n = 15 cups of cornstarch;
3. 2/3 = n/12, n = 8 pinches of salt;
4. 1/4 = 5/n, n = 20 drops of water

Unit 8 Test

1. C; 2. C; 3. A; 4. C; 5. D; 6. B; 7. B;
8. D; 9. A; 10. D; 11. C; 12. B; 13. A;
14. C; 15. B; 16. A; 17. C; 18. B; 19. C;
20. A; Constructed-response answers
will vary.

Final Review Test

1. C; 2. G; 3. C; 4. J; 5. B; 6. H; 7. A;
8. G; 9. C; 10. F; 11. D; 12. G; 13. C;
14. F; 15. C; 16. J; 17. C; 18. J; 19. A;
20. F; 21. C; 22. G; 23. A; 24. J; 25. B;
26. H; 27. A; 28. H; 29. B; 30. F

Page 5

1. forty thousand; 2. eight billion; 3. fifty million; 4. five thousand; 5. eight; 6. seventy thousand; 7. three million; 8. four hundred thousand; 9. seven hundred million; 10. two billion; 11. six; 12. two hundred; 13. three billion, four hundred twenty-one million, eight hundred thousand; 14. forty-five billion, nine hundred eighty-two million, four hundred six thousand, three hundred ninety-nine

Page 6

1. $400; 2. $600; 3. $600; 4. $1,000; 5. $600; 6. 8,000; 7. 5,000; 8. 10,000; 9. 6,000; 10. 7,000; 11. 60,000; 12. 50,000; 13. 80,000; 14. 40,000; 15. 30,000; 16. 20; 17. 350; 18. 700; 19. 500; 20. 6,480; 21. 750; 22. 700; 23. 3,400; 24. 700,000; 25. 360,000; 26. 70,000; 27. 300,000

Page 7

1. >; 2. >; 3. >; 4. <; 5. <; 6. <; 7. >; 8. >; 9. >; 10. >; 11. <; 12. <; 13. 192; 942; 6,597; 8,241; 14. 929; 1,382; 5,495; 8,297; 15. 42,394; 92,140; 92,149; 16. 340,384; 342,192; 928,191; 17. 8,298; 80,492; 849,142

Page 8

1. 13,368; 2. 8,272; 3. 11,386; 4. 9,299; 5. 9,413; 6. 9,501; 7. 10,144; 8. 13,719; 9. 9,065; 10. 6,452; 11. 8,629; 12. 6,680; 13. 59,613; 14. 400,997; 15. 212,615; 16. 106,135

Page 9

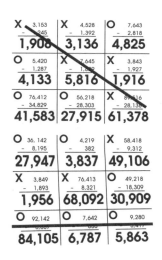

Page 10

1. 32; 2. 63; 3. 272; 4. 352; 5. 253; 6. 54; 7. 459; 8. 175; 9. 25; 10. 132; 11. 211; 12. 2,223; 13. 5,156; 14. 92; 15. 1,765; 16. 481,884

Page 11

1. $75.21; 2. $87.70; 3. $382.48; 4. $93.21; 5. $10.31; 6. $105.00; 7. $9.69; 8. $50.04; 9. $85.78; 10. $806.94; 11. $100.80; 12. $934.31; 13. $56.18; 14. $3.56; 15. $492.11; 16. $.65; 17. $66.62; 18. $4.54; 19. $491.87; 20. $68.85; 21. $54.69; 22. $2.64; 23. $9.11; 24. $21.65

Unit 1 Test

1. B; 2. A; 3. C; 4. A; 5. D; 6. B; 7. A; 8. C; 9. D; 10. B; 11. D; 12. C; 13. B; 14. A; 15. B; 16. B; 17. D; 18. C; 19. A; 20. A; Constructed-response answers will vary.

Page 16

1. Zero Property; 2. Associative Property; 3. Commutative Property; 4. Property of One; 5. Distributive Property; 6. Associative Property; 7. Commutative Property; 8. Associative Property; 9. Distributive Property; 10. 7; 11. 8; 12. 0; 13. 7; 14. 1; 15. 5; 16. 7

Page 17

1. 282; 2. 168; 3. 324; 4. 185; 5. 472; 6. 632; 7. 1,284; 8. 4,984; 9. 2,065; 10. 1,944; 11. 2,604; 12. 2,682; 13. 3,402; 14. 3,290; 15. 5,176; 16. 6,286; 17. 7,386; 18. 38,592; 19. 32,528; 20. 14,756

Page 18

1. 6,000; 2. 3,600; 3. 400; 4. 3,000; 5. 4,400; 6. 4,000; 7. 18,000; 8. 12,000; 9. 60,000; 10. 20,000; 11. 1,800; 12. 8,000; 13. 36,000; 14. 160,000; 15. 44,000; 16. 2,500; 17. 14,000; 18. 45,000; 19. 16,000; 20. 800,000

Page 19

1. 1,312; 2. 840; 3. 714; 4. 672; 5. 1,092; 6. 713; 7. 525; 8. 576; 9. 1,012; 10. 486; 11. 1,715; 12. 1,015; 13. 1,800; 14. 364; 15. 1,960; 16. 1,944; 17. 2,976; 18. 2,548

Page 20

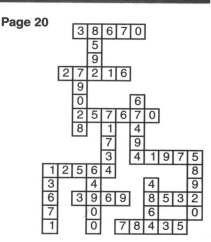

Page 21

1. 38,745; 2. 73,986; 3. 147,136; 4. 100,890; 5. 126,236; 6. 79,356; 7. 205,485; 8. 78,474; 9. 252,900; 10. 92,127; 11. 74,772; 12. 140,544; 13. 203,184; 14. 61,712; 15. 129,800

Page 22

1. $29.34; 2. $408.48; 3. $147.66; 4. $577.92; 5. $23.56; 6. $19.95; 7. $269.12; 8. $225.92; 9. $1,608.75; 10. $655.64; 11. $47.04; 12. $44.84; 13. $131.22; 14. $731.12; 15. $197.34; 16. $797.64; 17. $37.38

Page 23

1. $93.36, $80; 2. $59.01; $56; 3. $554.28, $540; 4. $25.11, $27; 5. $350.07, $340; 6. $389.76, $392; 7. yes; 8. no; 9. yes

Unit 2 Test

1. D; 2. B; 3. A; 4. C; 5. B; 6. A; 7. C; 8. B; 9. B; 10. C; 11. B; 12. D;13. C; 14. A; 15. B; 16. B; 17. D; 18. B; 19. B; 20. A; Constructed response: 61,056; Explanations will vary.

Page 29

1. 9 R1; 2. 6 R3; 3. 8 R4; 4. 5 R2; 5. 7 R3; 6. 8 R4; 7. 9 R3; 8. 8 R3; 9. 9 R5; 10. 8 R3; 11. 6 R2; 12. 8 R8; 13. 8 R4; 14. 9 R4; 15. 7 R3; 16. 7 R4

Page 30

1. 98; 2. 67; 3. 68; 4. 91; 5. 34; 6. 78; 7. 26; 8. 73; 9. 58; 10. 81; 11. 96; 12. 47; 13. 29; 14. 48; 15. 27; 16. 29; 17. 83; 18. 76; 19. 41; 20. 72

Answer Key

Page 31

1. 79 R1; 2. 58 R3; 3. 42 R4; 4. 63 R7; 5. 28 R4; 6. 39 R3; 7. 27 R4; 8. 96 R2; 9. 72 R3; 10. 28 R5; 11. 78 R6; 12. 97 R1; 13. 68 R5; 14. 85 R3; 15. 18 R8; 16. 63 R2

Page 32

1. 146; 2. 348; 3. 231 R1; 4. 172 R2; 5. 378; 6. 327; 7. 214; 8. 142 R4; 9. 317; 10. 136; 11. 413 R1; 12. 218 R2; 13. 416; 14. 181 R4; 15. 224 R1

Page 33

1. 50 R3; 2. 402; 3. 810; 4. 109; 5. 480 R1; 6. 103 R4; 7. 30 R8; 8. 309 R4; 9. 780; 10. 205 R5; 11. 90 R3; 12. 108 R2; 13. 680; 14. 109 R5; 15. 208 R2; 16. 150 R6; 17. 106 R2; 18. 207; 19. 301; 20. 102 R2

Page 34

1. $5.48; 2. $.78; 3. $6.21; 4. $3.59; 5. $6.24; 6. $1.05; 7. $7.12; 8. $3.79; 9. $5.88; 10. $1.87; 11. $4.11; 12. $3.56; 13. $.76; 14. $3.89; 15. $1.47; 16. $6.21

Page 35

1. 45; 2. 25; 3. 89; 4. 28; 5. 23; 6. 69

Page 36

1. 9; 2. 7 R6; 3. 6 R7; 4. 8; 5. 5 R40; 6. 4 R50; 7. 9; 8. 7 R7; 9. 8 R10; 10. 3 R37; 11. 6; 12. 9 R30; 13. 6 R4; 14. 9 R79; 15. 5

Page 37

1. 43; 2. 56 R6; 3. 29 R20; 4. 38 R38; 5. 14 R21; 6. 36; 7. 28 R40; 8. 21 R50; 9. 37; 10. 36; 11. 86 R18; 12. 15 R25; 13. 62 R40

Page 38

1. 312 R7; 2. 127 R19; 3. 154 R10; 4. 412 R15; 5. 141; 6. 113 R50; 7. 142 R12; 8. 114 R50; 9. 215 R20; 10. 124 R58; 11. 218; 12. 314 R20

Unit 3 Test

1. C; 2. A; 3. B; 4. C; 5. C; 6. C; 7. D; 8. A; 9. D; 10. C; 11. B; 12. A; 13. C; 14. C; 15. A; 16. A; 17. C; 18. B; 19. D; 20. A; Constructed-response answers will vary.

Page 43

1. 3.5; 2. 6.1; 3. 0.8; 4. 8.3; 5. 0.3;

6. 2.1; 7. 0.7; 8. 20.2; 9. 0.4; 10. 37.2; 11. 400.1; 12. 55.3; 13. 0.6; 14. 0.1; 15. three and nine tenths; 16. two and seven tenths; 17. twelve and eight tenths; 18. seven and three tenths; 19. 6/10; 20. 5/10; 21. 9/10; 22. 7/10; 23. 1 2/10; 24. 4 8/10; 25. 6 1/10; 26. 3 4/10; 27. 33 2/10; 28. 21 8/10

Page 44

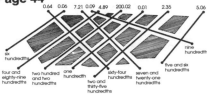

1. 8/100; 2. 6 9/100; 3. 2 12/100; 4. 21/100; 5. 7 34/100; 6. 55/100; 7. 16 8/100; 8. 300 24/100; 9. 25 4/100; 10. 600 49/100; 11. 72/100; 12. 22/100

Page 45

1. 300.07; 2. 15.045; 3. 218.004; 4. 0.002; 5. 67.631; 6. 0.012; 7. 49.099; 8. 5.845; 9. 0.008; 10. 10.602; 11. 0.003; 12. thirty-five thousandths; 13. eighty-nine and four thousandths; 14. three hundred twenty-four and eight thousandths; 15. seventy-two and forty-five thousandths; 16. 3 47/1000; 17. 289 78/1000; 18. 73 34/1000; 19. 556 345/1000; 20. 3 657/1000; 21. 900 2/1000; 22. 5/10; 23. 4 8/10

Page 46

1. <; 2. >; 3. <; 4. >; 5. >; 6. <; 7. <; 8. >; 9. >; 10. <; 11. <; 12. <; 13. <; 14. <; 15. >; 2.24, 4.19, 5.15, 6.07, 7.35, 8.38, 9.29

Page 47

1. 46; 3; 612; 90; 2. 2,346; 7; 1; 5; 3. 87; 43; 235; 1; 4. 567; 8; 6; 95; 5. 4.4; 2.8; 543.2; 0.5; 6. 56.1; 3.2; 78.0; 678.5; 7. 0.4; 36.2; 1.2; 0.3; 8. 34.2; 8.8; 16.7; 9.0; 9. 34.25; 5.25; 6.11; 45.81; 10. 5.21; 9.18; 23.68; 38.20; 11. 2.45; 9.02; 7.27; 435.46; 12. 6.32; 2,345.12; 6.24; 45.84

Page 48

1. 346.24; 2. 31.716; 3. 16.157; 4. 8.555; 5. 0.661; 6. 87.5; 7. 51.24; 8. 24.116; 9. 2.5; 10. 6.113; 11. 33.7; 12. 6.94; 13. 9.65; 14. 19.245; 15. 32.352;

16. 25.555; 17. 26.638; 18. 13.04; 19. 80.234; 20. 25.254

Page 49

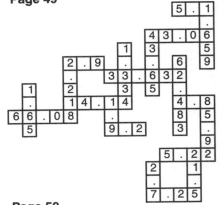

Page 50

1. 2 + 9 = 11; 2. 600 + 90 = 690; 3. 0.3 + 0.5 = 0.8; 4. 70 + 90 = 160; 5. 800 + 300 = 1,100; 6. 30 + 100 = 130; 7. 500 − 300 = 200; 8. 2,000 − 1,000 = 1,000; 9. 600 − 200 = 400; 10. 0.9 − 0.3 = 0.6; 11. 7,000 − 2000 = 5,000; 12. 600 − 400 = 200

Page 51

1. 5,949.5; 2. 0.56; 3. 1.22; 4. 1.075; 5. 20.06; 6. 1.56; 7. 67.64; 8. 1.12; 9. 47.97; 10. 30.68; 11. 0.018; 12. 11.48; 13. 8.64; 14. 1.506; 15. 1.74; 16. 21.28; 17. 238.35; 18. 2.808; 19. 5.04; 20. 32.492

Page 52

1. 0.02; 2. 0.08; 3. 0.03; 4. 0.07; 5. 0.3; 6. 0.04; 7. 2.7; 8. 0.14; 9. 1.45; 10. 2.47; 11. 3.56; 12. 1.89; 13. 2.58; 14. 3.4; 15. 4.26; 16. 0.27

Unit 4 Test

1. B; 2. D; 3. A; 4. C; 5. C; 6. B; 7. C; 8. B; 9. C; 10. A; 11. C; 12. C; 13. D; 14. B; 15. A; 16. B; 17. D; 18. B; 19. A; 20. A; Constructed-response answers will vary.

Midway Review Test

1. C; 2. H; 3. A; 4. J; 5. B; 6. G; 7. A; 8. H; 9. B; 10. J; 11. A; 12. H; 13. A; 14. G; 15. A; 16. H; 17. B; 18. G; 19. D; 20. G; 21. B; 22. H; 23. D; 24. F; 25. A; Constructed-response answers will vary.